Hegel, Logic and Speculation

Bloomsbury Studies in Continental Philosophy

Presents cutting-edge scholarship in the field of modern European thought. The wholly original arguments, perspectives and research findings in titles in this series make it an important and stimulating resource for students and academics from across the discipline.

Deleuze and the Diagram: Aesthetic Threads in Visual Organization, Jakub Zdebik
Derrida, Badiou and the Formal Imperative, Christopher Norris
Desire in Ashes: Deconstruction, Psychoanalysis, Philosophy, edited by Simon Morgan Wortham and Chiara Alfano
Early Phenomenology, edited by Brian Harding and Michael R. Kelly
Egalitarian Moments, Devin Zane Shaw
Ernst Bloch and His Contemporaries, Ivan Boldyrev
Jean-Paul Sartre's Anarchist Philosophy, William L. Remley
Why There Is No Post-Structuralism in France, Johannes Angermuller
Gadamer's Poetics: A Critique of Modern Aesthetics, John Arthos
Heidegger, History and the Holocaust, Mahon O'Brien
Heidegger and the Emergence of the Question of Being, Jesús Adrián Escudero
Hegel and Resistance: History, Politics and Dialectics, edited by Rebecca Comay and Bart Zantvoort
Husserl's Ethics and Practical Intentionality, Susi Ferrarello
Immanent Transcendence: Reconfiguring Materialism in Continental Philosophy, Patrice Haynes
Lacanian Realism: Political and Clinical Psychoanalysis, Duane Rousselle
Language and Being, Duane Williams
Merleau-Ponty's Existential Phenomenology and the Realization of Philosophy, Bryan A. Smyth
Mortal Thought: Hölderlin and Philosophy, James Luchte
Nietzsche and Political Thought, edited by Keith Ansell-Pearson
Nietzsche as a Scholar of Antiquity, Helmut Heit
Philosophy, Sophistry, Antiphilosophy: Badiou's Dispute with Lyotard, Matthew R. McLennan
Philosophy of Ontological Lateness, Keith Whitmoyer
The Poetic Imagination in Heidegger and Schelling, Christopher Yates
Post-Rationalism: Psychoanalysis, Epistemology, and Marxism in Post-War France, Tom Eyers
Revisiting Normativity with Deleuze, edited by Rosi Braidotti and Patricia Pisters
Schizoanalysis and Ecosophy: Reading Deleuze and Guattari, edited by Constantin V. Boundas
Towards the Critique of Violence: Walter Benjamin and Giorgio Agamben, Brendan Moran and Carlo Salzani

Hegel, Logic and Speculation

Edited by
Paolo Diego Bubbio
Alessandro De Cesaris
Maurizio Pagano
Hager Weslati

BLOOMSBURY ACADEMIC
LONDON • NEW YORK • OXFORD • NEW DELHI • SYDNEY

BLOOMSBURY ACADEMIC
Bloomsbury Publishing Plc
50 Bedford Square, London, WC1B 3DP, UK
1385 Broadway, New York, NY 10018, USA
29 Earlsfort Terrace, Dublin 2, Ireland

BLOOMSBURY, BLOOMSBURY ACADEMIC and the Diana logo are trademarks of
Bloomsbury Publishing Plc

First published in Great Britain 2019
This paperback edition published in 2021

Copyright © Paolo Diego Bubbio, Alessandro De Cesaris, Maurizio Pagano,
Hager Weslati and Contributors, 2019

Paolo Diego Bubbio, Alessandro De Cesaris, Maurizio Pagano, Hager Weslati have
asserted their right under the Copyright, Designs and Patents Act, 1988, to be
identified as Editors of this work.

For legal purposes the Acknowledgements on p. x constitute an extension
of this copyright page.

All rights reserved. No part of this publication may be reproduced or transmitted
in any form or by any means, electronic or mechanical, including photocopying,
recording, or any information storage or retrieval system, without prior
permission in writing from the publishers.

Bloomsbury Publishing Plc does not have any control over, or responsibility for, any third-
party websites referred to or in this book. All internet addresses given in this book were
correct at the time of going to press. The author and publisher regret any inconvenience
caused if addresses have changed or sites have ceased to exist, but can accept no
responsibility for any such changes.

A catalogue record for this book is available from the British Library.

A catalog record for this book is available from the Library of Congress.

ISBN: HB: 978-1-3500-5636-7
PB: 978-1-3502-4370-5
ePDF: 978-1-3500-5635-0
eBook: 978-1-3500-5637-4

Series: Bloomsbury Studies in Continental Philosophy

Typeset by Integra Software Services Pvt. Ltd.

To find out more about our authors and books visit www.bloomsbury.com
and sign up for our newsletters.

Contents

Notes on Contributors	vi
Acknowledgements	x
List of Abbreviations	xi

	Speculation and Hermeneutics of Effectual Reality *Maurizio Pagano and Hager Weslati*	1
1	Empowering Forms: Hegel's Conception of 'Form' and 'Formal' *Elena Ficara*	15
2	Essence as Reflection *Riccardo Dottori*	27
3	Effectual Contingency: The Ontological Problem of Modality in Hegel's *Science of Logic* *Alessandro De Cesaris*	43
4	Self-Consciousness and the Idea: From Logic to Subjective Spirit *Guido Frilli*	61
5	The Concept of Habit and the Function of Immediacy *Sean McStravick*	75
6	Singularity of the Concept – Singularity of the Will: The Logical Ground of Hegel's *Philosophy of Right* *Antonios Kalatzis*	89
7	Subverting Practical Philosophy *Myriam Bienenstock*	101
8	Work and Need, Particular and Universal *Campbell Jones*	117
9	Hegel's Conception of Personality and the Tension between Logic and Realphilosophy *Lauri Kallio*	135
10	Mind of God, Point of View of Man or Something Not Quite Either? *Paul Redding*	147
11	Logic and Theology in Hegel *Roberto Morani*	171
12	The Concept of Religion and Its Hermeneutic Function *Maurizio Pagano*	185
13	A Speculative Logic for Images in Hegel's Philosophy *Haris Ch. Papoulias*	201
14	The Silence of *Logik*: Hegel after Kojève *Hager Weslati*	217

Index	233

Notes on Contributors

Myriam Bienenstock is Professor Emeritus at the University of Tours after having held guest appointments at Frankfurt, Zürich, Münster and Berlin. Her fields of research are Hegel and German idealism, the practical philosophy of German idealism and Jewish thought in the nineteenth and twentieth centuries. Her major French publications include *Politique du jeune Hegel* (1801–1804) (Presses Universitaire de France 1992) and two editions of Hegel's *Philosophie de l'histoire*. She also co-edited (with A. Tosel) *La raison pratique au 20e siècle: trajets et figures* (L'Harmattan 2004). In English, she is the author of 'Between Hegel and Marx: Eduard Gans on the "Social Question"', in *Politics, Religion, and Art: Hegelian Debates*, edited by Douglas Moggach.

Paolo Diego Bubbio is Associate Professor of Philosophy at Western Sydney University, Australia. His research is mainly in the area of post-Kantian philosophy. In particular, he is interested in the relation of the post-Kantian tradition (from Kant to Nietzsche) to the later movements of European philosophy. His books include *Sacrifice in the Post-Kantian Tradition: Perspectivism, Intersubjectivity, and Recognition* (SUNY Press 2014) and *God and the Self in Hegel: Beyond Subjectivism* (SUNY Press 2017). He co-edited several collections of essays and authored numerous journal articles on nineteenth-century European philosophy in journals such as *British Journal for the History of Philosophy, Hegel Bulletin, International Journal of Philosophical Studies* and *International Journal for Philosophy of Religion*.

Alessandro De Cesaris is Postdoctoral Research Fellow at the University of Naples 'Federico II'. He studied in Naples, Vercelli, Freiburg im Breisgau and Berlin (thanks to a DAAD scholarship). He published essays and articles on Aristotle, Hegel, Natorp, contemporary metaphysics and the philosophy of technology. He also translated Paul Natorp's *Habilitationsschrift* on Descartes's philosophy (Aracne 2016). His doctoral thesis addresses the problem of singularity in Hegel's *Logic* and is about to be published in Italian.

Riccardo Dottori is Professor Emeritus at the University of Rome Tor Vergata. He studied philosophy at the University of Rome 'La Sapienza' and at the University of Tübingen. He was the holder of an Alexander von Humboldt scholarship that allowed him to study with Hans Georg Gadamer in Heidelberg (1968–1972). He also studied at the University Paris X, under the supervision of Paul Ricoeur. Some of his most recent publications include *A Century of Philosophy: Hans Georg Gadamer in Conversation with Riccardo Dottori* (Bloomsbury 2004), *Die Reflexion des Wirklichen* (Mohr Siebeck 2006), *L'art et le Jeu de l'existence* (Hermann 2018) and *Giorgio de Chirico: Immagini metafisiche* (La Nave di Teseo 2018).

Elena Ficara is currently Junior Professor at the University of Paderborn and Feodor Lynen Research Fellow at the Graduate Centre of the City University of New York. Her works include the monograph *Die Ontologie in der 'Kritik der reinen Vernunft'* (Königshausen & Neumann 2006), the edited collection *Contradictions: Logic, History, Actuality* (De Gruyter 2014) and the articles 'Dialectic and Dialetheism', in *History and Philosophy of Logic*, 34/1 (2013), and 'Contrariety and Contradiction: Hegel and the "Berliner Aristotelismus"', in *Hegel-Studien* 49 (2015).

Guido Frilli, former student of the University of Pisa and of the Scuola Normale Superiore in Pisa, has completed his PhD in 2015 at the universities of Florence and of Paris 1 Panthéon-Sorbonne, and is currently Postdoctoral Research Fellow in History of Philosophy at the University of Florence. His research and his main contributions focus on German idealism and on the connections between early modern philosophy and classical German thinking. He has recently published a book on reason and artifice in Hegel and Thomas Hobbes (*Ragione, Desiderio, Artificio*, Firenze University Press 2017) and is now investigating Friedrich Heinrich Jacobi's conception of reason and the relevance of Spinoza's philosophy for early Romanticism and Idealism.

Campbell Jones is Associate Professor of Sociology at the University of Auckland (New Zealand). He has published numerous works on Hegel, Marx and contemporary continental philosophy always in relation to concrete issues of political economy, such as entrepreneurship, the market, financialization, collective subjects, wealth taxes and the end of the world. He is currently writing a book to be entitled *The Work of Others*.

Lauri Kallio earned his PhD at the University of Helsinki in 2017. His dissertation (*J. V. Snellmans Philosophie der Persönlichkeit*) discusses the philosophy of the most remarkable Finnish Hegelian, J. V. Snellman (1806–1881). Kallio's research interests are focused on the history of late German idealism (1840–1880) in Germany and in the Nordic countries, the history of the Berlin journal *Der Gedanke*, the debate between F. A. Trendelenburg (1802–1872) and Hegelians Karl Rosenkranz (1805–1879) and K. L. Michelet (1801–1893), as well as Nordic Hegelianism.

Antonios Kalatzis is Research Fellow at the Martin Buber Society of Fellows in the Humanities and Social Sciences at the Hebrew University of Jerusalem. He is co-director of the interdisciplinary research group *Weltwissen und Erfahrungen des Globalen/Expériences et savoirs du global* at the Centre Marc Bloch, Humboldt-Universität, Berlin. His dissertation *Explikation und Immanenz. Das dreifache Argument der Wissenschaft der Logik* (completed at the Freie Universität, Berlin) was published in the Hegel-Jahrbuch Sonderband series (De Gruyter 2016). He is the co-editor of *From Ionia to Jena: Franz Rosenzweig and the History of Philosophy* (Neofelis, forthcoming) and *Into Life: Franz Rosenzweig on Knowledge Aesthetics and Politics*, to be published in the Supplements to *The Journal of Jewish Thought and Philosophy*.

Sean McStravick completed a master's degree in Philosophy (Panthéon-Sorbonne University) with a thesis on the notion of habit in Hegel's philosophy and a master's degree in Political Studies at the École des Hautes Études en Sciences Sociales with a thesis on Tocqueville and the reflexivity of modern societies. He is currently preparing the *agrégation* (Paris Sorbonne University) and works on a PhD project on the notion of immediacy in Hegel's philosophy.

Roberto Morani is Researcher at the University of Florence, Italy. He is the author of *Soggetto e modernità: Hegel, Nietzsche, Heidegger interpreti di Cartesio* (FrancoAngeli 2007), *Essere, fondamento e abisso: Heidegger e la questione del nulla* (Mimesis 2010) and *La dialettica e i suoi riformatori: Spaventa, Croce, Gentile a confronto con Hegel* (Mimesis 2015). He is also the author of several articles and essays on the philosophy of Hegel, Nietzsche, Heidegger, Croce and Gentile.

Maurizio Pagano is Professor Emeritus of Philosophy at the University of Eastern Piedmont (Vercelli, Italy), Director of the Centre of Philosophical and Religious Studies 'Luigi Pareyson' (Turin) and Director of the Hegel Studies Lab (Vercelli). He is the author of *Hegel: La religione e l'ermeneutica del concetto* (ESI 1992). He edited an Italian translation of some parts of the *Phenomenology of Spirit* and a French edition of the *Nachschriften* of Schelling's *Philosophy of Mythology* (with Luigi Pareyson). Pagano is the author of several essays on the question of cultural and religious pluralism and on the status of philosophical hermeneutics in the horizon of intercultural relationships.

Haris Ch. Papoulias is a founding member of HegeLab. He holds a PhD in philosophy and the history of philosophy (UPO, Italy) and won the award for the best doctoral research in the Humanities (2017) of the Advanced Research Institute of the University of Eastern Piedmont. He is a *Doctor Europaeus* (UMA, Spain), currently working with the International Research Project on Critical Hermeneutics 'HERCRITIA' Santander (UNED National University of Spain, Madrid). He is the author of *Iconoclastia Endogena: Una teoria dell'immagine nel sistema del sapere di G.W.F. Hegel* (Mimesis, forthcoming).

Paul Redding is Professor Emeritus of Philosophy at the University of Sydney. In publications stretching over four decades, including *Hegel's Hermeneutics* (Cornell University Press 1996), *Analytic Philosophy and the Return of Hegelian Thought* (Cambridge University Press 2007) and *Continental Idealism: Leibniz to Nietzsche* (Routledge 2009), he has advocated a reinterpretation of Hegel's philosophy as free of the first-order metaphysical commitments as traditionally understood. Hegel's idealism, he suggests, was more *meta*-metaphysical redefinition of Aristotle's original project, aimed at freeing metaphysics from Platonic assumptions so as to make it about the *actual world* with its historical and contingent features.

Hager Weslati is Senior Lecturer in Critical Theory and New Media Philosophy at Kingston University, London. She is the author of articles and book chapters on Kant and Derrida, Lacanian psychoanalysis, British cultural studies and travel writing in relation to coloniality and imperial cultural politics. She also translated Georges Bataille, Jean-Joseph Goux and Eric Alliez, and more recently Alexandre Kojève (*The Notion of Authority*, Verso 2014) and Daniel Bensaid (*In Praise of Profane Politics*, Brill 2019). Her main research interests are in the thought and philosophical system of Alexandre Kojève, the subject of her forthcoming monograph.

Acknowledgements

Most of the chapters included in this volume were presented at the conference of the HegeLab (*Laboratorio di Studi Hegeliani*, Vercelli) 'Hegel and Effectual Reality: Logic and Its Realizations' (15–16 December 2014), which was held at the University of Eastern Piedmont in Vercelli, Italy. The intellectual conversation that stemmed from that conference was then consolidated in another HegeLab conference, 'Hegel and the Concept of World History' (14–15 April 2016), which took place at Kingston University, London.

The editors would like to thank, aside from all the contributors to the present volume, the original participants, particularly Alfredo Ferrarin, who served as keynote speaker at the first conference, and George Di Giovanni, Jean-Francois Kervégan, Stefania Achella and Bruno Haas who served as keynote speakers at the second one.

We acknowledge the financial contribution of the Department of Humanities at the University of Eastern Piedmont, as well as the support of the Philosophy Research Initiative at Western Sydney University and the Centre for Research in Modern European Philosophy (CRMEP) at Kingston University.

Comments and suggestions from participants in both conferences are gratefully acknowledged. Thanks are also due to members of the Scientific Committee of the HegeLab, in particular Mario Farina and Gianluca Garelli, and to the director of CRMEP, Professor Peter Osborne. Last but not least, thanks are due to Liza Thompson at Bloomsbury Publishing for her patience and generosity, and for her efforts in seeing this project through.

List of Abbreviations

Contributions in this volume refer to the English editions of Hegel's work where available. When a German edition is cited, it follows the English citation if one is given: e.g. (*SL*, 37; *GW* XXI, 42)

Hegel's works are cited by page, section or paragraph (§) number; Hegel's remarks (Anmerkungen) to his sections are cited by an accompanying 'R' (e.g. *EI*, §140 R); Hegel's additions (Zusätze) with 'A' (e.g. *EI*, §140 A). Citations of additions, remarks and sections are separated with a comma. For example (*EI*, §140, R, A) would refer to a citation of the section, its remark and the addition. Where there are multiple additions to a single section, a number is placed after 'A' (e.g. *EI*, §136 A2).

Hegel's work in English translation

EI *Hegel's Logic: Part One of the Encyclopaedia of Philosophical Sciences (1830)*, trans. W. Wallace. Oxford: Oxford University Press, 1975.

EII *Hegel's Philosophy of Nature: Part Two of the Encyclopaedia of Philosophical Sciences (1830)*, trans. A.V. Miller. Oxford: Oxford University Press, 2004.

EIII *Hegel's Philosophy of Mind*, trans. W. Wallace and A.V. Miller, revised by M. Inwood. Oxford: Oxford University Press, 2007.

ETW *Early Theological Writings*, trans. T.M. Knox. Philadelphia: University of Pennsylvania Press, 1971.

FKL *Faith and Knowledge*, trans. H.S. Harris and W. Cerf. Albany, NY: State University of New York Press, 1988.

FPS *First Philosophy of Spirit (part III of the System of Speculative Philosophy 1803/4)*, in *Hegel's System of Ethical Life and First Philosophy of Spirit*, ed. and trans. H. S. Harris and T. M. Knox. Albany, NY: State University of New York Press, 1979.

JPS *Hegel and the Human Spirit: A Translation of the Jena Lectures on the Philosophy of Spirit (1805–6)*, trans. L. Rauch. Detroit: Wayne State University Press, 1983.

LA	*Aesthetics. Lectures on Fine Art*, 2 volumes, trans. T. M. Knox, Oxford: Oxford University Press, 1975.
LHP	*Lectures on the History of Philosophy 1825-6*, 3 volumes, trans., ed. Robert F. Brown, Oxford: Oxford University Press, 2009.
LLO	*Lectures on Logic*, trans. C. Butler. Bloomington, IN: Indiana University Press, 2008.
LMJ	*The Jena System 1804-1805: Logic and Metaphysics*, trans. J.W. Burbidge and G. Di Giovanni. Kingston and Montreal: McGill-Queen's, 1986.
LPG	*Lectures on the Proofs of the Existence of God*, trans. P.C. Hodgson. Oxford: Oxford University Press, 2011.
LPR	*Lectures on the Philosophy of Religion*, trans. by P.C. Hodgson. Oxford: Oxford University Press, 2006-2008.
LPS	*Lectures on the Philosophy of Spirit 1827-28*, ed. R. R. Williams, Oxford: Oxford University Press, 2007.
LPWH	*Lectures on the Philosophy of World History. Introduction: Reason in History*, trans. H.B. Nisbet. Cambridge: Cambridge University Press, 1975.
OPR	*Outlines of the Philosophy of Right*, trans. T. M. Knox. Oxford: Oxford University Press, 2008.
PS	*The Phenomenology of Spirit*, trans. A. V. Miller. Oxford: Oxford University Press, 1977.
PW	*Political Writings*, ed. L. Dickey and H.B. Nisbet, Cambridge: Cambridge University Press, 1999.
RR	'Report of Rosencrantz' in *Hegel's System of Ethical Life and First Philosophy of Spirit*, ed. and trans. H. S. Harris and T. M. Knox. Albany, NY: State University of New York Press, 1979.
SL	*Science of Logic*, trans. G. di Giovanni. Cambridge: Cambridge University Press, 2010.

German editions of Hegel's work

Briefe	*Briefe von und an Hegel*, 5 volumes, hrsg. J. Hoffmeister und Fr. Nicolin, Hamburg: F. Meiner, 1969-1981.
Hotho [1823]	*Vorlesungen über die Philosophie der Kunst*, hrsg. A. Gethmann-Siefert, Hamburg: F. Meiner, 1998.
GW	*Gesammelte Werke*, hrsg. im Auftrag der Deutschen Forschungsgemeinschaft, Hamburg: F. Meiner, 1968–

Kehler   *Philosophie der Kunst oder Ästhetik* nach Hegel. Im Sommer 1826.
[1826]   Mitschrift Fr.C.H.V. von Kehler, hrsg. A. Gethmann-Siefert und B. Collenberg-Plotnikov, München: W. Fink, 2004.
TWA   *Werke in zwanzig Bänden. Theorie Werkausgabe, hrsg. E. Moldenhauer und K.M. Michel, Frankfurt a.M.: Suhrkamp, 1970.*
VPR I   *Vorlesungen über die Philosophie der Religion. Teil I: Der Begriff der Religion*, hrsg. W. Jaeschke, Hamburg: F. Meiner, 1983.
VPR III *Vorlesungen über die Philosophie der Religion. Teil III: Die vollendete Religion*, hrsg. W. Jaeschke, Hamburg: F. Meiner, 1984.
VGP I   *Vorlesungen über die Geschichte der Philosophie. Teil I: Einleitung, Orientalische Philosophie*, hrsg. P. Garniron und W. Jaeschke, Hamburg: F. Meiner 1993.
VGP IV   *Vorlesungen über die Geschichte der Philosophie. Teil IV: Philosophie des Mittelalters und der neueren Zeit*, hrsg. P. Garniron und W. Jaeschke, Hamburg: F. Meiner 1986.

Speculation and Hermeneutics of Effectual Reality

Maurizio Pagano and Hager Weslati

In this Introduction, we aim to present the intellectual currents and critical perspectives underpinning the contributions to this volume; these are broadly framed with the notions of effectual reality, speculation and hermeneutics in approaches to the *Logic* and its realizations. These notions, which carry a 'foreign' resonance that some readers may not be familiar with in Anglo-American literature on Hegel or in Hegel's own work in English translation, are primarily, but not exclusively, in conversation with Hegel studies in Italy. We first clarify these intellectual links and conceptual threads, successively, in the first two parts of the Introduction. In the final section, we present an outline of the structure and contents of the book, highlighting the intersections and overlaps between the various chapters.

The inner rationality of the actual – its absence from, or coincidence with, actuality – is a prominent theme in critical interpretations of Hegel's philosophy. By contrast, the emphasis on the systematic function and pivotal role of Hegel's science of logic through the prism of the hermeneutic tradition is more concerned with the actual realizations of the concept in and as reality.

The focus of this book is Hegel's logic and its relation to the other parts of his mature system, which provides the speculative interpretation of reality. As the first science of the system, the logic becomes concrete only in the *Realphilosophie* where the fundamental structure of thought is confronted with effectual reality, considered in the manifold variety of experience. This interconnection of the logical-universal dimension with the hermeneutical dimension is interpreted in this volume as the core of Hegel's philosophical enterprise.

Wirklichkeit, one of the most pivotal concepts of Hegel's philosophy, is usually translated in English as 'actuality'; in Italian, it is usually translated as *realtà effettuale*, which could be rendered into English as 'effectual reality' – a translation that is closer to the original German. *Wirklichkeit* is 'effectual' reality insofar as it is the idea made actual or – precisely –'effectual' in the world. *Wirklichkeit* is 'reality in motion', that is, reality realizing itself, accomplishing itself and becoming actual.

The notion of effectual reality is omnipresent in the history of Hegelianism in Italian thought. While Hegel studies in other linguistic contexts often privilege either pure logic or its applications in the realm of objective or (more rarely) absolute spirit, the propensity to think the logic in conjunction with its realizations is a peculiar and distinctive feature of Italian interpretations of Hegel. As some readers may find this contention surprising, it is, therefore, useful to briefly consider the evolution and major articulation of Hegel studies in Italy in parallel with four phases that marked the reception of Hegel between the early decades following his death and the bicentenary of his birth in 1970 down to the present.

Italian Hegel studies

The first phase in the critical reception of Hegel, which spans from the time that immediately followed his death to the early twentieth century, mostly focused on the logic-systematic aspect of his thought. The debate among his disciples, which led to the generation of three factions – 'right', 'centre' and 'left' Hegelians (as testified by David Friedrich Strauß in 1837) – was centred on the overall meaning of the system. Readings were divided between interpretation of the system as reconciliation with reality and its consideration as a springboard for the transformation of such reality. Outside the 'Hegelian School', critical commentaries on Hegel's philosophy were notably concerned with the logic and the question of the beginning (*Anfang*).

The publication of an edited collection of Hegel's early writings by one of Wilhelm Dilthey's students, Hermann Nohl, alongside Dilthey's (1905) own work, arguably inaugurated a new phase in the history of the reception of Hegel's philosophy. Critical attention shifted from the overall meaning of the system to the journey of its maturation. The question of the decisive sources of the young Hegel's philosophical formation – whether they were to be retrieved in the Enlightenment or in the Romantic movement – and of the interests, whether religious or political, which guided his maturation, now became a subject of investigation. This phase, which came to be known as *Hegel-Renaissance*, marked the history of Hegelian scholarship in Germany, France and Italy, but had little impact on its Anglo-American counterpart.

Towards the mid-twentieth century, the approach that favoured Hegel's early writings weakened, and a new phase characterized by a renewed interest in Hegel's overall work began. The work undertaken in the second phase had, however, borne its fruits, and the attention towards the problematic aspects of experience facilitated the encounter with Hegel's philosophy in the context of existentialism and Marxism. The works by Lukács on the young Hegel, by Bloch on the subject/object relation, by Marcuse on reason and revolution, as well as Adorno's studies on the dialectic, all confirm the importance of the relation between Hegel and Marx along a line that, conversely, is contested in Italy by Della Volpe. The common presupposition of all these readings, which is almost taken for granted, is the consideration of Hegel's thought as having an entirely, or at least fundamentally, historical character. A different approach to Hegel emerged from Heidegger's reflection on the Hegelian concept of time and history, and his emphasis on the ontological dimension of Hegel's thought. In this vein, Gadamer was an important mediator of the third phase in Hegel's reception in and outside Italy. Gadamer turned back to Hegel's reflection on the historical experience, but opposed the idea of a closed system; at the same time, however, Gadamer emphasized the importance of the logic and, in particular, its relation to the logical instinct of language and its bond with Plato's dialogical model. With Gadamer's work, therefore, the relation of Hegel's thought to hermeneutics is explicitly thematized.

The bicentenary of Hegel's birth in 1970 led to a flurry of publications, inaugurating the most recent and most diverse phase in Hegel studies. Scholarly interest has now shifted to all aspects relevant to the making of the Hegelian system, from a more precise reconstruction of the so-called Jena period (Pöggeler, Henrich) and the re-evaluation of the philosophy of nature to his studies on the philosophy of right and history, as well as to those on the realms of absolute spirit. The critical edition of Hegel's works by the *Hegel-Archiv* and the publication, inspired by more accurate philological principles, of the *Nachschriften* of the lectures were a decisive contribution to the improvement and deepening of research towards a better understanding of the Hegelian system.

In our time, marked by globalization, by increasing inequalities and by ever-emerging conflicts, but also by an intense experience of cultural pluralism, the interest for an in-depth reflection on the structure of reality is growing. In this context, the most cherished source of inspiration seems to be (together, perhaps, with the contributions offered by the phenomenological school in general and by Husserl in particular) precisely Hegel's logical and speculative thought.

The Italian reception of Hegel offered its most significant contributions in the first and the last of the four phases mentioned above. In the nineteenth century, Hegel's legacy was developed, in a political progressive way, by a group of Hegelian scholars from Naples. The most important exponent of this group was Bertrardo Spaventa. In one of his writings (1864), Spaventa focused on the question of 'the beginning' (*cominciamento*), dealing with Trendelenburg's critique and with the works of German Hegelians such as Werder and Fischer. To make the path of logic coherent and sustainable, Spaventa argued, it was necessary to depart from the role of the subject, i.e. the act of thinking, which, alone, could explain the dialectical movement. With this move, Spaventa paved the way for Italian neo-idealism and anticipated the more radical solution advanced by Gentile.

In a general sense, and in their origin, Hegel studies in Italy were not immune from the divisive and extreme polarizations of left and right political agendas, polarizations which have marked Hegel's reception in virtually all linguistic and cultural contexts. As di Giovanni notes in his introduction to the most recent translation of *Science of Logic*, 'Benedetto Croce used [Hegel's Logic] in his defense of Italian political liberalism, and Giovanni Gentile drew upon it in defense of Italian fascism' (SL, iv).

In the thought of Giovanni Gentile, the 'reform' of the Hegelian dialectic was also the advancement of a new philosophy, *actual idealism* (*attualismo* in Italian), which intended to draw, in a radical and ultimate way, all the consequences from the development of modern thought on the subject's victorious opposition to the objective character of ancient thought. The movement of logic, Gentile argued, can be understood only if it is entirely traced back to the act of thinking, which resolves in itself every 'given'. Thus, Gentile produced a 'philosophy of absolute immanence' (Gentile 1913).

The philosophy of Benedetto Croce moved in a reverse direction. Croce stressed the need to affirm the autonomy of the intermediate moments of the system as an antidote to the monistic and hierarchical character of Hegel's philosophy. In that vein, Croce argued for the primacy of the relation of the distincts [*nesso dei distinti*] over the dialectic of opposites [*dialettica degli opposti*]. Croce's work was more attentive to the relation of the different spheres (art and philosophy, economics and ethics) where the life of spirit flows. This reading finds expression in the title of Croce's 1907 work, *What Is Living and What Is Dead of the Philosophy of Hegel*. In his later work, Croce identified in 'vitality' [*vitalità*] the source of the dialectic and of the distinct forms it takes (Croce 1952). Italian neo-idealism is also the cultural context in which the thought of Antonio Gramsci emerged. Gramsci was, however, rather sceptical about Croce's and Gentile's philosophical reforms, contending that both the latter and the former had made Hegel more abstract by overlooking the more realist and historicist part of his thought. It is with this 'more concrete' Hegel in mind that Gramsci presented 'the philosophy of praxis [as] a reform and a development of Hegelianism' (Gramsci 1971: 404).

In the context of the second phase of Hegelian scholarship (the so-called *Hegel-Renaissance*), the Italian 'school' offers a less decisive, but yet valuable, contribution. The most significant work was Galvano Della Volpe's 1929 book *Hegel romantico e mistico* (*Hegel the Romantic and Mystic*). Della Volpe, who was still close to Gentile's idealism, analyses the mystic sources of the formative years of Hegel's philosophy in an original way. From this period, it is also worth mentioning Enrico De Negri's work. In addition to editing an Italian translation of the *Phenomenology*, De Negri developed an interpretation that privileged Hegel's early writings and the Jena period over Hegel's mature works.

After his turn to Marxism, Galvano Della Volpe was also the protagonist of the third phase of Hegel studies in Italy. This change of perspective was mostly reflected in Della Volpe's radical critique of idealism, considered guilty of a dogmatic monism. Contrasting Marx's scientific method, based on the notion of determined abstraction, with Hegel's speculative method, Della Volpe thus moved in the direction opposite to the mainstream interpretative line of Italian Marxism, which tended to read Marx in continuity with Hegel's historicism.

Since the early 1970s, Hegel studies in Italy have been at the forefront of the post-bicentenary phase, featuring significant contributions especially in relation to the logical-systematic aspect of Hegel's thought. Representative of this phase is Remo Bodei's 1975 work *Sistema e epoca in Hegel: La civetta e la talpa* (*System and Epoch in Hegel: The Owl and the Mole*). Against more traditional interpretative lines that were still influential in the 1970s, Bodei showed that Hegel, with his mature works, had not narrowed his interests, but rather widened and scrutinized them.

In the context of the scholarship devoted to Hegel's logic, Italy has produced, in the last few decades, very significant studies. It is worth mentioning those by Leo Lugarini and Franco Chiereghin on Hegel's formative years. As for Hegel's logic, both interpreters, despite their differences, have identified its fundamental character in the self-movement of thought, which develops out of itself and hence does not require anything from the subject but 'to sit back and watch [*stare a guardare*]' (Lugarini 2005; Chiereghin 2011). Among other relevant scholars, we can at least mention Claudio Cesa and Valerio Verra.

Nowadays, Hegel is by far one of the most studied philosophers in Italy, generating a wide spectrum of research specialism on Hegel's formative years, his relation to ancient philosophy, his philosophy of nature and the different realms of the spirit. In this context, the systematic aspect of Hegel's philosophy, reading the logic in light of interpretations of experience, has been the subject of increasing attention.

In the broader context of neo-Hegelianism and the hermeneutic tradition, Hegel has also been a significant influence in the development of original philosophical theories in Italy from the post–Second World War period onwards. Italian political philosopher Norberto Bobbio devoted a collection of essays to Hegel (Bobbio 1981). Luigi Pareyson, probably the most important Italian philosopher in the post-war era, developed his own hermeneutics as an alternative to, and a 'way out' from, Hegel's definitive conclusion to the history of philosophy (Pareyson 1971). Pareyson was the mentor of Gianni Vattimo who, through a consideration of being as event (*Ereignis*) inspired by Heidegger, later somehow verged on the Hegelian reflection on time and history. Emanuele Severino developed a radical confrontation with Hegel's thought of identity and becoming (Severino 1995). Moreover, Hegel is also present in the most recent and widely known expressions of Italian philosophy. Giorgio Agamben tackled Hegel especially in the context of his reflections on the relation between language and death and on the connection between these two fundamental questions with the theme of negativity (Agamben 2006). Even for a thinker who is quite far from any Hegelian inspiration such as Roberto Esposito, a 'confrontation' with Hegel, as 'the greatest thinker of the negative' (Esposito 2018: 53), is deemed inevitable. In his most recent book, Esposito revisits the Hegelian articulation of politics to negation to elucidate the outlines of an 'affirmative philosophy'.

Overall, and across the four phases outlined in this section, the propensity to think the logic in conjunction with its 'realizations' features in virtually all variants of Hegel studies in Italy. More specifically, the intertwining of speculation and hermeneutics in the 'philosophical untranslatable' *realtà effettuale* (effectual reality) is perhaps one of the prominent aspects of this tradition, which we propose to explore in the next section.

Speculation and hermeneutics

In order to really understand the relation between logic and interpretation of reality, it is first necessary to address the notion of speculation, which for Hegel expresses the fundamental character of philosophy.

In medieval philosophy, *speculation*, as suggested in its Latin etymology *speculum* ('mirror'), considered the world as the reflecting mirror of divine order. Modern thought distanced itself from this medieval conception. In the *Critique of Pure Reason*, Kant writes that a 'theoretical cognition is speculative if it pertains to an object or concepts of an object to which one cannot attain in any experience' (A634/B662). Hegel is definitely opposed to the Kantian conception of speculation, without, however, recovering its medieval theological overtones.

It is possible to distinguish, in Hegel's philosophy, between two different uses of the term 'speculative' – uses that are, however, strictly interconnected. In a first sense, only logic is properly speculative, insofar as it draws from the dimension of pure thought (*OPR*, 32). In a second sense, however, not just logic but philosophy as a whole is speculative, insofar as it comprehends experience in its structural connection with the logical dimension.

Hegel clarifies the proper sense of the speculative in §82 of the *Encyclopaedia*. The speculative moment is that in which the oppositions generated by the understanding are sublated in a superior unity, but this unity is first of all unity with experience (*Erfahrung*) and with actuality, or effectual reality (*Wirklichkeit*) (*TWA* 8, 177).

In his Remark on 'The Sublation of Becoming', Hegel notes that 'for speculative thought, it is gratifying to find words that have in themselves a speculative meaning' (*SL*, R, 81–82). In contrast with the Latin *tollere*, the German *aufheben*, Hegel observes, retains in the notion of sublation the double meaning, on the one hand, of 'to keep', 'to preserve', and on the other hand, 'to cause to cease' and 'to put an end to'. This remark, which Hegel prepared for the second edition of the *Science of Logic*, is believed to be the philosopher's last word. For Nancy ([1973] 2001), Hegel's Remark on the speculative meaning of sublation denotes the 'restlessness' of the philosophical discourse, as well as its ability, after Hegel, to open language to the determinations of the concept.

The distinction between abstract, dialectical and speculative thinking is as important as thinking abstractly and dialectically in order to think speculatively. There are, however, numerous instances of contemporary philosophical projects where thinking dialectically and even using and applying the dialectic does not amount to thinking speculatively (Rose 1993). The seemingly oppressive dictate of speculative philosophy as that which forcefully brings within its fold other forms of thought, both 'keeping' and 'putting an end to' the abstract and dialectical, is indicative of the negative associations of the speculative. In this vein, Whitehead noted that speculation in philosophy has something to do with the inability of any philosophical enterprise to put an end to interpretation. Whitehead's cautionary words that speculation in philosophy should not exhaust everything in the world, nor aspire to being a theory of everything, are not antithetical to the spirit of speculative philosophy as described in Hegel's last words. These and other nuances of the Hegelian speculative are lost in the contemporary distinction between the linguistic turn and the speculative turn. Articulating concerns about thought's ability to 'think beyond itself' (Meillassoux 2008: 36), the linguistic and the speculative are not considered to be antithetical or mutually exclusive in the speculative hermeneutics of Italian Hegelianism.

The speculative is neither subjective nor objective; it is neither a totality conceived in definitive terms, and thus completely pacified in itself, nor the knowledge of something that goes beyond experience and that therefore can only be referred to as 'purely objective', or as the thing in itself. Following Hegel, the speculative consists in keeping together the unity and, at the same time, the distinction of subjective and objective. It, therefore, pertains to thinking the unity of thought and reality, of subject and object, *together* with their difference. To think speculatively is, in other words, to think the *Wirklichkeit*; it is to think the logic and its realizations – or, which is the same, to think the relation of the logic to the interpretations of reality. Therefore, at the core of Hegel's thought lies this fundamental idea of the tension inherent to the unity of thought and reality.

The guiding inspiration of the present volume, partly rooted in the relation between the logical-universal dimension and the concrete-hermeneutical dimension of Hegel's thought, is, admittedly, a hermeneutical reading. However, this does not amount to a hidden agenda that seeks to confine critical readings of Hegel to the perspective of a specific contemporary philosophical approach; a similar intention would be reductive and inappropriate.

In the present volume, the term *hermeneutics* is taken in the broad sense of 'expression' as in the Greek term *hermeneia*, i.e., expression in the sense of referring to something else, namely to the presence of a unity that is, at the same time, a difference, a 'swerve' – but a swerve that *constitutes* that unity rather than *denying* it.

What is of interest here is precisely the structural tension between logic and experience, the dynamic unity of identity and difference between these two poles. Interestingly, Gramsci defined and reflected on 'effectual reality' (*la realtà effettuale*) in very similar terms: as 'reality in motion, a relation of forces in continuous shifts of equilibrium'. Articulating this dynamic in the concrete sphere of political action, Gramsci explains:

> When applying one's will to the creation of a new equilibrium among really existing and active forces – basing oneself on the force with a progressive thrust in order to make it prevail – one is always moving on the stream of effectual reality, but for the purpose of mastering it and superseding it. (Gramsci 2007: 283)

In light of this tension, it is possible to provide a dynamic and vital reading of Hegel's thought in contrast with interpretations that present it as a closed and definitive system or the ones that relegate Hegel to the narrow confines of perspectivism.

In the conclusion to his lecture on speculative philosophy, Whitehead notes that in the same way speculation can be empowering and enabling, it can also turn into a hindrance, and even an affliction, calling for the need to 'balance […] speculative boldness […] by complete humility before logic, and before fact' (1978: 17). To many contemporary readers, Whitehead's reference to logic and facts may ring hollow, especially on the heels of successive recent assaults on facts in the so-called post-truth societies.

Outside the sphere of philosophy, here understood in the narrow disciplinary sense of the term, the engagement to think speculatively speaks to the alarming rise of radical polarization on a global scale: in political affiliation, in social and economic conditions, even in lifestyles and in numerous other spheres of life. And so in our time, it is the rise of the 'fake' and the 'deep fake' that we are witnessing, but not the reduction of error or the authority of logic and facts. There is, therefore, perhaps a renewed sense of urgency in the need to think abstractly in order to think dialectically and to think dialectically in order to think speculatively.

Structure and contents of the book

The majority of the contributions presented in this volume, by established and emerging authors, are informed by the intersection of speculation with the hermeneutic of effectual reality, which is prominent in the Italian tradition, and here shared by scholars belonging to many different linguistic traditions. The fourteen chapters of the book are thematically organized around three major strands. These are outlined below in the order of their appearance in the book.

I.

In the first three chapters, Ficara, Dottori and De Cesaris, respectively speaking from a 'soft' analytic, hermeneutic and continental perspective, depart from the *Science of Logic* and the dynamic elements in Hegel's logical forms to highlight a set of questions arising from their passage to essence and the concept.

Ficara presents five theses on the role of Hegel's logical forms in 'empowering' the principles of formal logic. The author invites a more discerning reading of Hegel's 'scornful' evocation of formal logic, which she interprets as a denunciation of its misuse in the disciplinary practice of logic in his time, rather than a definitive pronouncement on the incommensurability of formal logic as such with the Hegelian philosophical project.

By bringing to the fore the Aristotelian, Platonic and Kantian etymological layers stowed away in the logical moments of *positing* and *presupposing*, Dottori examines the passage to essence and the elusive articulation between metaphysics and logic, and the double-moment of their *turning*, rather than returning, in/to one another.

This line of thought is further resumed in the third chapter through the prism of 'modality' and its threefold deployment as 'singularity, objectivity and contingency' in the passage of essence to the concept. Teasing out the multilayered meanings of actuality and effectuality in the sections dedicated to the *Wirklichkeit* in the *Logic* and parts of the *Encyclopaedia*, De Cesaris argues that this is the place where reflexion finally overcomes the typical duality of the logic of essence.

II.

The five chapters placed in the middle part of the volume are concerned with the realization of different logical categories in Hegel's *real philosophy*. Consciousness, self-consciousness, immediacy and habit are explored in relation to the subjective spirit, while nineteenth- and twentieth-century variants of positivism and practical philosophy, constitutional and legal theories, and the political economy of work and need are revisited in light of the objective spirit.

Frilli relies on the *Logic* to examine the 'obscure' and 'tautological' passage of self-consciousness from the negative self-relation of life to the 'I' as an embodied activity of a living organism. The author underscores the tension between logic and reality in the vicious circle of the 'I', as realization of the identity of thought and the concept, and its return to difference in the guise of an unsurpassable Fichtian dualism.

McStravick explores the notions of habituation and habit as second nature, while highlighting their respective implications as materiality for the subject and as plasticity for spirit. McStravick follows the 'spiral structure' of spirit to deepen the question of immediacy *of* and *for* thought as they mediate one another. Reflecting on the relation of being and thought, the author contends that the correspondence of habit and immediacy is the condition of the 'onto-gnoseological' and the 'historico-epistemological' speculative dynamic that structures Hegel's philosophy.

Reading the opening sections of the *Logic of the Concept* as the subtext of Hegel's science of right, Kalatzis notes that from the standpoint of philosophical method, the latter is informed by the same presupposed necessity, which is at work in the former. The author goes back and forth between the two sciences, of logic and right, taking his bearings from Hegel's logical articulations of what is at stake in passages from, to and between the universal, the particular and the singular.

Bienenstock argues that the turn to different 'sciences' (*Wissenschaften*) in the three parts of Hegel's mature system – science of logic, philosophy of nature, philosophy of spirit – 'subverts' the traditional distinction between theory and practice. Revisiting Nicolai Hartmann's description of the Hegelian objective spirit as a 'discovery' in the proper sense of the term, the author shows what is at stake in a condition that may sound familiar to our contemporary ears, namely the fact that even though norms are 'in place' and objectively real, they do not 'motivate' us.

Drawing on Hegel's critique of the limited logic of the understanding, Jones underscores the primacy of 'the work of others' over the notion of 'working for oneself' or 'for others'. Situating those original elements of Hegel's political economy in his 'system of needs', the author draws important conclusions about the relevance of Hegel's science of logic and objective spirit to current debates on the future of work.

III.

The last six chapters are broadly concerned with the contentious subject of speculative theology from the standpoint of Hegel's *Logic* and the system as a whole. Kallio, Redding, Morani, Pagano, Papoulias and Weslati formulate different arguments on the subject, alternating the attribution of the point of view of the *Logic* and its realizations between the 'divine' and the 'anthropos', person and personality, the image and its disappearance, discourse and silence. Read together, the contributions situated in the third part of the volume provocatively speak to one another, inviting the reader to decide whether the notion of 'God's thinking before the creation of the world' evoked in the opening section of the *Logic* is to be taken literally or figuratively.

Kallio underscores the tension between different textual fragments on personality in Hegel's system, leaning towards their resolution 'in the path of God' towards concrete self-consciousness and the struggle of humans for universality.

Resuming this solution within the horizon of critical attempts to rid Hegel's speculative philosophy from its theologico-metaphysical elements, Redding departs from Longuenesse's treatment of the Hegel–Kant relation, which he labels as a 'qualified post-Kantian interpretation of Hegel', as opposed to a more 'conceptual realist' interpretation. Both interpretations, however, in Redding's view, share the same fear of theologizing Hegel. Redding forcefully demonstrates that we should not fear for the Kantian Copernican revolution and its philosophical achievement when engaging with Hegel's attempt to reconcile our human 'point of view' with 'the knowledge of God'.

Arguing for a god 'of the underworld, corporeality and the unconscious', Morani contests two extreme interpretations of the *Logic*: those in favour of the 'removal' of the divine from 'the created finite world' and those that relegate religion to 'feeling' and philosophy to 'thought'.

Pagano analyses the relation between the logical and hermeneutical dimensions in Hegel's philosophy of religion, showing that in all of his lecture series on the topic, Hegel's starting point is the spiritual crisis of his time, which is marked by the conflict between the autonomy of the rational subject and the reasons of the infinite content, that is, God. Contending that the point is to assume religion in all its aspects, to provide an interpretation of the religious experience and to demonstrate its truth, Pagano argues that the logic is nourished with hermeneutics, which allows the essential core of the spiritual experience to take shape.

Highlighting the ontological purport of Hegel's treatment of the image, Papoulias evokes its relevance to understanding the rhetorical nuances in Hegel's use of metaphor, simile and symbolism in his philosophical writings. Conceptualized as activity and as 'a frame' for action, rather than as object or permanent being, the Hegelian image is grasped in its appearance and disappearance, in its 'becoming diaphanous' and in its ability to 'acquire transparency that allows the gaze to pass through'.

In the final chapter of the book, Weslati argues that Kojève's lectures on Hegel were primarily articulated from the standpoint of the *Logic* rather than the *Phenomenology of Spirit*. In contrast with readings for or against the theologico-metaphysical elements in Hegel, Kojève considered the 'silence of logic' as a bigger 'threat' not only for a continued and productive engagement with Hegel but for philosophy in general.

At the end of this Introduction, we reiterate the guiding principles that enabled the collaborative work that went into the making of this book. The lived and the situated cannot be speculative in fossilized identity and coercive homogeneity; it is conceivable only *in relation* to the other and to its othered self in difference, in becoming and in discourse. The history (and future) of philosophical thought is inextricably intertwined with the concept of community, of intellectual exchange predicated on the richness of the 'untranslatable' as that which may have been articulated in one language, but whose vitality is resumed and invigorated in translation (Cassin 2015). The contributions assembled in the present volume, although presented in English, perform philosophical thinking, and the thinking activity in general, in many languages (Italian, German, Finnish, French, Greek, Arabic) and *speak from* different parts of the world. The deliberate editorial choice to retain the *foreign* resonance of the volume's individual chapters reflects the (Hegelian) speculative as *de*centring and *orient*ation, overcoming and preservation.

References

Agamben, G. (2006), *Language and Death: The Place of Negativity*, trans. Karen E. Pinkus with Michael Hardt, Minneapolis: University of Minnesota Press.

Bobbio, N. (1981), *Studi hegeliani: Diritto, società civile, stato*, Turin: Einaudi.

Bodei, R. (1975), *Sistema ed epoca in Hegel: La civetta e la talpa*; 2nd augmented edition 2014, *La civetta e la talpa: Sistema ed epoca in Hegel*, Bologna: Il Mulino.

Cassin, B., ed. (2015), *Dictionary of Untranslatables: A Philosophical Lexicon*, trans. E. Apter, J. Lezra, and M. Wood, Princeton and Oxford: Princeton University Press.

Chiereghin, F. (2011), *Rileggere la* Scienza della logica *di Hegel*, Rome: Carocci.

Croce, B. (1907), *Ciò che è vivo e ciò che è morto nella filosofia di Hegel*, Bari: Laterza; trans. D. Ainslie, *What Is Living and What Is Dead of the Philosophy of Hegel*, London: Macmillan and Co., 1915.

Croce, B. (1952), *Indagini su Hegel e schiarimenti filosofici*, Bari: Laterza.
Della Volpe, G. (1929), *Hegel romantico e mistico*, Florence: Le Monnier.
Dilthey, W. [1905] (1921), 'Die Jugendgeschichte Hegels und andere Abhandlungen zur Geschichte des Deutschen Idealismus', in Id., *Gesammelte Schriften*, vol. IV, 1914–2006, H. Nohl (ed.), Göttingen: Vandenhoeck & Ruprecht.
Esposito, R. (2018), *Politica e negazione: Per una filosofia affermativa*, Turin: Einaudi.
Gentile, G. (1913), *La riforma della dialettica hegeliana*, Milan: Principato.
Gramsci, A. (1971), *Selections from the Prison Notebooks*, trans. Q. Hoare and G. N. Smith, New York: International Publishers.
Gramsci, A. (2007), *Prison Notebooks, Volume III*, New York: Columbia University Press.
Lugarini, L. (2005), *Orizzonti hegeliani di comprensione dell'essere: Rileggendo la* Scienza della logica, Milan: Guerini.
Meillassoux, Q. (2008), *After Finitude*, trans. Ray Brassier, London: Continuum.
Nancy, J.-L. (2001), *The Speculative Remark (One of Hegel's Bons Mots)*, trans. Céline Surprenant, Stanford, California: Stanford University Press.
Pareyson, L. (1971), *Verità e interpretazione*, Milan: Mursia; trans. R. Valgenti, *Truth and Interpretation*, Albany, NY: State University of New York Press, 2013.
Rose, G. (1993), 'From Speculative to Dialectical Thinking – Hegel and Adorno', in *Judaism and Modernity*, 53–63, Oxford: Blackwell.
Severino, E. (1995), *Tautótes*, Milan: Adelphi.
Spaventa, B. (1864), 'Le prime categorie della logica di Hegel', in F. Valagussa (ed.), *Opere*, 327–397, Milan: Bompiani.
Whitehead, A. N. (1978), *Process and Reality*, ed. David Ray Griffin and Donald W. Sherburne, New York: The Free Press.

1

Empowering Forms: Hegel's Conception of 'Form' and 'Formal'

Elena Ficara

The meaning of 'form' and 'formal' is the subject matter of many debates in the history of logic and in contemporary philosophical logic.[1] Usually, Hegel's view is not considered in these debates. In what follows, I present five theses about logical forms and formal logic stressed by Hegel in the Preface to the second edition of the *Science of Logic* and ask about their role within the history and philosophy of logic.

Many authors stress that Hegel's attitude towards formal or common logic is irretrievably critical (Ritter et al. 1971ff., vol. 5: 358; Peckhaus 1997: 120). Others, such as Krohn (1972: 57), highlight that Hegel's standpoint is 'ambivalent', since Hegel not only criticized formal (intellectual) logic but also considered it as a fundamental endeavour. By contrast, I highlight that the critical views that are usually traced back to Hegel are not Hegel's own views, but rather common theses Hegel recalls in order to present the diffused scorn of logic typical of the philosophy of his times, a scorn that Hegel himself does not share at all. Hegel defines it 'barbaric' (*TWA* VI, 375).[2] Formal, intellectual logic is not per se despicable for Hegel.[3] Its content are the forms of truth, forms that are at the very basis of our life, thought and action:

> The several forms of syllogism constantly exert influence on our knowledge. If any one, when awaking on a winter morning, hears the creaking of the carriages on the street, and is thus led to conclude that it has frozen hard in the night, he has gone through a syllogistic operation – an operation which is every day repeated under the greatest variety of complications. (*EL*, §183, 166)

This chapter is part of a project, generously supported by the Alexander von Humboldt Foundation.

Hegel even recalls that being aware about the forms we always use is important, for many reasons, first of all for pedagogic reasons, for educating human beings to the evaluation of arguments and to critical thought. In the *Subjective Logic*, he writes:

> But without going into this aspect of the matter which concerns the education [...] and, strictly speaking, pedagogics, it must be admitted that the study of the modes and laws of reason must in its own self be of the greatest interest – of an interest at least not inferior to an acquaintance with the laws of nature. (*SL*, 605)

What Hegel sharply criticizes is, by contrast, the way in which the subject of formal logic (the syllogistic forms) is dealt with in the handbooks of his times:

> The most merited and most important aspect of the disfavor into which syllogistic doctrine has fallen is that this doctrine is a *concept-less* occupation with a subject matter whose sole content is the *concept* itself. (*SL*, 607)

It is an arid, 'concept-less' treatment – the syllogistic forms *are* the conceptual realm and are presented without any trace of conceptual thought. For this reason, Hegel states that the forms are reduced to an 'ossified material', and logic is a 'ruined building'. In what follows, I examine these Hegelian views in more detail.[4]

Five theses on logical forms

Logical forms are dynamic

In the Preface to the second edition of the *Science of Logic*, Hegel writes that the forms produced by Aristotelian and earlier logic 'must be regarded as an extremely important source [of the *Science of Logic*], indeed as a necessary condition and as a presupposition to be gratefully acknowledged' (*SL*, 12). In this respect, the task of Hegel's *Wissenschaft der Logik* is what I call an operation of 'empowering' the forms traditionally studied by logic and metaphysics (the realm of thought, *das Logische*) 'to exhibit the realm of thought philosophically, that is, in its own immanent activity or what is the same, in its necessary development' (*SL*, 12). This is the idea of *the dynamic nature of forms or, what amounts to the same, of the 'dynamics' introduced into the forms (fixed in Aristotle and in the handbooks of Hegel's times) by philosophy*, i.e. by a reflexive and critical consideration about them.

In the *Lectures on the History of Philosophy*, when Hegel discusses Aristotle's view about the syllogism, this idea about the necessity of introducing dynamicity into the forms is clarified. Here Hegel not only praises Aristotle but also emphasizes that the syllogistic forms in Aristotle are just enumerated and fixed without any reflection about their relations to each other and without any explanation of what they are and that to which they are to be referred. They have lost their use. Thus Hegel also writes:

> The form of an inference, as also its content, may be absolutely correct, and yet the conclusion arrived at may have no truth, because this form as such has no truth of its own, but from this point of view these forms have never been considered. (*LHP* II, 222; *TWA* XIX, 240)[5]

So one could say that introducing a consideration about the question 'Are the syllogistic forms true?' within the Aristotelian logic of Hegel's times is, for Hegel, a way of rendering forms dynamic, so as to make them apt to grasp truth. The second thesis is coherent to this insight.

Logical forms are expression of the essence of things

In the Introduction to the *Science of Logic*, Hegel remarks that *the forms of thought are the expression of the peculiar essence and substance of individual things*. Logic assumes, rightly, that 'the determinations contained in definitions [...] are determinations of the object, constituting its innermost essence and its very own nature' (*SL*, 30) and that

> if from given determinations others are inferred, [...] what is inferred is not something external and alien to the object, but rather that it belongs to the object itself, that to the thought there corresponds being. (*SL*, 30)

This idea is further articulated in the third thesis.

Logical forms have a predicative nature

In the Preface to the *Science of Logic*, second edition, Hegel writes:

> If the nature, the peculiar essence, that which is genuinely permanent and substantial in the complexity and contingency of appearance and fleeting manifestation, is *the concept of the thing*, the *immanent universal*, and [if] each human individual though infinitely singular has the most fundamental of all his singularities in being a man, exactly like each individual animal has it in being an animal: if this is true, then it would be impossible to say what such an individual could still be if this foundation were removed, no matter how richly endowed the individual might be with other predicates, if, that is, this foundation can equally be called a predicate like the others. (*SL*, 16; my emphasis)

The passage addresses the view about the *conceptual (predicative) nature of logical forms*. Predicates stand for properties, such as 'being a man' or 'being an animal', the concept is the essential predicate and is for Hegel the very condition of expressing things and their singularity.[6]

Logical forms are forms of truth

Logical forms, insofar as they express both the essence of things and the concept that makes our knowledge of things possible, *have an alethic, i.e. truth-implying, nature*. That is, they are conditions of our grasping things and thinking truthfully. In the Preface to the second edition of the *Science of Logic*, Hegel points to the generalized 'scorn' of logic typical of his times. Everyday thought has

> so much lost its respect for the school which claims possession of such laws of truth [the law of identity and the law of contradiction] that it ridicules it and its laws and regards anyone as insufferable who can utter truths in accordance to such laws: the plant is – a plant, science is – science. (*SL*, 18)

Hegel also recalls a further reason of complaint. The inference rules

> quite as well serve impartially error and sophistry and […] however truth may be defined, they cannot serve higher, for example, religious truth […] they concern only correctness […] and not truth. (*SL*, 18)

Hegel's famous distinction between *Wahrheit* (truth properly speaking, higher philosophical or religious truth) and *Richtigkeit* (correctness) (*EI*, §172) is here connected to the problem of logic. What is important to focus on now is that philosophical (and religious) truth goes beyond the idea of correctness established by *Verstandeslogik*, i.e. a logic that does not critically reflect upon its forms. Such truth has different conditions and requires different forms.

The common understanding of 'formal' in the expression 'formal logic' is inaccurate

The connection between forms and truth introduces a *criticism of 'formal logic'* as it is usually intended. In the Introduction to the *Science of Logic*, Hegel criticizes the view of logic typical of his times. He writes:

> When logic is taken as the science of thinking in general, it is understood that this thinking constitutes the *mere form* of a cognition, that logic abstracts from all *content* and that the so called second *constituent* of a cognition, namely its *matter*, must come from elsewhere; and that since this matter is absolutely

independent of logic, this latter can provide only the formal conditions of true knowledge [original German wahrhafter Erkenntnis/original translation: genuine cognition] and cannot in its own self contain any real truth, nor even be the *pathway* to real truth because just that which is essential in truth, its content, lies outside logic. But [...] it is quite inept to say that logic abstracts from all *content*, that it teaches only the rules of thinking without any reference to what is thought or without being able to consider its nature. For as thinking and the rules of thinking are supposed to be the subject matter of logic, these directly constitute its peculiar content; in them, logic has that second constituent, a matter, about the nature of which it is concerned. (*SL*, 24)

Hegel criticizes here the formalistic conception of logic.[7] In particular, he discusses the inference from the claim that logic studies the most general forms of thought, obtained abstracting away from particular contents, to the theses that logic has no content and therefore 'cannot contain truth'. Some authors interpret these and similar passages as statements against formal logic[8] and infer from them that Hegel's logic is not a formal logic.[9] But this reading risks being misleading. What I suggest instead is that Hegel does not discuss the formal nature of logic, but rather the philosophy of logic in his times, i.e. the interpretation that postulates the 'abstract' (separate) nature of logical forms.[10] In other words, the theses considered above, i.e. the dynamic, ontological, conceptual and truth-implying conception of forms, introduce the last aspect, the criticism of the inference from 'logic is interested in the form of sentences and arguments' to 'forms have no content, and have nothing to do with truth, i.e. with the relation of thought to content'.

Logic, for Hegel, *is* formal in the sense of interested in the underlying structure of sentences and arguments, but this does not mean that logic does not have content (its content are the same forms) or that logic does not express real truth. Importantly, as soon as we admit that forms are logic's subject matter, the questions must be asked: 'Are these forms expression of reality? Are they true?'. If we question the validity of the forms in this way, we are fulfilling, for Hegel, two important desiderata: first, we are shaking (introducing dynamicity into) the logical building, and second, we are beginning to practise and conceive logic as the pathway to real truth. The 'living' nature of forms (of any kind of form) is the same skepsis we address to the forms and what makes the forms our guide to truth. Thus, what is wrong is not formal logic in itself, but rather the way in which philosophers may think about it: 'If logic is supposed to lack content, then the fault does not lie with [logic's] subject matter but solely *with the way in which this subject matter is conceived*' (*SL*, 28; my emphasis).

One hypothesis

There are now non-classical conceptions of logic that are particularly close to the Hegelian view of forms and the formality of logic. Hegel's critique of the incapability of traditional logic to convey truth anticipates relevant logic's critique of classical logic.[11] As we have seen, Hegel writes that 'the true cannot be found in these [Aristotelian logical] forms', that 'the form of an inference may be absolutely correct, and yet the conclusion arrived at may be untrue', and that this is the sign that 'this form as such has no truth of its own. But from this point of view' Hegel concludes 'these forms have never been considered' (*LHP* II, 222–223; *TWA* XIX, 240).

One could argue that now logical rules are being considered precisely from this point of view. In a more traditional perspective, that classically valid forms fail to express sound (i.e. true, relevant, fruitful, strong) arguments is simply taken to mean that logic is merely formal and has nothing to do with the content of thought. By contrast, in contemporary philosophical logic a more Hegelian point of view has come to prominence. According to it the inability of classical logical forms to convey sound arguments is the sign of a *failure* in classical logical forms, the source of a critical reflection on the same forms and of the need of revising or enlarging classical logic.[12]

Furthermore, Hegel's critique of formalisms is, as we have seen, connected to truth. Logic in a contemporary sense deals with truth (since validity is anyhow defined as truth-preservation), though not properly with the effective, realistic truth of our usual inquiries, but rather with the assumption of truth, as related to abstract domains, or to axioms, or to possible worlds. In this respect, Hegel's logic is not formal in the sense of being 'uninterested in the content', but rather in the sense that it aims at individuating the valid form of philosophical, conceptual reasoning. And this is a kind of 'formal' admitted by contemporary non-classical logics, such as relevant logics. However, Hegel's conception of logical forms also differs from the standard one in some important respects.[13]

Logical forms are generally intended to be linguistic structures that can be repeated and on whose basis we establish the validity of arguments (Sainsbury 2001: 44). For example, the arguments

'Berlin is in Germany and Berlin is in Europe, hence Berlin is in Europe'

and

'Giacomo loves Silvia and Silvia is a teacher, hence Silvia is a teacher'

and

'Rome is in Italy and today the sun shines, thus the sun shines today' have the same form: p and q, therefore q. The form is valid insofar as, for every substitution of the non logical terms 'p' and 'q', it conveys conclusions that cannot be false, given that the premises are true.

In the case of sentential forms, such as 'S is P' or 'for all x, x is P', we establish the truth or falsity of the sentence on the basis of the substitution of 'S' and 'P' or 'x' and 'P' (if S = cat and P = animal then we have a true sentence, if S = Donald Trump and P = Democratic candidate then we have a false sentence).

All this stated, two aspects concerning Hegel's view of logical forms mark its originality with respect to contemporary views. First, in a standard account the substitutions are given on the basis of domains (Tarski 1999: 115–143). In this conception, which goes back to Tarski, we fix the domain of entities that can take the place of 'p' and 'q' (or S and P) in our inferences and sentences and establish on that basis the truth and falsity of our sentences, and the validity or invalidity of our inferences. For Hegel the substitutions are given by the world and by the use and meaning of words in our natural or scientific language.

Second, for Hegel the form of sentences and inferences depends on the form of concepts. The guarantee of truth and validity is given by the conceptual content, and the conceptual content is given in the definition or conceptual determination. This means that the forms of inferences and sentences are to be rooted, according to Hegel, in the form of conceptual thought which, for Hegel, is the only adequate expression of truth.[14]

Notes

1. For an overview of current debates on the subject, see Dutilh Novaes (2011: 303–332). See also Mac Farlane (2000) and, from a historical point of view, Peckhaus (1997) and Gabriel (2008: 115–131). Dutilh Novaes (2011: 306) distinguishes between two basic meanings of the adjective 'formal' in the expression 'formal logic': formal as pertaining to forms and formal as pertaining to rules, whereby she identifies five declinations of the first meaning, all based on the insight that 'what is form, and formal, is what remains once matter is removed (abstracted from)' and that there are five basic meanings of 'matter' (as thing, subject matter, meaning, content, subclass of the terms of an argument). Cook (2009: 177) reduces the different meanings of 'formal' to two: 'formal' as 'pertaining to the structure of sentences or arguments' and 'symbolic'. Read (1995: 61) underlines that the use of 'formal' as synonym of 'symbolic', though common, is inappropriate. In what follows, I do not discuss the relationship of Hegel's notion of 'form' and 'formal' to 'symbolic'.
2. On Hegel's critique of the romantics' critique of intellectual, syllogistic logic, see Krohn (1972: 56).

3   For an analysis of the relation between Hegel and 'common' (or formal) logic, see Krohn (1972), Hanna (1986: 305–338), Nuzzo (1997), Nuzzo (2014: 257–273), Redding (2014: 281–301). Hanna claims that Hegel neither merely criticizes common logic nor denies its legitimacy. He rather 'preserves the entire edifice of common logic while still using the critique of the latter as a motivation for its own self-development towards a more comprehensive and radically new sense of logic. Many of the misunderstandings of Hegel's logic are based precisely on confusions concerning the equally critical and conservative character of Hegel's treatment of the common logic' (306). Hanna also remarks that Kant, by contrast, did not see the common logic as ontologically naïve and undeveloped, but rather as a well-grounded, necessary propaedeutic and foundation of his transcendental logic (307). What it means that Hegel's logic is science of the 'absolute form' is clarified by Nuzzo (1997: 50ff.). See also De Vos (1983 and 2006: 210). Nuzzo (1997: 50ff.) claims that Hegel rejects the idea of logic as abstract and formal discipline. If 'the logical' is conceived as form separated from every content, then forms are deprived of truth and formal logic is reduced to a logic of falsity and has no scientific value. In this context, I show that what Hegel criticizes is not the formal character of logic or the discipline 'formal logic', but rather the formalistic philosophies of logic of his times.

4   See for a detailed reconstruction of Hegel's standpoint on syllogistic forms Schick 2003: 85–100.

5   'Die Form eines Schlußes, so wie sein Inhalt, kann ganz richtig sein und doch sein Schlußsatz ohne Wahrheit, weil diese Form als solche für sich keine Wahrheit hat.' I have substituted 'the form of a conclusion' in the English translation with 'the form of an inference' because by *Schluß* Hegel means here, evidently, 'argument' or 'inference' and not the conclusion of an argument. For the conclusion of the argument he uses *Schlußsatz*.

6   In the third chapter of the present volume, De Cesaris presents a more detailed analysis on the role of singularity in Hegel's *Science of Logic*. For an analysis about the relationship between logic and singularity in Hegel's *Science of Logic*, see also De Cesaris (2016: 122–159).

7   In the *Subjective Logic*, Hegel traces this view back to Kant (SL, 523ff.). Litt (1961: 261) criticizes the formalistic approach in terms that are reminiscent of the Hegelian ones: 'Whether it is possible to separate form and matter in this way is not only a question that needs to be answered in a clear and objective manner; it is also and above all a *logical* question. If logic considers itself in these [formalistic] terms, then it makes the cardinal mistake to dispose once and for all of a question it should explicitly deal with.'

8   See, for example, Krohn (1972: 107) who interprets what Hegel says on *the theories on logic* of his times as statements on formal and Aristotelian logic.

9   According to Ritter et al. (1971ff. 5: 358), '[Hegel's *Wissenschaft der Logik*] radically rejects formal logic and substitutes it with a dialectic that is the product of

speculative metaphysics'. Butler (2012: 81) writes 'dialectical logic is not a formal system of axioms with rules of inference abstracted from any particular content'. However, he also states that Hegel's dialectic is 'applied formal logic about a particular content'. See also Mittelstraß (1980ff. 2: 57ff.).

10 In this respect, Nuzzo (1997: 52) remarks that Hegel argues against the notion of formality as abstractedness and proposes a more complex notion of formality linked to a dialectical view of 'form'. For Litt (1961: 269) formal traditional logic is concerned with thought's determination of objects; dialectical logic, by contrast, could be called a logic of thought's self-awareness (*die Logik des selbstbesinnlichen Denkens*).

11 For an overview on relevant logics from the point of view of the controversy on the Law of Non-Contradiction, see Berto 2007, Chapter 9.

12 In this spirit, Read (1995: 2) complains about 'a widespread but regrettable attitude towards logic, one of deference and uncritical veneration. It is based on a mistaken belief that since logic deals with necessities, with how things must be, with what must follow come what may, that in consequence there can be no questioning of its basic principles'. Berto (2007: 187) writes that 'the notion of relevance goes beyond the mere realm of pragmatics; it fully belongs to logic, and it can be supplied with a rigorously formal treatment'.

13 I do not discuss in this context the meaning of 'formal' as 'symbolic' and Hegel's critique of formalisms. See for a first account Ficara (2014: 59–65). On Hegel's critique of Leibniz' *calculus ratiocinator* and *lingua characteristica*, see Peckhaus (1997: 120ff.) as well as Kirn (1985: 40ff.).

14 See Käufer (2005: 259–280) on the role and meaning of concepts in twentieth-century logic. Merker (1996: 92) highlights that 'form' and 'concept' for Hegel overlap. Both are conceived in dynamic terms and refer to the activity of 'distinguishing what is identical and rendering identical what is different' (see also *Encyclopaedia* §314). Also chapter 3 in Stekeler-Weithofer (2005) examines the connection between concept and form in Hegel, with special reference to its Platonic origins. Hegel's view on the conceptual realm (*der Begriff*) implies for Stekeler-Weithofer (1992: 40) the idea of an interplay between syntax and semantics. Logical forms are for Hegel 'conceptual, i.e. syntacto-semantic forms'.

References

Berto, F. (2007), *How to Sell a Contradiction. The Logic and Metaphysics of Inconsistency*, London: College Publications.

Butler, C. (2012), *The Dialectical Method. A Treatise Hegel Never Wrote*, New York: Prometheus Books.

Cook, R. (2009), *A Dictionary of Philosophical Logic*, Edinburgh: Edinburgh University Press.
De Cesaris, A. (2016), 'Logica della singolarità. Genesi e struttura del singolare nella Scienza della logica di Hegel', *Annuario Filosofico* 32: 122–159.
De Vos, L. (1983), *Hegels Wissenschaft der Logik: Die absolute Idee. Einleitung und Kommentar*, Bonn: Bouvier.
De Vos, L. (2006), 'Form', in P. Cobben, P. Cruysberghs, P. Jonkers and L. De Vos (eds), *Hegel Lexikon*, 209–211, Darmstadt: Wissenschaftliche Buchgesellschaft.
Dutilh Novaes, C. (2011), 'The Different Ways in Which Logic Is (Said to Be) Formal', *History and Philosophy of Logic* 32 (4): 303–332.
Ficara, E. (2014), 'Hegel on the Mathematical Infinite', *Siegener Beiträge zur Geschichte und Philosophie der Mathematik* 4: 59–65.
Gabriel, G. (2008), 'Wie formal ist die formale Logik? Friedrich Adolf Trendelenburg und Gottlob Frege', in P. Bernhard and V. Peckhaus (eds), *Methodisches Denken im Kontext. Festschrift für Christian Thiel*, 115–131, Paderborn: Mentis.
Hanna, R. (1986), 'From an Ontological Point of View. Hegel's Critique of the Common Logic', *Review of Metaphysics* 40 (2): 305–338.
Käufer, S. (2005), 'Hegel to Frege: Concepts and Conceptual Content in Nineteenth-Century Logic', *History of Philosophy Quarterly* 22 (3): 259–280.
Kirn, M. (1985), *Der Computer und das Menschenbild der Philosophie. Leibniz' Monadologie und Hegels philosophisches System auf dem Prüfstand*, Stuttgart: Urachhaus.
Krohn, W. (1972), *Die formale Logik in Hegels 'Wissenschaft der Logik'. Untersuchungen zur Schlußlehre*, München: Hanser.
Litt, T. (1961), *Hegel. Versuch einer kritischen Erneuerung*, Heidelberg: Quelle & Meyer.
MacFarlane, J. (2000), '*What Does It Mean to Say That Logic Is Formal?*' PhD Dissertation: University of Pittsburgh.
Merker, N. (1996), 'Forma', in N. Merker, *Hegel. Dizionario delle idee*, 92, Roma: Editori Riuniti.
Mittelstraß, J., ed. (1980ff.), *Enzyklopädie Philosophie und Wissenschaftstheorie*, Mannheim/Wien/Zürich: B.I. Wissenschaftsverlag.
Nuzzo, A. (1997), 'La logica', in C. Cesa (ed), *Hegel*, 39–82, Roma Bari: Laterza.
Nuzzo, A. (2014), 'Dialektisch-spekulative Logik und Transzendentalphilosophie', in A. F. Koch, F. Schick, K. Vieweg and C. Wirsing (eds), *Hegel – 200 Jahre Wissenschaft der Logik*, 257–273, Hamburg: Meiner.
Peckhaus, V. (1997), *Logik, Mathesis universalis und allgemeine Wissenschaft. Leibniz und die Wiederentdeckung der formalen Logik im 19. Jahrhundert*, Berlin: Akademie Verlag.
Read, S. (1995), *Thinking about Logic*, Oxford: Oxford University Press.
Redding, P. (2014), 'The Role of Logic "Commonly So Called" in Hegel's *Science of Logic*', *British Journal for the History of Philosophy* 22 (2): 281–301.

Ritter, J., K. Gründer and G. Gabriel, eds. (1971ff.), *Historisches Wörterbuch der Philosophie*, Basel: Schwabe.

Sainsbury, M. (2001), *Logical Forms. An Introduction to Philosophical Logic*, Oxford: Blackwell (first edition 1991).

Schick, F. (2003), 'Begriff und Mangel des formellen Schliessens. Hegels Kritik des Verstandesschlusses', in A. F. Koch, A. Oberauer and K. Utz (ed.), *Der Begriff als die Wahrheit. Zum Anspruch der Hegelschen 'Subjektiven Logik'*, 85–100, Paderborn: Schöningh.

Stekeler-Weithofer, P. (1992), *Hegels Analytische Philosophie. Die Wissenschaft der Logik als kritische Theorie der Bedeutung*, Paderborn: Schöningh.

Stekeler-Weithofer, P. (2005), *Philosophie des Selbsbewusstseins. Hegels System als Formanalyse von Wissen und Autonomie*, Frankfurt a.M.: Suhrkamp.

Tarski, A. (1999), 'The Semantic Conception of Truth and the Foundations of Semantics', in S. Blackburn and K. Simmons (eds), *Truth*, 115–143, Oxford: Oxford University Press.

2

Essence as Reflection

Riccardo Dottori

The transition from being to essence

The *Science of Logic* is, as Hegel himself maintains, an ontological logic – namely it is metaphysics. It was Kant who turned metaphysics into logic, even though he 'gave to the logical determinations an essentially subjective significance out of fear of the object' (*SL*, 30; *GW* XXI, 35). However, thought is not to be separated from its object – this is Hegel's semantic thesis and the core of his philosophical project, since 'the forms of thought are first set out and stored in human language' (*SL*, 12; *GW* XXI, 10). Hence, he denounces that 'what is commonly understood by logic is considered with a total disregard of metaphysical significance' (*SL*, 27; *GW* XXI, 31–32) and that 'the concept of logic has hitherto rested on a separation, presupposed once and for all in ordinary consciousness, of the *content* of knowledge and its *form*, or of *truth* and *certainty*' (*SL*, 24; *GW* XXI, 28). The unity of these two elements was already present in Kant's notion of the transcendental, which leads to the systematic unity of knowledge and thus to the idea of a supreme being. Yet he had reduced this idea to a mere *hypothesis*, to a *presupposition* of pure reason. This is an important source for the interpretation of the opening paragraphs of the *Logic of Essence*, and it is useful to analyse them in more detail.

In these paragraphs, Hegel describes the movement of knowledge that leads to essence by using a word of Platonic origin: 'inner recollection' (*Erinnerung/Anamnesis*) (*SL*, 338; *GW* XI, 341). While knowledge goes beyond what is immediately at hand, in order to inquire about its authentic being, it is 'being's nature to recollect itself', and 'it becomes essence by virtue of this

---

Translated from German by Alessandro De Cesaris with Paolo Diego Bubbio.

interiorizing'. Recollection, as the interiorization of being, also has another meaning in addition to the one related to the *anamnesis* of the soul: it is a path of being that thought must follow and which leads to the 'purification' of being, just like the path of experience in the *Phenomenology of Spirit* led to the purification of the soul. This is the reason why recollection and interiorization are so closely connected: they both are paths to the inner. The inner was considered by the entire traditional ontology until Kant as the inner ground of the determination of the thing. Kant does not abandon the idea of essence, but distinguishes between *logical* and *real* essence. The former is the first cause of all the logical predicates of a thing and thus the inner reason of that which is included in the concept, whereas real essence is the first cause of all the determinations of a thing (*Ding*) and thus the inner reason of what belongs to the thing (*Sache*). Moreover, Kant defined logical essence as the concept that is the principle of the possibility of a thing, while real essence is the nature of the thing, namely the principle of the reality of the thing; the former is *principium essendi*, the latter is *principium fiendi*. Now, the question is whether it is possible to know the inner reason of the thing, its real essence; and the answer, even though formulated in various ways, is univocal. 'Now the inner ground of all this is the nature of the thing. We can infer the inner principle only from the properties known to us; therefore the real essence of things is inscrutable to us' (Kant 1997: 319). If we wanted to grasp the logical essence together with the real essence, the latter would be reduced to impenetrability, extension and form, namely to the transcendental 'something' in general, to an object of reflective thought. This is simply the Aristotelian *hypokeimenon*, which Aristotle first, and then Kant, describes as *matter*. This concept is the first step to the determination of essence, and for both Aristotle and Kant it is inadequate as such, because if we take all determinations away from the substrate, nothing is left for us to know.

At the end of the *Doctrine of Being*, Hegel focuses precisely on matter in the context of his discussion about the resolution of measure. Measure is the unity of quality and quantity; eventually quality crosses over to quantity and from there to the measureless. What is missing here is the principle of the specification of the measure-relations, namely the Concept, and therefore only the mere substrate (a matter, a thing) is left to account for their continuity (*SL*, 325; *GW* XXI, 372). Therefore, whereas Hegel at the beginning of his interpretation of measure begins with Plato's motto 'God is the measure of all things' (*SL*, 285; *GW* XXI, 326), at the end of the section on measure as the relation of quality and quantity (the first group of categories, which Kant calls mathematical) he finds the logical conclusion in the transition to the measureless. The abstract indifference of the totality of being that results from this transition is the mere substrate, the *hypokeimenon*, which Hegel calls absolute indifference (*SL*, 333; *GW* XXI, 381). This is not a negative result, but rather a positive one, since it sets up the concepts upon which the analysis of the dynamic categories in the *Doctrine of Essence* is based. This is stated quite clearly: 'This reciprocal transition into the other of the qualitative and the quantitative moments occurs on the basis of their unity, and the meaning of this process is only the *existence* which is the *demonstration* or the *positing* [*Setzen*] that such a substrate does underlie the process and is the unity of its moments' (*SL*, 324; *GW* XXI, 371).

Here we have a clear definition of 'positing': positing is the demonstration of the underlying substrate of the unity of the categories of being, which is the ground of a further determination of their inadequate unity. The indifference of being as immediate, posited as it is, namely as incompatible with itself, is the repulsion from itself (*SL*, 334; *GW* XXI, 382). At the end of the *Doctrine of Being*, Hegel finally defines the whole sphere of being as immediately presupposed totality (*SL*, 335; *GW* XXI, 382–383), which through the sublation of this presupposition must become the original self-identity, i.e. essence. In this way, Hegel provided another notion that is associated with positing, namely *presupposition*. Whereas positing becomes a demonstration of the ground of a further determination of the unity of being, namely essence, presupposition is the simple assumption of the totality of being, whose negation provides only the first ground of that which must be posited.

Kant defines such a way of positing *suppositio per thesin* or *suppositio absoluta* and distinguishes it from the *suppositio per hypothesin*, also called *suppositio relativa*, which is the presupposition.[1] But he also means that we have to start from a *suppositio relativa* in order to reach a *suppositio absoluta*. This fundamental methodological distinction of philosophical demonstrations traces back to Plato's *Republic* (Books VI and VII).[2] What is to be kept in mind is the final objective of this path, the absolute identity of essence.

The preliminary concept of reflection in the introduction to the *Logic of Essence*

Essence, as negation of the presupposed totality of being, is merely the simple unity void of determination (*SL*, 338; *GW* XI, 241). This unity is the result of a mediation that has purified Existence (*Dasein*) and turned it into pure being. Insofar as essence is the abstraction of every determination, essence might be thought as originated and sublated through an external reflection and abstraction, but this would mean to think of essence in terms of the Kantian notion of reflection. Conversely, here Hegel aims at determining essence according to the inner reflection of thought and therefore summarizes the outcome of the *Logic of Being* as follows: essence is what it is, not through a negativity foreign to it, but thanks to the infinite movement of being (*SL*, 338; *GW* XI, 242). But this is the point zero of the *hypokeimenon*: 'Essence, as the complete turning back of being into itself, is thus at first the indeterminate essence.' Now we hear for the first time the expression 'turning back into itself [*Rückkehr in sich*]'. Through this expression, all determinations of being are included in the essence, but simply 'in themselves', not as they were posited *in being itself*. This means, according to the concept of positing discussed above, that the unity of this coming out of itself and turning back into itself has not yet been demonstrated. The demonstration happens with the process through which being-in-itself becomes being-for-itself. With the negation of itself as unity without determination, essence receives a first preliminary determination and, as the unity with itself in this difference between essence and its own negation demonstrates, *posits* its infinite being-for-itself (*ibidem*). Therefore, we have two different pathways for the self-determination of essence. The first path starts from the negative relation to itself (the self-repulsion to itself), a determination that it possesses as being-in-itself, but which is not yet posited, because its *ground* has not yet been given. The second path is the turning back into itself from being-other and the positing, that is, the demonstration of itself as infinite being-for-itself in the demonstrated determination. Each of the pathways succeeds through the negation of itself and the negation of the other than itself. The two pathways, therefore, mirror each other, the former being reflected into the latter and hence Hegel can conclude with this statement: 'The negativity of essence is *reflection*, and the determinations are *reflected* – posited by the essence itself in which they remain as sublated' (*SL*, 339; *GW* XI, 243).

Shine

Reflection is dealt with in the first section of the volume, which is entitled 'Essence as reflection within itself'. This section is divided into three chapters, and the first is entitled 'Shine'. This chapter, in turn, consists of three parts: the first ('The essential and the unessential') is merely an introduction to the second ('Shine'), where the core of the section is discussed. Just after the clarification of what shine is, in the third part ('Reflection') the thought of reflection is developed according to its three forms: positing, external and determining reflection.

Now, what has to be explained through the thought of shine is the relation between being and essence. From ancient philosophy onwards, the problem of *phainomenon* has exacerbated the question of the determination of essence, of the *ti esti*, and has become, for Plato, the problem of the understanding of shine, which he describes with the metaphor of the hunt for a wild beast in the *Sophist*. For Hegel, shine is connected with the problem of scepticism (a relevant concern for Hegel), but also with the problems of modern philosophy and of his own time, including issues emerging from Kant's and Fichte's philosophies. But if essence is the absolute negativity of being, where being sublated itself, then it is not possible to understand being as something unessential contrasted with the essential; rather, being should be understood as a non-essence, shine (*SL*, 342; *GW* XI, 245–246): a non-being that somehow *is*, without having an identifiable being.

Now the question is the following: How does shine originate?

The second part of the chapter, 'Shine', begins in fact with the expression: 'Being is shine.' Shine is the sublatedness of being in the essence. Further, it is the nothingness of being, which has the essence in itself, so that, without essence, it is nothing (*SL*, 342; *GW* XI, 246). Later we read that 'shine is all that remains of the sphere of being'. In order to save this 'residue', and in order to obtain the concept of shine, Hegel must consider shine for itself as the non-self-subsistent [*das Unselbständige*] that exists only in its negation. This immediacy that being has in shine is a 'reflected immediacy' because it is 'one which is only *by virtue of the mediation* of its negation and which, over against this *mediation*, is nothing except the empty determination of the immediacy of non-existence' (*ibidem*). The reflected immediacy is thus only the holding of negated being in the process of mediation. This is how shine originates.

Shine is therefore the phenomenon of ancient scepticism, according to which the whole appearance of the sensible world is admitted, and yet it is not admitted to say that 'it is'. The same applies to the representations of Leibniz's monad, which rise up inside it like froth; to the phenomenon of modern idealism, according to which knowledge cannot be a real knowledge of things in themselves; or also to the infinite check (*Anstoß*) of Fichte's idealism, which does not presuppose a thing in itself and yet recognizes an immediate determination, a limit, which includes the nothingness of the I. If shine is an immediate determinate, then 'it can have this or that content; but whatever content it has, it has not posited it but possesses it immediately' (*SL*, 343; *GW* XI, 247). This is Hegel's criticism against all these philosophies: all being is only shine, if it is not possible to posit and demonstrate its ground. In fact, positing means this, the demonstration (*zeigen*) of the ground that precedes a process or a thing. In this sense the ancient scepticism was more coherent than modern idealism, because on this point it abstained from the judgement concerning being. The thing in itself and Fichte's infinite check are limitations of knowledge and of the subject; for such limitations no justification can be given, and nonetheless they are kept in the process of thought.

Now we come to the second point of the chapter: shine still possesses an immediate presupposition, an independent side against essence. Here Hegel remarks that the problem is not to demonstrate how shine sublates itself into essence, but rather to demonstrate that the determinations that distinguish shine from essence are determinations of essence itself and that this *determinateness of essence*, which shine is, is sublated into essence itself (*SL*, 344; *GW* XI, 247). But how can shine, which is in itself nothing, produce a determinateness of essence? It is necessary to make a further step, which is included in the concept of essence: 'In essence, being is non-being. Its inherent *nothingness* is the *negative nature of essence itself*'. The manifold content of shine is obtained only when it is known in its nothingness, thus negated and turned into a determination of essence. That which is only *pros heteron* is turned back into *kath'auto*. In this consists the negative nature of essence, in which the determinateness of shine is only a moment. Hegel can thus conclude:

> These two moments – nothingness but as subsisting, and being but as moment; or again, negativity existing in itself and reflected immediacy –these two moments that are *the moments of shine*, are thus *the moments of essence itself*; it is not that there is a shine of being *in* essence, or a shine of essence *in* being: the shine in the essence is not the shine of an other but is rather *shine as such, the shine of essence itself*. (*SL*, 344; *GW* XI, 248)

Thus, Hegel preserves in the logical process both the continuity of being and essence and their difference. In fact, essence is also immediacy, but not the 'being immediacy' of what is immediately at hand, but the reflected immediacy that shine is 'the determinateness of being as against mediation; being as moment'. This determinateness, which is included in essence as its necessary condition, is only an immediacy reflected in itself, which can be obtained only through the mediation of essence as shine: 'For essence is what stands on its own: it *exists* as self-mediating through a negation which it itself is. It is, therefore, the identical unit of absolute negativity and immediacy' (*SL*, 344; *GW* XI, 248). In this way, according to a generally accepted interpretation the immediacy of being becomes a second immediacy, since it includes mediation, and there is a displacement of meaning, albeit inconsequential in the logical process, because mediation destroys the simple immediacy of being.[3] But here Hegel does not speak of the simple immediacy of being, but rather of the reflected immediacy of shine, which had dissolved being, existence and the inessential in the essence. It is precisely through the revised concept of being as shine that essence reaches its own determinateness.

In fact essence, as negativity related to itself, is that which stands on its own, which constitutes the *on kath'auto* compared to the various *onta*, whereas the determinateness of shine is only 'being as moment' in this process. This determinateness is nonetheless essential to essence, because it is the decisive moment of definition (*ti esti*), without which according to Aristotle there can be no essence. Without determinateness, namely without the *ti esti*, essence is only *hypokeimenon*, substrate, which is discussed at the end of the *Logic of Being*.[4] The question '*ti esti*' ('what is this') belongs to the essential determinations of *ousia*, and the answer is expressed in the past tense with the expression *to ti en einai*. This form exposes being (*to einai*) to the question *ti esti*; in the answer, after the discussion, the *ti esti* has become *ti en*.[5] Or, following Aristotle again, essence is what the thing had already always been. According to Hegel essence is in fact 'past – but timelessly past – being' (*SL*, 337; *GW* XI, 241).

As long as the determinateness remains autonomous for itself, it is only disappearing shine. In the negative process of essence, nonetheless, this determinateness is 'being as moment' of the shine of essence in itself. 'The *determinateness* that shine is in essence is, therefore, infinite determinateness' (*SL*, 345; *GW* XI, 248). The same happens, for instance, in the case of the actual substance, the genus, which becomes infinite being-for-itself through the disappearance of the finite things.

At the end of the chapter Hegel focuses again on the difference between essence and being, that is, between the unessential and shine as residue of being, in order to argue that essence, as it had been grasped at the beginning, is only an immediate and not yet immediacy as pure mediation or absolute negativity. Therefore in essence there is a first immediacy against the pure mediation, but it is not the first immediacy of being, but rather the reflected immediacy of determinateness and thus infinite determinateness; conversely, being at the beginning of the *Seinslogik* is only the indeterminate immediate. This is clearly stated by Hegel:

This first immediacy is thus only the *determinateness* of immediacy. The sublating of this determinateness of essence consists, therefore, in nothing further than showing that the unessential is only shine, and that essence rather contains this shine within itself. For essence is an infinite self-contained movement which determines its immediacy as negativity and its negativity as immediacy, and is thus the shining of itself within itself. In this, in its self-movement, essence is *reflection*. (*SL*, 345; *GW* XI, 249)

The transition from shine to reflection as the autonomous movement of essence is, again, the demonstration of the process through which shine becomes the movement of absolute reflection. Through this demonstration essence is shown as reflection: it is *posited*.

Reflection: Positing, external and determining reflection

The concept of shine must be replaced with the concept of reflection. Hegel begins the new part concerning shine with a famous 'linguistic coquetry': 'Shine is the same as what *reflection* is; but it is reflection as *immediate*. For this shine, which is internalized and therefore alienated from its immediacy, the German has a word from an alien language, "*Reflexion*"' (*SL*, 345; *GW* XI, 249). With reflection, conceived as shine alienated from itself, the topic of the otherness of being and essence is dealt with once more in order to consolidate the pure self-reference of essence, that is, the pure identity with itself.

But while Hegel uses the formula of negativity for shine, intended as subsistence, and for being, intended as moment, now for the self-reflective movement of essence he chooses the formula – completely unintelligible for Adorno (Adorno 1963) – of the movement from nothing to nothing and thereby back to itself (*SL*, 346; *GW* XI, 250). This movement from nothing to nothing and then back to itself is performed through Plato's concept of otherness (*to heteron*), already introduced in the *Logic of Being*. Hegel distinguishes three moments of this concept: 'The other which is such for itself is the other within it, hence the other of itself and so the other of the other' (*SL*, 42; *GW* XXI, 106).[6] So the movement of reflection that leads from being to essence is performed in three steps:

1. 'Reflective movement is by contrast the other as *negation in itself*, a negation which has being only as self-referring' (*SL*, 345; *GW* XI, 249). In this first step we have the movement of *the other in itself*, the 'negation in itself'.

2. Moreover, since the other is in relation to itself, so it is the negation of negation, something that has being as being-negated – shine. It is the '*other than itself*', being as shine of essence.
3. Nonetheless, since it is in *negative* relation to itself, the other is not being with negation, or limit, like it was in the sphere of being, but rather the negation with negation, or better negation as negation (through the first form of negation in itself). It is '*the other of the other*', and thereby identity with itself, that here is still called 'self-equality'.

The inference is thus the following: 'But the *first* over against this other, the immediate or being, is only this self-equality itself of negation, the negated negation, the absolute negativity' (*SL*, 346; *GW* XI, 249). In this last step it appears like we are exposed again to the previously criticized identity between the first immediacy of being and the second immediacy of essence, which has gone through absolute negativity and mediation. But this is not the case. If being is determined as 'the other of the other', then being against this other is the absolute negativity that essence is. Being as 'the other against essence' is 'the movement of nothingness to nothingness, and so it is essence'. Essence is the movement of reflection that begins from the other as other and thereby it is absolute negativity. Therefore, Hegel can determine this absolute negativity as positing reflection.

Now, the only hermeneutical pathway to overcome Adorno's incomprehension that is still feasible leads back to an 'essential' Platonic source, in the already mentioned *Sophist*, which is the first philosophical work where shine is properly considered. When the stranger from Elea is faced with the alternative between the ontology of Parmenides or that of Heraclitus, namely between the unmoved Being or being as pure movement, he points to a third option, that is, the mixture or participation of both in Being. But if being is at the same time rest and movement, then this third option leads him to the biggest aporia: 'that rest moves and movement rests'. He sees only one way out of this dilemma, a way that he chooses with decision:

'τίθεμαι γὰρ ὅρον ὁρίζειν τὰ ὄντα ὡς ἔστιν οὐκ ἄλλο τι πλὴν δύναμις' ('For I set up as a definition which defines being, that it is nothing else than power').[7]

Being is not the simple being at hand of τὰ ὄντα ὡς ἔστιν, namely of the ὄντα which are resting or moving, but rather the nothing of that which is instead understood for being, and therefore also the nothing of motion and rest, which are the two other supreme genera along with them: insofar as it is 'other than being', *dynamis* is the movement from nothing to nothing (since it is at the same time motion and rest) and thereby back to itself, because what lies at the end of this negating movement is only *dynamis* itself, posited essence. Here Hegel translates the metaphysical thought of *dynamis* through the logical thought of negation as negation and through the thought of the movement from nothing to nothing, and this is clear from the structure of both these thoughts. It is also Hegel's aim to turn metaphysics into logic.[8] If essence is such a 'nothing else than *dynamis*', then the true being of *ousia* with reference to rest and motion can be understood in its truth. Essence can explain the processes of bodies and sensible things in their movement, as well as the processes of thought and knowledge of ideas, which instead rest. We could surely understand this 'nothing else than *dynamis*' as a repulsion of *ousia* from itself, or as a recoil in itself, through which its other is posited – and from this other, *ousia* turns back to itself. With the definition of *dynamis* is posited the *ti esti* of the supreme genus of being, which is the essence of *ousia*. Through this movement we have the third meaning of essence mentioned by Aristotle: the first is the substrate; the second is the determination or the *ti esti*; the third meaning is the relation of both, which is *cause*,[9] a word that for us expresses the *dioti*, the reason for which the substrate (or matter) is so determinate. We find the same line of reasoning in Plato: only after we have conceived *dynamis* as the essence of *ousia*, we know the cause, *aitia*, that is, the participation of being, rest and motion. In addition to this we still need two supreme genera: the identical (*to auto*) and the different (*to eteron*) as principles of the relation and differentiation between the genera. And it is the work of dialectic not to confuse the identical with the different or the different with the identical.[10]

Let us now go back to the interpretation of the *Science of Logic*, and specifically to absolute reflection, which is first determined as positing reflection. Once more, we start from the thought of the immediacy of equality with itself, which is again the self-coinciding of negation; but then this immediacy is the equality of the negative with itself, and thus self-negating equality, 'the negative of itself: its being is to be what it is not' (*SL*, 347; *GW* XI, 251). This negative relation to itself has been conceived until now as a repulsion from itself, and thus as the reference to the other or the presentation of the other of itself. Conversely, now Hegel tells us that the relation of the negative to itself is its turning back to itself – and this, prima facie, might seem strange. Until now, reflection was positing reflection: essence does not transition into an immediate determinateness, but rather it is in its transition the sublation of transitioning; it posits, manifests itself in a determinateness that is infinite determinateness. This is the positedness, the 'immediacy purely as *determinateness* or as self-reflecting' (*SL*, 347; *GW* XI, 251). Positing must be understood from the beginning as the reflection of essence in itself, rather than the turning back from a being. It is nothing else than 'the immediacy which constitutes the determinateness of shine, and from which the previous reflective movement seemed to begin', but this immediacy is only in the reflection – as long as this is the movement of essence – and thus only in the turning back in itself. Thus Hegel comes to the essential passage: 'Reflection is therefore the movement which, since it is the turning back, only in this turning is that which starts out or returns.'

In this circular movement, reflection is at first positing reflection: 'It is a *positing*, inasmuch as it is immediacy as a turning back.' The turning back into the unity of essence is the positing of it, and therefore at first this is just a being-posited. But it is also possible to turn the discourse around and see reflection not as negation of the immediate, but rather as negation of itself. Therefore, positing reflection is turned into presupposing reflection. In order to take itself seriously, reflection must let the immediate emerge in its own right, namely as the presupposition of reflection itself, and not understand it just as second immediacy, namely as reflected immediacy. Hegel claims this explicitly: 'Reflection, in positing, immediately sublates its positing, and so it has an *immediate presupposition*' (SL, 349; GW XI, 253). And also: 'In presupposing, reflection determines the turning back into itself as the negative of itself, as that of which essence is the sublating' (SL, 347; GW XI, 251). True positing only succeeds through the negation of that which is presupposed, namely when the *thesis* is considered as a *hypothesis*, hence as a mere presupposition. Every being-posited is a being-presupposed. Positing sublates itself only through the sublation of its being-presupposed. It is possible to come out of the circularity of reflection only by reflecting, namely as long as an essential reflection is performed and the *phainomena* are led back to essence. In fact, essence is always already posited, or better, essence has presupposed itself since it is the sublation of the presupposition of the immediate. Yet, this sublation of the presupposition is again presupposition; in fact, it is essence itself that presupposes itself as the negation of negated being. But this does not mean that if this ontological structure was transferred to the reflection of conscience, this reflection would not be a serious enterprise (that is, that it would just be a circle of a lazy reason, as Kant would say). What Hegel writes here already sounds like an anticipation of the circular structure of understanding later discussed by Heidegger and Gadamer:

> It is only by virtue of the sublating of its equality with itself that essence is equality with itself. Essence presupposes itself, and the sublating of this presupposing is essence itself; contrariwise, this sublating of its presupposition is the presupposition itself. – Reflection thus *finds* an immediate *before it* which

it transcends and from which it is the turning back. But this turning back is only the presupposing of what was antecedently found. This antecedent *comes to be* only by being *left behind*; its immediacy is sublated immediacy. (*SL*, 347–348; *GW* XI, 251–252)

We have now reached the end of the section, where the outcome of the movement of positing reflection is again criticized as absolute recoil. Positing reflection is the movement that reverses itself and becomes self-movement, because it becomes presupposing reflection and this becomes positing reflection again. Here the determinateness of being rises in the turning of essence back in itself through the dialectic of positing and presupposing reflection. In fact the being-posited is a being-presupposed and is therefore determined as a negative, 'as immediately in opposition to something, and hence to an other'. As long as reflection is determined, it has a presupposition in this determination. If reflection starts from the immediate as an other, it is *external* reflection. Yet, in the section dedicated to external reflection nothing new is said about essence and reflection, because there is no other external reflection except the one between positing and presupposing reflection. In external reflection, which starts from the immediate as its presupposition, Hegel still wants to let the first immediacy appear by highlighting the difference between positing and presupposing reflection in order to get to their unity as *determining reflection*. He defines this reflection in itself as the cornerstone of his conception of reality and the intermediate step between being immediately at hand and concept.

In the remark to the section about external reflection, there is a criticism against Kant with reference to reflective judgement. Gadamer thought that Hegel here wanted to show that it is not possible to distinguish between determining and reflective judgement. That may be right, but my opinion is that Hegel trivializes Kant's reflective judgement.[11] It is not the aim of this chapter to deal with this topic; therefore, I will not analyse it in more detail. Rather, let us go back to the section on determining reflection, where the transition to the determinations of reflection – identity, difference, opposition and contradiction – is easily introduced. Elsewhere, I have suggested that it is here that the real discussion between Kant and Hegel takes place.[12] I have also shown that the starting point for it is the chapter on the amphiboly of the concepts of reflection in the *Critique of Pure Reason*, where Kant confronts Leibniz. The concepts of reflection, which are discussed there, are sameness and diversity, agreement and opposition, form and matter, inner and outer. The first four – identity (Kant calls it *Einerlei*), diversity, agreement and opposition – come again from the dialectic of the *megista gene* in Plato's *Sophist*. In the subsequent chapter of the *Logic of Essence* they are called 'essentialities' and 'determinations of reflection'. The other four – form and matter, inner and outer – will be considered in the third chapter of the second section of the *Logic of Essence*, which is focused on ground [*Der Grund*].

In conclusion, we can refer again to Kant's distinction between *suppositio per thesin* (or *suppositio absoluta*) and *suppositio per hypothesin* (or *suppositio relativa* – the presupposition), which can be understood as a distinction between logical and real essence as, respectively, *principium essendi* and *principium fiendi*. It is clear that Hegel in the *Logic of Essence* cannot accept the difference between these two principles precisely because of the Platonic dialectic between *thesis* and *hypothesis*. Book VII begins with the myth of the cave, and at the end of the description – where the idea of the Good is introduced by way of comparison through the analogy with the Sun – Socrates addresses again the double meaning of 'hypothesis' in order to differentiate the two parts of knowledge (*dianoia* and *nous*)[13] When we go beyond *dianoia* and reach the other part of knowledge, which is obtained by reason with the power of dialectic, then hypotheses are not principles anymore, but rather presuppositions and starting points. In this way it is possible to start from them and go towards something that is not hypothetical anymore, but rather is the principle of the whole and from there go back to sensible things again in order to know them only through the ideas.[14] This is noetic knowledge, which is performed, thanks to dialectic, and which allows to know the essence of things in all their relations.[15] This is the sense of dialectic that Hegel gets from Plato while abandoning Kant, who saw dialectic only as apparent knowledge because reason has a tendency to hypostatize when it abandons the reference to experience and therefore becomes volatile. This is the reason why the position of external reflection, whereby positing becomes presupposing and presupposing must prove itself again as a positing, and by which the hypothesis proves to be an absolutely valid thesis, is of fundamental significance.

Notes

1 Kant himself underlines this distinction in the appendix to the transcendental logic, which is entitled 'On the final aim of the natural dialectic of human reason', where idea and reality seem to diverge: 'I can have a satisfactory reason for assuming something relatively (supposition relative) without being warranted in

assuming it absolutely (supposition *absoluta*). This distinction is pertinent when we have to do merely with a regulative principle, which we recognize as necessary, but whose source we do not know, and for which we assume a supreme ground merely with the intention of thinking the universality of the principle all the more determinately, as, e.g., when I think as existing a being that corresponds to a mere and indeed transcendental idea' (Kant 1998: 608 /A676; B704).

2   In the *Republic* Plato 2006 (VI, 510b 5–511 e 6), the notion of 'hypothesis' is taken in two different meanings. On the one hand, an hypothesis is a thesis or a postulate, just like geometrical figures, numbers and musical chords are postulates and principles of their corresponding sciences; on the other hand, in its proper sense an hypothesis is the initial ground of the supreme science, which is dialectic. See *Rep.* VII, 510c-d, 511b-c. 534b-c.

3   This is the reason why Dieter Henrich talks about a displacement of meaning in the concept of immediacy and identifies in this the interpretative problem of this passage, since it is not possible to think the first immediacy (which Hegel wants to save in order to preserve the continuity of the logical process) together with the second one. See Henrich 1971: 110. Stephen Houlgate objects that in the sphere of being mediation is already included, but this is not an appropriate criticism, since the kind of immediacy meant by Henrich is the undetermined immediacy of being, which constitutes the beginning of logic and precedes any mediation.

4   Aristotle 1994, Book Z.

5   This is the interpretation of the expression that Gadamer offered in a seminar on Hegel's logic of essence in Heidelberg in 1969.

6   Although in the *Logic of Being* the other is understood as the other of spirit, e.g., physical nature (that is, 'that which alters'), its logical determinations are exactly the same of the *Logic of Essence*: 'but that which alters itself is not determined in any other way than in this, to be an other; in *going over* to this other, it *only unites with itself*. It is thus posited as reflected into itself with sublation of the otherness, a self-*identical* something' (*SL*, 92; *GW* XXI, 106). The something is not the other in itself, but just a being for other.

7   Plato 1921 247e. This passage had not been taken under consideration in Gadamer's seminar in 1969. This interpretation of *Sophist* concerning appearance is my own.

8   In the discussion of chemical elective affinities at the end of the chapter on real measure, Hegel interprets the theory of the Swedish scientist J.J. Berzelius, author of the notation of chemical elements, who wrote in his *Textbook of Chemistry* (1802–1828) that these affinities take place through the symmetry of atoms and the relation by determinate proportion. Hegel's stance is that the experiment presented by Berzelius can demonstrate neither the existence of atoms nor the symmetry of atoms in their position and disposition, and remarks that 'corroboration could come only by a consideration of these representations themselves, that is, by metaphysics, which is logic' (*SL*, 313; *GW* XXI, 358). Berzelius had also defined 'the

speculative philosophy of certain German schools' as 'dynamic philosophy' and had rejected it.
9 Aristotle 1994, 17, 1041 a 27–29; 1041 b 4–6.
10 Plato 1921 253 d 1–4.
11 See Dottori 2006: 80–93.
12 Dottori 2006: 33ff.
13 *Republic* 510 c-d.
14 *Republic* 511 b-c.
15 *Republic* 543 b-c.

References

Adorno, Th.W. [1963] (1993), *Hegel: Three Studies*, trans. Shierry Weber Nicholsen, Cambridge, MA: The MIT Press. Originally appeared in German under the title *Drei Studien zu Hegel*, Frankfurt a.M.: Suhrkamp.

Aristotle (1994), *Metaphysics, Book Z and H*, trans. Dabid Bostock, Oxford: Clarendon Press.

Dottori, R. (2006), *Die Reflexion des Wirklichen*, Tübingen: Mohr-Siebeck.

Henrich, D. (1971), *Hegel im Kontext*, Frankfurt a.M.: Suhrkamp.

Kant, E. (1997), *Lectures on Metaphysics*, trans. Karl Ameriks and Steve Naragon, Cambridge: Cambridge University Press.

Kant, E. (1998), *Critique of Pure Reason*, trans. Paul Guyer and Allen W. Wood, Cambridge: Cambridge University Press.

Plato (1921), *Plato with an English Translation: Theaetetus; Sophist, Volume 2*, trans. Harold North Fowler. London: Heinemann.

Plato (2006), The Republic, trans. R.E. Allen, New Haven: Yale University Press.

3

Effectual Contingency: The Ontological Problem of Modality in Hegel's *Science of Logic*

Alessandro De Cesaris

Contingency is at the core of today's philosophical sensibility, but it is also a pivotal element in the development of modern thought. Niklas Luhmann has argued that contingency is the 'Midas' gold' of modernity, since every theoretical effort and every search for the necessary and the eternal only seem to lead to the contingent and the relative (Luhmann 1998: 44ff.). Despite its renewed popularity over the last decades, Hegel's thought is still considered by some to be quite distant from this kind of sensibility. The view according to which Hegel's philosophy is interpreted as a closed system – whose aim is, supposedly, to embrace the totality of knowledge in a teleological, determinist conception of history and of nature, offering a secularized version of some sort of optimistic providentialism – is a traditional one and one that has not yet been completely abandoned (Brassier 2007: 70ff.; Meillassoux 2008: 107–108; Mordacci 2015: 27ff.).

Hegel's thought has been often interpreted as a philosophy of universality, of subjectivity and of necessity; however, from the twentieth century onwards, several scholars and philosophers have read it as an attempt to radically rethink singularity, objectivity and contingency. This new direction in Hegel's interpretation has been pushed further by scholars belonging to different traditions over the last twenty years (Houlgate 1995; Malabou 2005; Burbidge 2007; Žižek 2012; Mabille 2013), but has not yet managed to show the close intersection of these three concepts. A systematic reinterpretation of Hegel's philosophy should show that it manages to rethink contingency only by redefining objectivity and that its new account of contingency leads to a new theory of singularity. In this chapter, I will focus specifically on the notion of contingency in the *Science of Logic*, but at the same time I will show the close relation between these three themes in Hegel's thought. In particular, I will make three points. First, Hegel systematically rethinks the category of contingency by starting a critical dialogue with the philosophical tradition. Second, contingency is at the same time the core and the culminating point of the section on *Wirklichkeit*, which is also the acme of the whole logic of essence. Finally, I will argue that the natural development of Hegel's account of contingency is his discussion of the notion of singularity at the beginning of the *Subjective Logic*. This close correlation between contingency and singularity is pivotal for the logical development of the notion of freedom.

From logic to ontology

The problem of modality acquires more and more importance through the development of Hegel's system. In one of the earliest formulations of his philosophy, dating back to the Jena period (1804–1805), modal categories were included in the discussion about the *Relation of Being* and were considered as different ways of being of the sole Spinozian substance (which is the true subject of the section, *LMJ*, 43–45). At this stage of Hegel's philosophy, substance was possibility, actuality or necessity in virtue of expressing different kinds of relation among its own determinations. As simply posited – *positively* – it was *possibility* (and not something possible). Then it changed into a *negative* relation, in which a determination was always posited together with the negation of its opposite and was then *actuality*. Finally, *necessity* was the unity of these two former moments, concluding the speculative account of substance.

The same exposition can be found, almost identically, in the lectures on logic that Hegel delivered in the Nuremberg's gymnasium in 1810–1811 (*TWA* IV, 178–180). Possibility, actuality and necessity are the three steps through which the true essence of substance manifests itself in relation to its accidents. In both texts it is possible to find some references to the question of accidentality or of the contingent (*Zufälliges*), but contingency itself does not belong to the list of modal categories.[1] Their exposition is closely entwined with the categories of relation (substance, causality and reciprocal action), as they already featured in the Kantian table of categories. There, contingency was already included as the opposite of necessity but was not analysed in detail.

This implicit reference to Kant already shows an attempt to rethink his theory of modality and to criticize it. In the *Critique of Pure Reason*, specifically in the section about the 'Postulates of Empirical Thought in General', Kant writes that 'the categories of modality have this peculiarity: as a determination of the object they do not augment the concept to which they are ascribed in the least, but rather express only the relation to the faculty of cognition' (A219; B266; Kant 1988: 322). Conversely, in Hegel's analysis, the fusion of the modal categories with the categories of relation suggests exactly that the formers are moments of the development of substance itself.

In his *Encyclopaedia* (1830), Hegel explicitly refers to the Kantian passage mentioned above and argues that the statement is correct only if it is applied to formal possibility. It is correct to state that possibility is 'the empty abstraction of the reflection-in-itself' and that it is a 'simple modality' belonging only to subjective thought. However, 'actuality and necessity are, by contrast, truly anything but a mere sort and manner for an other; rather, they are precisely the opposite, posited as the not merely posited but instead as the concrete [dimension] that is complete in itself' (*EI*, §143). However, Hegel had already completely changed the general structure of his account of modality. In the *Logic of Essence* of 1813, modality was in fact no longer entwined with substantiality or with the other categories of relation, but was an independent phase of the logical development. Modal categories are moments of the development of the category of *Wirklichkeit*, whose meaning – far from that of Kant's *Dasein* – is explicitly ontological. *Wirklichkeit* is actuality as absolute manifestation, an overcoming of the contraposition between internal and external and of the duality typical of the whole *Logic of Essence* (*SL*, 477ff.; *GW* XI, 380).[2] *Wirklichkeit* is in fact at the same time the title of the whole section, which culminates with the passage to the *Concept*, and the title of the second chapter of the section itself, which is the intermediate step between the *absolute* and the *substance*. That alone should guarantee the crucial importance given by Hegel to modality in the development of the system. Modal categories are in a first stage a *formal* moment of the absolute, that is, its reflection in itself (*SL*, 478; *GW* XI, 381). This formality is progressively removed during the speculative movement, leading to the full development of the category of effectual reality and its further transformation into substantiality.

This explains Hegel's partial agreement with Kant's choice to consider modal categories as a simple expression of the subject's relation with the object of experience: the chapter on *Effectual Reality* is at the same time a genetic and systematic rethinking of the whole categorial implant (which in Kant still lacks foundation that is not merely empirical) and a criticism against the way modality had been traditionally understood. By criticizing it, though, Hegel agrees with the pre-Kantian tradition about the fundamental ontological meaning of modality itself. In this sense his analysis is deeply related to the Leibnizian and post-Leibnizian metaphysical tradition.[3] In Wolff's philosophy, the discussion of the difference between necessary and contingent belongs to ontology, that is, to the discipline that studies the nature of any being *independently* from its existence without proving the actual reality of any determinate being (Wolff 2001: §8–9; De Boer 2011: 53–58). That does not allow us to consider Hegel's thought as a return to a pre-Kantian notion of modality; rather, we should consider it as the attempt to overcome two views he tried to prove equally incorrect: rationalist dogmatism and transcendental logic. It could be said that this overcoming requires the foundation of an ontological and metaphysical but not dogmatic perspective, according to which the reality of the objects of experience cannot be deduced starting from pure notions, but it is rather investigated in its condition of thinkability.

The different meanings of contingency

There are many occurrences of the notion of *Zufälligkeit* in Hegel's work from the early writings up to the latest lectures. The term is usually adopted in order to refer to that which can be otherwise than it is: in this meaning it was used during the Middle Ages, often as a synonym of 'accidental'.[4] Understood in such a way, *Zufälligkeit* is at the core of Hegel's ontology, since it is the main property of finite beings, that is, of anything that is subject to becoming and therefore doomed to disappear. The most comprehensive account of *Zufälligkeit* can be found in the *Lectures about the Proofs of the Existence of God*, where Hegel analyses the cosmological proof and discusses the problem of the relation between God and the world. Here he also deals with the problem of contingency and gives an etymological explanation of the deeper meaning of the term:

> Individual things do not come from themselves or proceed by themselves. As contingent they are destined to pass away: this is something that does not happen to them simply contingently but is constitutive of their nature. *(LPG, 102; TWA XVII, 448)*

From this angle, any finite being, that is, any thing existing (*Dasein*) in the simple form of natural exteriority, is contingent. That the finite is contingent is not itself something contingent, but rather essential and determining for its own nature: the contingency of finite being is necessary. Hegel's account of contingent being can thus be found in the *Objective Logic*, in the categorial analysis that leads from the *Dasein* to the *Ding* (Houlgate 1995: 46–48; Illetterati 2014: 140–146). And yet in the *Science of Logic* the category of contingency plays a specific role and acquires a technical meaning it does not have in other works. This meaning, moreover, is further analysed in three different moments, which we should now consider.

Formal modality

Contingency appears as the title of the section A in the chapter about *Wirklichkeit*: it is then the core concept of the first (purely *formal*) moment of reflection about modal categories. The beginning of the analysis shows us the first, more immediate understanding of the category of actuality, which now no longer refers to the totality of modal forms to become a particular moment of its dialectical development.

In a first, immediate sense, actuality (*Wirklichkeit*) cannot be distinguished from being (*Sein*) or existence (*Dasein*) (*SL*, 478; *GW* XI, 381–382). And yet, since the logical development does not allow an exterior return to a previous step, the peculiar feature of *Wirklichkeit* consists in being the formal unity of exteriority and interiority, that is possibility. The actual is thus immediately designated as *possible*.

In this first step, possibility is immediately identified with the category of identity (or with non-contradiction, which – as stated in the chapter about the 'Determinations of Reflection' – is just the negative version of the former). The possible is everything that does not contradict itself. This understanding of possibility corresponds to the way it had been thought by the modern philosophical tradition and yet appears to incur in two different contradictions. In the first place:

> Possibility is this mere essentiality, but so *posited* as to be only a moment, to be disproportionate with respect to the absolute form. It is the in-itself, determined as only a *posited* or, equally, as *not to be in itself*. Internally, therefore, possibility is contradiction, or it is *impossibility*. (*SL*, 479; *GW* XI, 382)

The possible is contradictory because, on one hand, it is something in-itself, but, on the other hand, its determinacy can be found only in the relation to something else, namely to *Wirklichkeit* (Burbidge 2007: 20). The possible is a *moment* of the form, not its totality, precisely because it leaves actuality outside itself, while at the same time referring to it. This is why the possible is described as *only* possible: what distinguishes it from pure essence is the *Sollen*, namely the constant tension – according to the structure of the bad infinite – towards an actualization never to be accomplished. This is the reason why Hegel can argue that possibility is like essence without being: since it is determined by this contradictory tension, the possible is effectively *impossible*. This dialectical process reminds of the ancient Aristotelian question about a possibility that never becomes actual (*Metaphysics* 1047b3-6; Bechler 1995: 102–107; Massie 2011: 127).

Similarly, the second contradiction of formal possibility relates back to the Aristotelian discussion about contingent futures: even if the possible is determined as non-contradictory, it necessarily entails contradiction, since the possibility of A is at the same time the possibility of non-A (*De Interpretatione*, IX, 18a34-b9). Thus, the possible manifests itself at the same time as an impossible, because the possibility for everything to become actual is at the same time the impossibility for *everything* to become actual.[5]

This implicit reference to ancient thought becomes stronger in the following passage, where contingency finally comes into play. If the contradiction of possibility is removed with the passage to actuality, the latter is also very weak, since it is the simple unity of possibility and actuality itself. By stating that reality is not really different from being or existence – a further proof of the role of ancient philosophy throughout this section – reality is at the same time described as *contingent*.

Here we find the common meaning of contingency: something that is actual, but can be other than it is or not be at all (*EI*, §145).[6] And yet Hegel already gives the notion a further determination. First of all, contingency is the union of actuality and possibility not just from the side of actuality but also from the standpoint of possibility. The possible itself, as possible, is *actually* possible and so it is contingent. Contingency is at the same time the possibility of the actual being to be other and the actually-being-possible of the possible being; in this twofold conception it is possible to find the Aristotelian notions of possibility as *accidentality* and *dynamis*.[7]

Furthermore, contingency shows in this phase a brand new feature:

> The contingent thus presents these two sides. First, in so far as it has possibility *immediately* in it, or, what is the same, in so far as this possibility is sublated in it, it is *not positedness*, nor is it mediated, but is *immediate* actuality; it has *no ground*. – Because this immediate actuality pertains also to the possible, the latter is determined no less than the actual as contingent and is likewise groundless. (*SL*, 480–481; *GW* XI, 384)

Contingent being manifests itself as immediate being, which – as immediate – does not have any reason to be. This meaning of contingency is quite different from the modern one, as it had been formulated by Leibniz. In Leibniz's thought, in fact, the distinction between contingent and necessary had a metaphysical foundation: it was rooted in the difference between a finite series of conditions, in the case of necessity, and an infinite one in the case of contingency, something that made it impossible to deduce a predicate starting from the simple concept of the subject.[8] Nevertheless, it remained possible for God to bring a contingent proposition to its analytical necessity: contingency is still subject to the principle of sufficient reason, exactly as happens for necessity. The Hegelian introduction of the notion of *Grundloses*, on the contrary, recalls the Aristotelian notion of chance, the ancient conception of an event or of a being that emerges spontaneously, without any cause.[9]

And yet, as mediated by the category of possibility, the contingent is at the same time grounded in the possible, that is, it finds its reason in possibility itself.[10] According to Hegel, contingent being is exactly this restlessness, this steady transition from possibility to actuality and vice versa, a tension between absence of ground and groundedness in possibility. At this point, it is really important to remark that it is only from the resolution of this tension that the category of necessity emerges. In the Jena writings, as in the Nuremberg lectures, necessity was immediately deduced from the union of possibility and actuality, now it is instead produced only from contingency, establishing a relationship that will never lose its significance in Hegel's subsequent writings (Houlgate 1995: 41).

In this first stage of the critical discussion of modal categories, the most immediate notion of necessity is discussed: something is necessary just because it is actual and hence because its opposite is not possible anymore. Hegel describes this process as a sublation of the relation to possibility, recalling once again the ancient debate between Aristotle and the Megarians: all that has been just because it has been – namely because it has removed its own possibility – is necessary (*Metaphysics* IX, 1046b29-33; Burbidge 2007: 28). At the end of this first subsection, the discussion about formal modality seems to rediscover, and at the same time to criticize, ancient modal thought, providing a new meaning of contingency aside from the classical, Leibnizian-Wolffian one.

Real modality

In the second stage of the analysis, which focuses on real modality, the reference to Leibniz and Wolff comes into play again: section B is dedicated to the critical discussion of the modern conception of modality – at least with regard to the relation between necessity and contingency.

Hegel starts by emphasizing that the necessity discovered in the first step is just formal: and yet, as a unity of different moments that is also indifferent to them, necessity reveals itself as real *Wirklichkeit*. It is difficult to provide a good translation of this expression, since it is important not to lose the difference between *Realität* and *Wirklichkeit*, a difference already present in the previous philosophical tradition and fully developed by Hegel in the *Science of Logic*. As Hegel himself remarks (*SL*, 85; *GW* XXI, 99), the concept of *Realität* is quite vague and has different meanings. It can also be used as a synonym of *Wirklichkeit*, but its specific features are determined in the section about *Quality* where the two distinctive traits of what is *real* refer to a qualitative property and the positive nature of the latter – that is, the absence of negativity in it. *Realitas* refers to the *content* of the notion of an object in general, as is evident in some passages, where Hegel uses the adjective 'real' in order to point out this relation to content.[11] This use of the term 'real' is reminiscent of the Kantian statement according to which existence is not a 'real predicate', that is, it is not a predicate that increases the *realitas* of the concept of its object (Heidegger 1984: 215–216; Rosen 2014: 383). With this expression, then, Hegel points out that now effectual reality is not just formal but has content.

Effectual reality is actual because it lasts and stays identical despite the multiplicity of its manifestations – its properties or its activity in the world (*wirken*). It still embraces possibility within itself, but this possibility is also no longer formal, but real. This means that, unlike what happened in the earlier phase, it does not consist in the simple non-contradiction, but rather in the set of conditions that make something actually possible. This conception seems to be related to the Aristotelian concept of *dynamis*, as it is discussed in the book IX of *Metaphysics*.[12] In Aristotle's writings, the purely logical conception of 'possible' as 'not necessary' is surely present, but it is at the same time kept separated from the metaphysical notion of 'potentiality'. Something is potential not just when its actualization is not contradictory but only when the conditions of its actualization are effectually present (*Metaphysics*, IX, 1048b35-1049a18). These conditions are themselves something actual insofar as the real possibility of something consists in a set of conditions that, in order to actualize that possibility, have to be actual themselves.

That which is actually possible still obeys the conditions of formality: it must not contradict itself, but at the same time it has to be consistent with the set of its own conditions. And yet the notion of real possibility turns out to be contradictory too, and not just because the existence of a multiplicity (namely of the conditions) entails some sort of contrast between the elements of that manifoldness but also for another, specifically logical, reason. The possible is not really possible until all its conditions are actual, and yet, once they are all actual, the possible is not possible anymore, but it is immediately actualized. This was also remarked by Aristotle, though he did not consider it as a paradox: a potential being, whose conditions are all actual, is necessarily actual.

This is what Hegel means when he states that 'real possibility and necessity are, therefore, only *apparently* distinguished' (*SL*, 484; *GW* XI, 388). Real possibility and actuality are both brought back to real necessity (the titular section B). Also this category, though, immediately appears to be only relative, or formal, real necessity is in fact necessary only from the formal point of view according to which necessary is what cannot be otherwise. However, with regard to the content, the necessary being remains conditioned by something external, that is, by that set of conditions which, singularly considered, are themselves something contingent (*EI*, §147):

> The relativity of real possibility is manifested in the content by the fact that the latter is at first only the identity indifferent to form, is therefore distinct from it and a *determinate content* in general. A necessary reality is for this reason any limited actuality which, because of its limitation, is in some other respect also only something *contingent*. (*SL*, 485; *GW* XI, 389)

This subordination regards the *what*, but also the *how* of necessity: *that* something is necessary is only determined by a set of conditions, but at the same time these conditions determine externally *what* is necessary, what the content of this necessity will be. Real necessity describes a reality still limited, because its conditions are outside of itself. This is why Hegel can make two statements that are apparently contradictory. On one hand, necessary being is itself a simple contingent, since its existence is subject to a series of external conditions. This identity of necessity and contingency can be compared to what Wolff writes in his *Ontology*, where he states that contingent is what is hypothetically necessary (Wolff 2001: §318).[13] On the other hand, though, real necessity is incomplete precisely because it '*has not yet determined itself out of itself into contingency*', namely because it keeps contingency as something external and simply posited. The way modernity understood necessity is for Hegel absolutely insufficient, since this necessity reveals itself as something contingent. Section B, as well as section A, ends up with the unity of necessity and contingency as a result more specifically with the affirmation of the contingency of necessity.

Absolute modality

The first two sections of the chapter seem to consider the main ways in which tradition had considered modality from a metaphysical standpoint: the twine of ancient and modern philosophy, from Aristotle to Wolff, reveals the insufficiency of the classical formulation of the categories of possibility, actuality, contingency and necessity, as well as their essential logical instability. Contingency has turned out to be the core of both sections, representing the category all others fall into eventually.

In the third section of the present chapter, the relation between necessity and contingency has to be radically reshaped. The aim is to think the unity of necessity and contingency, preventing the former from being reduced to something contingent and contingency itself from falling out of necessity. The title of this section suggests that the dominant category is now 'absolute necessity': it rises from the simple remark that in real modality contingency is already somehow included into necessity. This relation is reshaped through a new categorial development, in which the formal and the real understanding of modality are finally united:

> Absolute necessity is therefore the truth in which actuality and possibility in general as well as formal and real necessity return. – As we have just seen it is being which in its negation, in essence, refers itself to itself and is being. It is equally simple immediacy or *pure being* and simple immanent reflection or *pure essence*; it is this, that the two are one and the same. – The absolutely necessary only *is* because it *is*; it otherwise has neither condition nor ground. – But it equally is pure *essence*, its *being* the simple immanent reflection; it is *because* it is. (*SL*, 487; *GW* XI, 391)

In this passage the fundamental significance of modal categories for the whole logical development is as clear as possible. With the notion of absolute necessity we do not just reach the unity of possibility and actuality, as stated in the former versions of the system, but also – and for the first time – the unity of *being* and *essence*: absolute necessity reveals itself at the same time as an immediate and a mediated, showing simultaneously – but in a new form – the main features of formal and real necessity. On one hand, in fact, that which is absolutely necessary has no reason to be, that is, it is a *Grundloses* (as shown in the section of this chapter); on the other hand, however, it is something reflected and grounded, because it has its own reason within itself. The expression 'the necessary is because it is' holds the unity of these two aspects, depending on what part of the sentence one chooses to emphasize, the '*because*' or the verb '*to be*'.

Stephen Houlgate remarked how being is at the core of this final part of the modal process: the union of necessity and contingency expresses an ontological truth, since it makes of the latter the only content of the former. True necessity is contingency and not because necessary being, as necessary, has no reason to be – whether it is a right understanding of Hegel's thought or not, it is not what Hegel writes in this passage[14] – but rather because the only true necessity of finite being is change, the rising of beings from nothing and their coming back into it. This is why Hegel specifies, later, that 'absolute necessity is not so much the *necessary*, even less *a* necessary' (*SL*, 489; *GW* XI, 393). Hegel's discussion about modality does not end up with the proof of the existence of one or more necessary beings – there's no cosmological or theological climax – but remains purely ontological: that's how Hegel's logic shows itself as a speculative (in Kantian sense) but non-dogmatic philosophy. The aim is not the demonstration of the existence of anything, but rather the dialectical elaboration of modal categories and their development in a more consistent and philosophically relevant form.[15] Absolute necessity, which as absolute is not anymore limited by anything, entails a new relation to totality: it is totality itself, since it does not leave anything outside (Burbidge 2007: 47; Rosen 2014: 365–366). Absolute necessity does not only coincide with contingency – it is exactly the necessity *of contingency* – but is also a necessity produced only by the whole set of what is contingent:

> Absolute necessity is thus the *reflection or form of the absolute*, the unity of being and essence, simple immediacy which is absolute negativity. *On the one hand*, therefore, its differences are not like the determinations of reflection but *an existing manifoldness*, a differentiated actuality in the shape of others independently subsisting over against each other. *On the other hand*, since its connection is that of absolute identity, it is the *absolute conversion* of its actuality into its possibility and its possibility into its actuality. (*SL*, 487; *GW* XI, 391)

Wirklichkeit is finally adequate to describe the absolute: absolute necessity is still a somehow formal understanding of it, but thanks to absolute necessity the absolute already shows itself not as a *thing*, as some determinate being, but rather as a *relation*. This is how the inessential formality of real modality can be sublated (Wölfle 1994: 480). The moments of the absolute do not just belong to external reflection but are actual beings. Their determination is the steady passage from possibility to actuality and from actuality to possibility; individually considered, they are contingent, but as a whole, they constitute what Hegel describes as absolute necessity.[16] The sublation of the last formal element in the discussion requires a better understanding of the new concrete relation between the whole and its elements: the sublation of real modality does not express yet the internal dynamic of the absolute.

Therefore, the analysis of modality logically leads to the account of relation: the nexus between these two sets of Kantian categories is justified by the role of modality in Hegel's logic. In the chapter about the absolute relation the problem of the relation between necessary and contingent being is accounted for starting from the necessity to think the relation between the absolute and its determinations. Spinozian substance, the causal relation and the notion of reciprocity of action are the three stages through which this relation is freed of its one-sidedness. As soon as we have properly understood this unity, we find ourselves already in the domain of the concept. Without going through this new step, it is important to remark that in the last sentence of the 'Objective Logic', Hegel writes that the concept is the domain of *subjectivity* and *freedom*. Concept and subject come to the point of being synonyms, as Hegel shows in the chapter 'Of the Concept in General':

> But this consummation is no longer the *substance* itself but is something higher, the *concept*, the *subject*. The transition of the relation of substantiality occurs through its own immanent necessity and is nothing more than the manifestation of itself, that the concept is its truth, and that freedom is the truth of necessity. (*SL*, 511; *GW* XII, 14)

This overcoming takes place, as we saw, thanks to a new relation between the Whole and its moments:

> The concept is the free [actuality] as the substantial power that is for itself, and it is the totality since each of the moments is the whole that it is, and each is posited as an undivided unity with it. So, in its identity with itself, it is what is determinate in and for itself. (*EI*, §160)

This new relation's ultimate result is freedom. Now we need to specify what sense of freedom is accounted for in the *Science of Logic*.

Contingency and freedom

Hegel describes absolute necessity as 'blind necessity' (*EI*, §147): this notion corresponds to the ancient notion of 'destiny', discussed by Hegel in various works (*TWA* XVII, 487; *EI*, §147 A). Contingent beings are characterized as *essentially free*, but at the same time as necessary in themselves (*SL*, 487–88; *GW* XI, 391–92). *Prima facie*, it could seem that freedom comes into play together with absolute necessity. On the other hand, however, the problem of contingency is important also – and particularly – because the accountability of free agency depends on its solution. For there to be something like a free action, the world cannot be completely determined by some sort of all-embracing necessity, and there has to be something that can actually be otherwise than it is.

A better understanding of the relation between freedom and contingency can be reached by reading an *Addition* to the *Encyclopedia*, where the difference between the ancient and modern notion of freedom is taken into account. At a first glance the notion of destiny seems to exclude the possibility of freedom. And yet, Hegel remarks, 'this lies in the fact that the lack of freedom is grounded in clinging to an opposition of the sort that we regard what is and happens as standing in contradiction to what should be and happen' (*EI*, §147). In ancient philosophy this contradiction did not subsist, and thus it was still possible to understand freedom as consistent with an all-embracing fate. This conception, continues Hegel, seems valid only if we conceive subjectivity as the part of individuals dominated by passions, by exteriority and by matter; in this sense, the 'freedom' of cosmic events seems to be higher and better:

> Furthermore, however, the subjectivity is not merely the bad and finite subjectivity, standing opposite the basic matter, instead it is, in keeping with its truth, immanent to the basic matter and, accordingly as infinite subjectivity, is the truth of the basic matter itself. (*EI*, §290)

Hegel's philosophy features a higher understanding of subjectivity, whose logical foundation can be found only in the *Doctrine of Concept*. The historical setting of this new conception is modern and Christian thought, expressing the idea that instead of blind fate there is a personal god, rational and capable of teleological agency (*EI*, §147).

If freedom is the process of coming-together with itself in an other (*EI*, §159 R), the domain of freedom coincides with the one of the concept. Subjectivity, concept and freedom are thus three strictly entwined signifiers leading the logical process towards its new stage, conceived by Hegel as a true sublation of abstract and dogmatic thought. The concept is free not because it possesses a subjective character, some sort of conscience or the capacity to act intentionally: freedom is in the first place a logical structure, whose essence emerges through the dialectical development of modal categories.

The new sense of freedom – subjective not in an empirical or personal, but rather in a structural and logical sense – emerges in fact from the fusion of necessity and contingency. This emergence, in turn, corresponds to the transformation of these two categories in the new categories of universality and singularity (*SL*, 504ff.; *GW* XI, 408ff.). This means that in the economy of the whole system, contingency plays a quite complex role. On one hand, in fact, necessity and contingency are still useful in order to give a proper account of finite being; on the other hand, though, the fact that they have been sublated requires a brand new account of reality itself, which can no longer be reduced to those categories. The products of freedom, as part of the world, are still subject to the general structure of formal, real and absolute modality, and yet this is not enough, since a new step of the logical development is required in order to define their nature properly.

This new step does consist in rethinking not just substance as a relationship but also the nature of this relationship itself. That is why Hegel's logic is a sublation of ontology: not because it does not refer to being or to the fundamental structure of reality but rather because it does not start from the typical assumption of ancient and modern (Christian) philosophy, namely that the absolute must be some sort of *being (ens)*.

Contingency and singularity

Dieter Henrich addressed the relation between the problem of contingency and the question of individuality. In his renowned essay about the problem of chance in Hegel's philosophy, contingency is shown as a necessary moment of the logical process and thus of the structure of reality, with reference to both the natural and human – practical and historical – sphere (Henrich 1971).[17] Henrich's main point is that throughout his account of contingency, Hegel endorsed some sort of neo-Aristotelian perspective, according to which individuals are basically excluded from the range of philosophical knowledge because they are undeducible from the pure concept (Henrich 1971: 159). This would also be, in Henrich's view, Hegel's response to Krug's famous provocation, when Krug asked Hegel to deduce the pen he was using to write in order to prove the truth of his absolute idealism (Henrich 1971: 157–158; *EI*, §250 R). According to Henrich, the necessity of the *whole of being* does not necessarily entail the necessity of *every thing*. Absolute idealism holds even if we admit – together with necessity – the existence of the multiplicity of undeducible individuals, which are thus *zufällig*, in the sense of *random*.[18]

And yet this reading shows some problematic aspects. First, according to Henrich, contingent being – on both natural and historical/practical levels – lies next to necessary being outside of it. In this way the domain of the necessary and the contingent is simply juxtaposed, and there is just an exterior relationship between them. Henrich affirms that Hegel's solution is not trying to fight contingency, but to leave it be as leftover of a system able to prove the necessity of something somehow external to it (Henrich 1971: 172). On the basis of this neo-Aristotelian reading, Hegel's system would be able to deduce the existence of some determinate beings – for example Napoleon or Africa – but just because they are more like essences, *eide* in the Aristotelian understanding (Henrich 1971: 170).

Furthermore, according to this interpretation it is difficult to understand how being as a whole can be necessary. As Henrich himself remarks, if the existence of both necessary and contingent beings is assumed, a necessary whole cannot emerge from them. It is not by chance that Henrich suggests to understand the whole as necessary from a *practical* point of view by interpreting absolute necessity as an ethical and not theoretical moment (Henrich 1971: 185–187).

In contrast with this interpretation, in this chapter, I argued for an interpretation of Hegel's account of contingency that directly leads to the need to theoretically rethink totality in its relation with singularity. Henrich is forced to bring the whole on an ethical level precisely because he still employs a conception of individual being that he describes as Aristotelian.[19] It is surely true that Hegel admitted the existence of a multiplicity of contingent beings – in particular in nature and through history – which are subtracted from the domain of reason, and the reason for it is that objective logic remains the categorial structure of the nature of finite being. And yet, as Henrich himself remarks, the great novelty of Hegel's thought consists in thinking contingent being not only as a limit of the system but as an element of it.

It follows that the ontological problem of contingency naturally leads to the ontological question of singularity. The entire subjective logic shows the way Hegel provided his own solution to the problem underlined by Henrich: how to reconcile totality with the subsistence of individual and contingent being, the rationality of history with the existence of freedom, the eternity and universality of logical categories with the creativity of spirit and the authenticity of a future that does not obey any external necessity.[20]

Hegel's account of modal categories only leads to the statement that such categories are not sufficient in order to answer these questions in a satisfactory way. Any *ontic* answer to them, any distinction between things that are necessary and things that are contingent, is doomed to leave many logical, ontological and practical problems unsolved. Only by radically thinking the dynamic mediation between singularity and universality, and thus by opening to the domain of life and history, Hegel's ontology shows its radical attempt to reshape our understanding of the future, of free agency and of the human's place in the cosmos.

Notes

1. Dieter Henrich remarks how Hegel pays more and more attention to the problem of contingency (Henrich 1971: 160–161).
2. See also Henrich 1971: 182, where the ontological problem is strictly connected to the problem of totality as unity of being and essence. See also Zander 2012: 179–188.
3. In Kant's philosophy, contingency, even though it is included in the set of modal categories without playing any special role, is discussed in the Transcendental Dialectic, during the discussion of the Fourth Conflict of the Transcendental Ideas (B480–489). That constitutes another proof of the Leibnizian-Wolffian legacy, even though the Kantian account of contingency does not play a significant role in Hegel's analysis of modality.
4. This is already evident in Aquinas 1991, XIII: 17. In the Nuremberg lectures, and later in the *Lectures on the Proof of the Existence of God*, the notion of 'accident' already appears together with the notion of 'contingent' (*TWA* IV, §65; *TWA* XVII, 419).
5. It also has to be mentioned that Hegel used the notion of 'contradiction' in many different ways. In this case, contradiction could also be considered as the simple *compresence* of opposite determinations in a concept, something that does not entail in itself a violation of the law of non-contradiction.
6. On contingency as mutability, see also Wolff 2001: §295.
7. And yet in Aristotle's thought, as in general during the Middle Ages, contingency had a privileged relation to the future, as shown in chapter IX of *De Interpretatione*.
8. Leibniz, *On Contingency*, in Leibniz 1989: 28–30; Id., *Discourse of Metaphysics*, in Leibniz 1989: 44–46.
9. Aristotle, *Physics*, II, 195b31-198a14; Id., *Prior Analytics*, 32b4-13; On this theme, see Mabille 2013, 205. Mabille suggests a comparison between the two Aristotelian senses of possibility and the two Hegelian meanings of contingency. This remark does not seem completely correct, but it is useful to recognize the Aristotelian inspiration of Hegel's analysis, despite the absence of a specific account of contingency in Aristotle's works. The notion of '*endechomenon*', which is present in chapter XIII of *De Interpretatione*, appears in fact identical to the notion of *dynaton*. See Aristotle, *De Interpretatione*, XIII, 22a14-32.
10. Houlgate (1995: 41) comments this passage in the same way, but at the same time he gives an extremely positive connotation to the 'reality of possibility'. It is actually disputable that Hegel already wanted to underline the actuality of possibility as

something positive, since in this passage he is criticizing an extremely abstract notion of possibility.
11 See, for example, section B of the chapter about *Ground* or the section about Quality. In the paragraph about real modality, the reference to content is immediately next to the first occurrence of the term *Realität*.
12 The influence of Aristotle's thought on Hegel's account of modality was already briefly remarked by Mure (1950: 134 and 149). See also *TWA* IV, 179 (§65): '*actu* und *potentia*. Unterschied von Macht und Möglichkeit; – ich mag nicht'.
13 See also Leibniz's essay *On Contingency*, where contingent being is characterized as the one in which existence is not entailed by essence.
14 This is, for example, Burbidge's interpretation (2007: 47), already criticized by Houlgate.
15 In this sense, Hegel's philosophy seems to meet perfectly the needs expressed by Quentin Meillassoux's 'speculative materialism', despite his negative judgement about Hegel's proposal. See Meillassoux 2008: 47–48.
16 Burbidge understands the absolute identity of necessity and contingency as if Hegel stated the contingency of the whole. It is a rather strong interpretation that does not find further confirmation in other writings, as the Nuremberg lectures or in the early Jena system.
17 The title of the paper already shows a rather problematic aspect of Henrich's reading, namely the distinction between *Zufall* and *Zufälliges*: if the former can be translated as 'chance', the latter possesses a variety of meanings that I have tried to clarify in this chapter, since it is not entirely accounted for in Hegel's text. See also Ferrarin 1999: 182.
18 I hence agree with Ferrarin's translation (1999: 177). Henrich understood contingency as 'indeducibility', as in Leibniz's philosophy, and did not take into consideration Aristotle's concept of chance.
19 It is disputable, though, that Aristotle really understood individuality as Henrich describes it. See, e.g., Ferrarin 1999: 177–178.
20 Folko Zander underlines the absence in Hegel's thought of a deterministic notion of necessity and the presence of a necessity that is only *a posteriori* (see *EI*, 147 A). See also Zander 2014, 188. The same direction is followed by Žižek, who however does not give a specific analysis of modal categories. See Žižek 2012: 463–473.

References

Aquinas, Thomas. (1991), *Summa Contra Gentiles, Book One: God*, Notre Dame: University of Notre Dame Press.
Bechler, Z. (1995), *Aristotle's Theory of Actuality*, New York: SUNY Press.

Brassier, R. (2007), *Nihil Unbound. Enlightenment and Extinction*, New York: Palgrave Macmillan.
Burbidge, J. W (2007), *Hegel's Systematic Contingency*, New York: Palgrave Macmillan.
De Boer, K. (2011), 'Transformations of Transcendental Philosophy: Wolff, Kant, and Hegel', *Bulletin of the Hegel Society of Great Britain*, 63: 50–79.
Ferrarin, A. (1999), *Hegel and Aristotle*, Cambridge: Cambridge University Press.
Heidegger, M. (1984), *Die Frage nach dem Ding*, in Id., *Gesamtausgabe*, Band: Vittorio Klostermann Verlag, 41.
Henrich, D. (1971), *Hegels Theorie über den Zufall*, in Id., *Hegel im Kontext*, Frankfurt: Suhrkamp Verlag.
Houlgate, S. (1995), 'Necessity and Contingency in Hegel's Science of Logic', *The Owl of Minerva*, 27, 1 (Fall): 37–49.
Illetterati, L. (2014), 'Limit and Contradiction in Hegel', in E. Ficara (ed.), *Contradiction. Logic, History, Actuality*, Berlin-Boston: De Gruyter.
Kant, I. (1998), *Critique of Pure Reason*, trans. P. Guyer and A. W. Wood, Cambridge (Mass.): Cambridge University Press.
Leibniz, G. W. (1989), *Philosophical Essays*, ed. R. Ariew, E. D. Garber, Indianapolis: Hackett Publishing Company.
Luhmann, N. (1998), *Observations on Modernity*, trans. W. Whobrey, Redwood City: Stanford University Press.
Mabille, B. (2013), *Hegel, L'épreuve de la contingence*, Paris: Hermann.
Malabou, C. (2005), *The Future of Hegel. Plasticity, Temporality and Dialectic*, London-New York: Routledge.
Massie, P. (2011), *Contingency, Time, and Possibility: An Essay on Aristotle and Duns Scotus*, Plymouth: Lexington Books.
Meillassoux, Q. (2008), *After Finitude. Essay on the Necessity of Contingency*, trans. R. Brassier, London: Continuum.
Mordacci, R. (2015), *Il dovere di fare la storia*, in I. Kant (ed.), *Idea per una storia universale in prospettiva cosmopolitica*, trans. S. Baccin E. F. Pongiglione, Milano-Udine: Mimesis.
Mure, G. R. G. (1950), *A Study of Hegel's Logic*, Oxford: Clarendon Press.
Rosen, S. (2014), *The Idea of Hegel's Science of Logic*, Chicago: Chicago University Press.
Wolff, Ch. (2001), *Philosophia prima sive Ontologia*, in Id., *Gesammelte Werke*, herausgegeben von J. École, Hildesheim: Olms Verlag.
Wölfle, G. M. (1994), *Die Wesenslogik in Hegels Wissenschaft der Logik. Versuch einer Rekonstruktion und Kritik unter besonderer Berücksichtigung der philosophischen Tradition*, Stuttgart: Frommann-Holzboog.
Zander, F. (2012), 'Die Logik des Zufalls. Über die Abschnitte A und B des Kapitels Wirklichkeit der Wesenslogik', in A. F. Koch, F. Schick, K. Vieweg, and C. Wirsing (eds), *Hegel – 200 Jahre Wissenschaft der Logik*, Hamburg: Meiner.
Žižek, S. (2012), *Less Than Nothing. Hegel and the Shadow of Dialectical Materialism*, London: Verso.

4

Self-Consciousness and the Idea: From Logic to Subjective Spirit

Guido Frilli

In this chapter, I discuss Hegel's account of self-consciousness from the standpoint of the relationship between logic and the philosophy of subjective spirit. I contend that while representation reduces the 'I' to the finitude of my particularity, self-consciousness in its truth is in fact an infinite form of the Idea. I submit that outright self-consciousness is the subjectivity of the Idea emerging from life. Yet, I also maintain that the universal 'I' of pure thought must necessarily realize itself in the finite form of an embodied 'I', that is, of my own spiritual subjectivity. Finally, I challenge the assumption that, pace Hegel himself, this correlation between the Idea and its spiritual realization would be ultimately able to elude the form of dualism Fichte introduced between transcendental and empirical self-consciousness.

Self-consciousness between representation and thought

What is the 'I'? How does self-consciousness emerge from nature? Why does Hegel connect it to desire and recognition? How can self-consciousness be the beginning of the 'native realm of truth' (*PS*, 104) and – with Luther and Descartes – of free subjective thought and at the same time the source of formal subjectivism and of moral particularism? Such questions are at the heart of some of the most innovative and influential interpretations of Hegel, both classical and recent: from Wahl (1929) and Kojève (1947) to Pippin (1989, 2011) and Pinkard (2012).[1] Scholarly literature has paid much attention to Hegel's account of self-consciousness as presented in the *Phenomenology of Spirit* (in its 1807 and later *Encyclopaedia* versions: Marx 1986; Jaeschke 2009; Pluder 2013) in the realms of moral and religious philosophy, as well as with regard to Hegel's critique of Kantian and Fichtean transcendentalism. However, smaller efforts have been made to account for the more general connection between the 'I' and thought (Düsing 1976, and more recently Ferrarin 2016) and for the 'I' as a logical category. The aim of this contribution is to examine self-consciousness from the perspective of the intricate link between pure thought and its realization, that is, between logic and subjective spirit.[2] My main assumption here is that if the truth of a thing is only its apprehension in pure thought (*EI*, §§21–22), then only by starting from the primary standpoint of logic one could claim to grasp spiritual self-consciousness in its full significance.

From the outset, such an investigation has to deal with a set of preliminary difficulties. First, the place of self-consciousness in the development of logical categories is, to say the least, ambiguous; and this may lead to the conclusion that self-consciousness is not a logical category, but only a category of spirit – that is to say a manifestation of the Idea as a concrete spiritual activity. Second, even granting that self-consciousness does possess a logical consistency, it would be easy to claim that it has neither an ontological priority nor any grounding status with respect to the other categories. Logical thought is essentially thought *without an 'I'* (*SL*, 53ff.), which, however, does not obviously mean that it is unconscious or disorganized thought.

On this point, the following preliminary picture can be drawn. The activity of thought, for Hegel, can as a matter of fact be unconscious; as I will emphasize in the conclusions, Hegel describes *Denken* as an instinct pervading all our activities. We are always thinking; that is, our flow of feelings, representations and desires is always structured by logical categories, even if we are not aware of their presence and efficacy. Hegel goes as far as to say that categories keep us in their possession, and not vice versa (*SL*, 14ff.). More to our point, according to Hegel, many things are *selves* without being self-*conscious*; that is, they are self-centred activities exhibiting an internal finalism, even if they do not express their subjectivity in a conscious way (e.g. *EII*, §350). Concepts are selves because they are like objective impulses; they are present in things as immanent activities (*PS*, 20). In other words, thought is not the operation of a presupposed consciousness; it does not have a fixed ego as its presupposition – be this ego *my* empirical awareness, as in Descartes or Jacobi, or a transcendental synthetizing (or self-intuitive) consciousness, as in Kant and Fichte. Quite to the contrary, Hegel would maintain that self-consciousness is one way in which pure thought determines itself; in other words, the 'I' is a form in which thought specifies its infinite activity. How can we make sense of this anti-subjectivist conception of thought? Is it plausible to maintain that self-consciousness is not a primitive basis of thought, but the result of its self-determination? How is the relationship between the activity of thought and self-consciousness to be conceived?

In the 1831 *Lectures on Logic*, Hegel repeatedly stresses an important point, which contributes to a first articulation of his controversial account. One should distinguish, he insists, between the 'I' as found in immediate consciousness and representation, and the 'I' as grasped by thought (*LLO*, 39, 110). Representational self-consciousness, so to speak, is what we usually associate to selfhood; empiricism, critical philosophy and Jacobi's immediate certainty (the second and third positions of thought towards objectivity) uncritically assume the 'I' in this representational sense. As it is immediately found by representation, indeed, self-consciousness is finite. It is opposed to an external world; it tries to grasp its objects through concepts reduced to empty or formal instruments. True, the 'I' in this sense is not mere consciousness but also *self*-consciousness; that is to say, it is the movement of assimilating externality into its own activity.[3] Yet, while destroying the independence of its objects in order to gain self-certainty, the finite 'I' remains essentially bound to them. On the contrary, the 'I' of thought is infinite; it is no more opposed to an object, but is free in its otherness; it is a universal self that pervades particularity (*LLO*, 7–8). On this score, we can notice, there is no difference between thought and the thinker – between the objective logos displaying itself in the *Science of Logic* and the thinking subject that articulates it. As a 'speculative' or infinite self, the thinker simply becomes its object – it *is* the thoughts that he or she is thinking (*EI*, §25). We can say that insofar as I enter into pure thought, my self-consciousness becomes identical to the self-consciousness of the Idea.[4]

Yet this claim, however enlightening, leads us to further questions. Are we entitled to say that something like *my* self-consciousness, as distinguished from universal thought, exists in the first place? And if we answer in the affirmative, are particular and representational self-consciousness two synonymic expressions for the same reality? Or else, is the finite 'I' of representation a sheer misleading illusion? To my mind, it is clear that, while criticizing its alleged immediacy or fixedness, Hegel regards the finite 'I' as a necessary determination of the activity of thought, just as, we can add, *my* particular self is a necessary determination of the universal concept. The above distinction might therefore need further specification. The finite 'I' of representation is not merely opposed to the infinite 'I' of thought; it is also a self-determination or particularization of thought. To put it differently, while the infinite 'I' is identical to the whole process of thought – it is, in the end, the logical Idea itself as *Denken*'s self-knowing subjectivity –

the finite 'I' is a specification of this process. Representation is thus partly true; its falseness consists in the fact that it non-dialectically stiffens self-consciousness in a rigid form; it severs the 'I' from the movement of thought that substantiates it and unilaterally affirms it as an ungrounded and primitive phenomenon. True actuality is instead achieved by my particular 'I' only as a moment of the dialectical-speculative life of thought.

I suggest, moreover, that we expand this picture by means of the following observation. When we ask ourselves what sort of thing the 'I' is, we usually tend to see it – as does representation – as an immediate and private phenomenon, a phenomenon, moreover, whose simplicity cannot be analysed or described without being dissolved.[5] Conversely, Hegel states that thinking the 'I' is a very complex action, which involves the deployment of a whole range of simpler logical categories – most directly those of being-for-itself and negative self-relation. I believe, in this regard, that Hegel's view is not incompatible with Dieter Henrich's contention according to which self-consciousness cannot be the product of language, nor can it properly be *explained* – in the sense of resulting from an antecedent principle, for example intersubjectivity – without circularity (see Henrich 1982). Yet Hegel's point concerns less an *explanation* of the 'I' as a private singularity than the indication of the path of its self-knowledge – of its full actuality.[6]

In order to *know* ourselves or to be truly self-conscious (*EIII*, §377), we must in fact think, and thinking means employing universal categories. Indeed, it is only by abstracting from all my particular feelings, inclinations and representations that I can conceive myself as an 'I' – that is, as a universal point that contains all my determinate experiences. In order to focus this all-embracing universality, we need to employ simpler determinations, like negation and being-for-itself. But more importantly, once we have grasped it, we come to utter *contradiction* in its purest form (*LLO*, 8). Being a universal abstracted from particular feelings and representations, the 'I' is devoid of any determinacy. As famously showed by the dialectics of self-certainty, while employing the word 'I' to refer to myself, I cannot but express *all* the selves (*PS*, 62). Hence, the 'I' is simultaneously the most universal – everyone is an 'I' – and the most particular. But for this very reason, the 'I' is the unity of universality and particularity; it is singularity, that is, an infinite self-relation that tolerates contradiction. As such, it is the whole movement of the concept expressed in a simple determination.

It is precisely in these terms that self-consciousness makes an entrance as thought-determination [*Denkbestimmung*] in the logic. After having introduced it as an illustration of *being-for-itself* (*SL*, 127) and *quantum*,[7] Hegel – in the introductory section of *Subjective Logic* 'On the Concept in General' – presents the I as an exemplification of the concept itself. Here we read that 'the concept, when it has progressed to a concrete existence which is itself free, is none other than the "I" or pure self-consciousness'. More precisely:

> The 'I' is the pure concept itself, the concept that has come into *determinate existence*. It is fair to suppose, therefore, when we think of the fundamental determinations which constitute the nature of the 'I', that we are referring to something familiar, that is, a commonplace of ordinary thought. But the 'I' is *in the first place* purely self-referring unity, and is this not immediately but by abstracting from all determinateness and content and withdrawing into the freedom of unrestricted equality with itself. As such it is *universality*, a unity that is unity with itself only by virtue of its *negative* relating, which appears as abstraction, and because of it contains all determinateness within itself as dissolved. *In second place*, the 'I' is just as immediately self-referring negativity, *singularity, absolute determinateness* that stands opposed to anything other and excludes it – *individual personality*. (*SL*, 514ff.)

Like the concept, the 'I' is 'immediately self-referring negativity'. Yet the 'I' is not the concept as such, but the concept 'that has come into *determinate existence*'. The concrete or determinate existence gained by the concept as self-consciousness is posited by the concept itself; that is to say, self-consciousness is a logical form of the Idea, the unity of the concept and its realization.[8]

Indeed, the genuine logical place of the 'I' is the Idea – specifically, the Idea of cognition. '*Thought, spirit, self-consciousness* are determinations of the Idea inasmuch as the latter has itself as the subject matter, and its *existence*, that is, the determinateness of its being, is its own difference from itself' (*SL*, 689). Self-consciousness is the dialectical *Aufhebung* of life. Whereas life is the only immediate Idea, cognition elevates the Idea above its own existence as genus: this *Erhebung* is first accomplished by self-consciousness, since self-consciousness is the Idea in its immediate *subjective* form. Life is a dynamic unity of universal genus and particular existence, but one that remains exterior to particularity itself; the living organism achieves its destination only by dying, and its death reaffirms the universality of genus. Cognition, on the contrary, is the genus per se: universality conscious of itself in and through particularity. Self-consciousness is hence 'absolute self-reference', an immediate self-partition (*Ur-teilung*) of universality. The 'I' is object to itself; it has an object which is immediately identical to it. As such, it is both particular – *my* self-consciousness – and truly universal, finite and infinite.[9] Thus, self-consciousness is a circle:

The awkwardness, the circle, is in fact the relation by which the eternal nature of self-consciousness and of the concept is revealed in immediate, empirical self-consciousness – is revealed because self-consciousness is precisely the existent and therefore empirically perceivable pure concept; because it is the absolute self-reference that, as parting judgment, makes itself into an intended object and consists in simply making itself thereby into a circle. (*SE*, 691)

Embodied self-consciousness: From logic to subjective spirit

In the 1807 *Phenomenology*, Hegel already describes self-consciousness as emerging dialectically from life. Life, though in an exceedingly dense and difficult passage, is conceptualized by Hegel in almost the same way as it will be in the 1816 *Subjective Logic*: indeed, it is not a part of consciousness's experience, but it is anticipated as a true determination of infinity (*PS*, 106ff.). Life is the inner rational movement that pervades reality; it is an unconscious 'pulsation', a 'simple fluid substance of pure movement within itself'. Self-consciousness, by contrast, still appears as a phenomenal and finite determination; it is not grasped by thought in its truth, but exposed in the way in which it is first experienced by consciousness – hence, by means of representation. As such, the 'I' is shown as disconnected from life and infinity; it strives to affirm its particularity at the expense of external objects. Again, this disconnection exhibits a partial truth. Struggling for the truth of its self-certainty, self-consciousness practically demonstrates its independence from life; it announces the superiority of spiritual universality with respect to the natural universality of genus. Like living beings, self-consciousness is essentially negativity and desire (*Begierde*) – still, it is no more a corporeal need only, but a desire for self-certainty and recognition. Yet, since it is unilaterally committed to validate its own particularity against life, self-consciousness faces loss, fear and slavery; it glimpses infinity – in the abstract form of the reciprocal recognition between two separate individuals – but cannot hold to it in a stable relationship.

In all the three versions of the *Encyclopaedia*, as is well known, Hegel reiterates a good part of the analysis of the 1807 *Phenomenology*. Yet the perspective is different in many respects.[10] The point is no longer how consciousness makes experience of truth, but how spirit becomes concrete in turning its own natural givenness into freedom. Hence, Hegel no longer puts emphasis on the shortcomings of a phenomenal representation of self-consciousness, but – it is a subtle yet important difference – on the genuine concept of self-consciousness as it operates in the concrete context of spirit. The logical concept of the 'I', which we outlined in the first section, is now the presupposition of the whole investigation; this is why the dialectics of self-consciousness, contrary to its 1807 version, is now capable of leading to universality and reason (*EIII*, §436). Whereas self-consciousness in the 1807 *Phenomenology* was the *appearance* of the true concept of the 'I', in the *Encyclopaedia* Hegel shows the *realization* of this concept.

The infinite concept of self-consciousness – that is, the 'I' as a circle of self-negating universality – can be easily detected as the driving thrust of the dialectics of desire and recognition. Self-consciousness, at its beginning, is still a practical desire, but such desire closely resembles the *Trieb* of the subjective Idea, which already constitutes a form of infinity. As we read in the *Science of Logic*:

> At first the subjective idea is *impulse*. For it is the contradiction of the concept that it has itself for the *subject matter* and is to itself the reality without, however, the subject matter being an *other* that subsists on its own over against it, or without the differentiation of itself from itself having at the same time the essential determination of *diversity* and of indifferent existence. The specific nature of this impulse is therefore to sublate its own subjectivity, to make that first abstract reality a concrete one, filling it with the *content* of the world presupposed by its subjectivity. (*SL*, 697)

Correspondingly, the 'I's desire in the *Encyclopaedia* is more the expression of spirit's inner split into particularity and universality than an individual's longing for self-certainty. Self-consciousness is both spirit's own self-division into conscience and object,[11] and the drive to overcome this very division into a concrete unity:

> The 'I' is for itself, is free, through the fact that it excludes this immediacy from itself. The freedom of spirit means that it knows, it has this totality in itself, it acquires this totality, makes it its own possession; it means that it is its own representations, thoughts, determinations. But at first the 'I' is the abstract; the 'I' is the act of excluding, and takes what it excludes as the negative of itself. (*LPS*, 168)[12]

In other words, self-consciousness is now presented as both a contradiction and the very overcoming of this contradiction into infinity. The consequence that I would like to discuss brings us to the relationship between logic and subjective spirit. In what sense is the logical category of the 'I' realized as a spiritual activity? How does such realization differ from an only exterior application of an already affirmative infinity into a more tangible sphere?

I wish to suggest that self-consciousness is an apt standpoint for the investigation of the systemic link between pure thought – the logical Idea – and its manifestation as nature and spirit; besides, this link is key to the understanding of Hegel's overall understanding of the 'I'. Self-consciousness, as it emerges in subjective spirit, exhibits both its logical ground – the 'I' as a self-negating universality, i.e. as the subjective form of the Idea – and the insufficiency of this ground. I would like to reformulate this crucial aspect in the following terms: the pure thought of the 'I' is the logical soul and grounding principle of every individual human being, but a soul or principle is not enough: it has to finitize itself as an embodied self-consciousness. Speaking of a necessary embodiment of the 'I', in this context, is not a metaphor: self-consciousness is *real* only as an embodied individual.[13]

The 'I', as we read in the text just quoted from the 1827–1828 *Lectures on the Philosophy of Spirit*, is first found as immediate: 'the "I" in its immediacy includes everything we have treated as the soul in the Anthropology'. As anthropological soul, spirit is an unconscious or instinctive self, which permeates and individualizes the body before becoming expressly self-aware. Thanks to the pre-intentional work of habit, spirit shapes the whole of our corporeal sensations, feelings, passions and preconscious activities. Only after having idealized an individual natural body, spirit is capable of opposing itself to itself.[14] As a consequence of this self-opposition, the natural unity of the soul is irrevocably split into subjectivity and objectivity, into a consciousness and its body; and consciousness becomes a properly self-conscious individuality as soon as it interrupts its spontaneous immersion in external objects and turns back to itself as the source of their value.

As a logical truth, the 'I' is a result of life from which it awakens; yet the real manifestation of this awakening occurs with the shaping of an individual body. It is true that self-consciousness overcomes the soul and its passive idealization of the body. Only by opposing its natural substance, spirit gains individuality and freedom. Such opposition, however, does not come abstractly from above; self-consciousness is a result of nature, since nature itself is permeated by the instinctive work of logos. Unlike Descartes's ego, the Hegelian 'I' is a living part of the world; it is rooted in a previous organized natural activity that shapes each one's corporeality before becoming conscious of itself as a singular subjectivity.[15]

Conclusion: Self-consciousness and the Idea as instinct

The systemic link between logic and subjective spirit sheds much needed light on Hegel's account of self-consciousness; the 'I' must be taken not only as a moment of the logical Idea but also as the embodiment of the Idea in a spiritual individuality. I wish to reformulate this contention in the following way: truly thinking the 'I' – that is, grasping self-consciousness as a determination of the Idea – involves a double movement of (1) universalization and (2) exteriorization of thought.

First, I find myself immersed in the determinacy of particular feelings and representations. As long as I perceive this determinacy as *mine*, I am a particular ego bounded to particular experiences. By *thinking* myself as an 'I', by contrast, I rise up to a purified universality[16]; I access something that is common to all individuals. Since I am a self-relating universal, objective thought becomes my true self – I *am* the subjective form of the Idea, the whole concept in a 'determinate existence'. Second, the Idea is not only pure thought but thought exteriorized in nature and spirit. Paradoxically, then, my self-consciousness becomes actually *mine* only as a moment of the Idea's exteriorization in the world – I am neither a merely particular 'I', nor simply the concept expressed in a 'concrete existence', but rather spirit individualized in a body and awakened to conscious freedom. Individual self-consciousness, when abstractly opposed to universality, is the origin of evil. But its conceptualization as a dialectical moment of the Idea, that is to say of the infinite self-consciousness of logos, does not involve its dissolution into the uniformity of a rarefied universality. The Idea is exteriorized in nature; it exists everywhere as an instinct towards self-presence, and it becomes self-conscious by determining its instinctive life as a spiritual individuality, as my 'I', that is, in a particular body. Thought, in other words, both overcomes my finitude and at the same time confirms finitude as permeated by the Idea – as an immanent finitization of logos.[17]

Finally, I wish to conclude my reconstruction by anticipating one possible objection. We have seen that self-consciousness, grasped in its truth, is a circle of universality and particularity. When understood as a spiritual realization of the Idea, however, the circularity of the 'I' runs the risk of becoming vicious. How can the 'I' arise from corporeality, except by being already presupposed as the logical *telos* to be realized by the unconscious work of the soul? If we want to avoid such an external teleology, the only option seems to be a Fichtean one: that is, the assumption of a duality between thought and experience, and hence between a transcendental and an empirical 'I'. Both horns of this alternative are unpleasant for Hegel, but the path between them might prove too narrow.

Hegel's answer has already been foreshadowed and, I believe, consists in accounting for the Idea as an all-pervasive instinct to self-knowledge. In the chapter on the absolute idea, method is described as the most universal and comprehensive expression of the activity of thinking, the rational essence of the world (SL, 737)[18]; it is 'a concrete existence that is the concept itself', 'the *universal absolute activity*', or again the rational pulsation intrinsic both to the 'manner of cognition' and to 'the *substantiality of things*'. As this instinctive rationality, the Idea is exteriorized in the world in nature as well as in spirit. It is 'instinctive act' that moves thought to overcome negativity and to achieve satisfaction and self-presence. In this sense, each one's real self-consciousness emerging from the soul is nothing but thought that awakens from its only natural and instinctive life; the 'I' is one with the soul to which it is opposed, since thought is one and the same 'erotical' force, both in its unconscious and in its conscious forms. Logical categories exist everywhere as self-movements and instincts.[19] The 'logical task' of philosophy, Hegel argues, consists in bringing to consciousness the instinctive activity of thinking intrinsic to every logical and real determination. As a logical category, hence, the 'I' as well is a moment of the instinctive life of reason in the world.

Yet, I think that this answer might eventually be unsatisfactory. If, as a moment of the Idea, self-consciousness is a rational instinct, yet it is the only instinct that leads thought beyond instinctiveness. Thought is everywhere as an immanent soul or life-pulsation; still, paradoxically, self-consciousness is the only life that affirms instinctively the self-conscious form of thought – that is, thought in its wholeness and perfection. The 'I' must be both identical and other with respect to the Idea's realization as soul; even granting that such partial otherness is but a different form of a single rational substance, it seems to reintroduce the kind of duality that Hegel's anti-Fichteanism wanted to refute.

Notes

1 See also, among others, Düsing (1986), Butler (1987), Honneth (1992), Brandom (2007).
2 This direction is not investigated in Ferrarin (2016). For a critical discussion of this book, which however is close to the exegetical perspective that I will defend here, see Frilli (2018).

3   *SL*: 127: 'Consciousness is thus phenomenal, or it is this dualism: on the one side, it knows an external object which is other than it; on the other side, it is for-itself, has this intended object in it as idealized, abides not only by this other but therein abides also with itself. Self-consciousness, on the contrary, is being-for-itself brought to completion and posited; the side of reference to another, to an external object, is removed. Self-consciousness is thus the nearest example of the presence of infinity – granted, of a still abstract infinity, but one which is of a totally different, concrete determination than the being-for-itself in general, whose infinity still has only qualitative determinateness.'
4   For a similar claim, see Rosen (1974).
5   See, with reference to Hegel, Henrich (1970) and Cramer (1974).
6   For this distinction, see Ferrarin (2018).
7   *SL*, 156. See also the critical discussion of Kant and Fichte in the paragraph on "quantitative infinite progress": *SL*, 194ff.
8   Hegel's argument in the paragraph 'On the Concept in General' contains an explicit praise of Kant's doctrine of apperception, yet with a crucial restriction: even if Kant has seized the concept (the unity of apperception) as the immanent synthesis of objectivity, he has not conceived this objectivity as the objectivity *of* the concept; one may say that, for Hegel, Kant has not reached the thought of self-consciousness as Idea.
9   *PS*, 102: 'I distinguish myself from myself, and in doing so I am directly aware that what is distinguished from myself is not different. I, the selfsame being, repel myself from myself; but what is posited as distinct from me, or as unlike me, is immediately, in being so distinguished, not a distinction from me.' In the 1827–1828 *Lectures on the Philosophy of Spirit* we read, in a similar vein, that 'everything is a contradiction, but a contradiction that has been resolved. I am the whole, pure, simple, and universal, and at the same time I am immediately the opposite, an individual, a "this". I am the resolution of this contradiction' (*LPS*, 166).
10 For a discussion of the differences between the 1807 and the *Encyclopaedia's Phenomenology*, see Schalhorn (2000), Ferrarin (2016), chap. 1.
11 It is the upshot of the 'judgement by which spirit constitutes itself as *I*, as free subjectivity in contrast to determinacy', such as 'spirit emerges from substance, and philosophy, when it makes this judgment the absolute determination of spirit, emerges from Spinozism' (*EIII*: §415 R, 145).
12 Still more concisely: 'the being of spirit is the soul. It is something for me' (ibid.).
13 It seems to me that Ferrarin (2018) takes instead embodiment, in this context, to be a metaphorical expression.
14 On the more general problem of the soul–body connection, see Wolff (1992).
15 The same process has an objective side as the juridical appropriation of one's own body as private property.
16 Self-consciousness is 'the universal in the form of universality' (*LPS*, 166).

17 In the Absolute Spirit chapter (see esp. §574 of *EIII*, 275), Hegel writes that the self-thinking Idea is now 'the universality verified in the concrete content as in its actuality. In this way science has returned to its beginning, and the logical is its result as the spiritual [*das Geistige*]'. Hegel points clearly to the difference between logical and spiritual reason in the Remark to § 437 (*EIII*, 163): 'reason as the Idea (§213) appears here in the following determination: the general opposition between concept and reality, which are unified in the Idea, has here taken the specific form of the concept existing for itself, of consciousness and, confronting it, the externally present object'.

18 Method is 'not only the highest *force* of reason, or rather its *sole* and absolute *force*, but also reason's highest and sole *impulse* to find and recognize *itself through itself in all things*' (ibid.).

19 *SL*, 17: 'as impulses the categories do their work only instinctively; they are brought to consciousness one by one and so are variable and mutually confusing, thus affording to spirit only fragmentary and uncertain actuality. To purify these categories and in them to elevate spirit to truth and freedom, this is therefore the loftier business of logic'.

References

Brandom, R. (2007), 'The Structure of Desire and Recognition: Self-Consciousness and Self-Constitution', in R. Bubner and G. Hindrichs (eds), *Von der Logik zur Sprache. Stuttgarter Hegel-Kongress 2005*, 426–449, Stuttgart: Klett-Cotta.

Butler, J. (1987), *Subjects of Desire*, New York: Columbia University Press.

Cramer, K. (1974), *Erlebnis. Thesen zu Hegels Theorie des Selbstbewußtsein mit Rücksicht auf die Aporien eines Grundbegriffs nachhegelscher Philosophie*, Hegel-Studien Beiheft 11, 537–603, Bonn: Bouvier.

Düsing, E. (1986), *Intersubjektivität und Selbstbewußtsein: Behavioristische, phänomenologische, und idealistische Begründungstheorien bei Mead, Schütz, Fichte und Hegel*, Köln: Dinter.

Düsing, K. (1976), *Das Problem der Subjektivität in Hegels Logik*, Hegel-Studien Beiheft 15, Bonn: Bouvier.

Ferrarin, A. (2016), *Il pensare e l'io. Hegel e la critica di Kant*, Roma: Carocci.

Ferrarin, A. (2018), 'Il pensare e l'io: a reply to Magrì and Frilli', *Critique*, https://virtualcritique.wordpress.com/2018/02/19 (last visit: 09- 03-2018).

Frilli, G. (2018), 'Alfredo Ferrarin's "Il pensare e l'io": a critical discussion', *Critique*, https://virtualcritique.wordpress.com/2018/02/19/guido-frilli-on-alfredo-ferrarins-il-pensare-e-l'io (last visit: 09- 03-2018).

Henrich, D. (1970), 'Selbstbewußtsein. Kritische Einleitung in einer Theorie', in R. Bubner, K. Cramer and R. Wiehl (eds), *Hermeneutik und Dialektik. Aufsätze I*, 257–284, Tübingen: J. C. B. Mohr.

Henrich, D. (1982), *Selbstbewußtsein und spekulatives Denken*, in Id., *Fluchtlinien. Philosophische Essays*, Frankfurt a. M.: Klostermann.

Honneth, A. (1992), *Der Kampf um Anerkennung*, Frankfurt a. M.: Suhrkamp.

Jaeschke, W. (2009), *Das Selbstbewußtsein des Bewußtsein*, in T. S. Hoffmann (ed.), *Hegel als Schlüsseldenker der modernen Welt*, 15–30, Hamburg: Meiner.

Kojève, A. (1947), *Introduction à la lecture de Hegel*, Paris: Gallimard.

Marx, W. (1986), *Das Selbstbewußtsein in Hegels Phänomenologie des Geistes*, Frankfurt a. M.: Klostermann.

Pinkard, T. (2012), *Hegel's Naturalism*, Oxford: Oxford University Press.

Pippin, R. (1989), *Hegel's Idealism. The Satisfaction of Self-Consciousness*, Cambridge: Cambridge University Press.

Pippin, R. (2011), *Hegel on Self-Consciousness. Desire and Death in Hegel's Phenomenology of Spirit*, Princeton: Princeton University Press.

Pluder, V. (2013), *Die Vermittlung von Idealismus und Realismus in der Klassischen DEutschen Philosophie*, 467–550, Stuttgart-Bad Cannstatt: Frommann-Holzboog.

Rosen, S. (1974), 'Self-consciousness and self-knowledge in Plato and Hegel', *Hegel-Studien*, 9: 109–129.

Schalhorn, C. (2000), *Hegels enzyklopädischer Begriff von Selbstbewußtsein*, Hegel-Studien Beiheft 43, Hamburg: Meiner.

Wahl, J. (1929), *Le Malheur de la conscience dans la philosophie de Hegel*, Paris: PUF.

Wolff, M. (1992), *Das Körper-Seele-Problem. Kommentar zu Hegel, Enzyklopädie 1830, § 389*, Frankfurt a. M.: Klostermann.

5

The Concept of Habit and the Function of Immediacy

Sean McStravick

In the present chapter, I wish to *explore* the correspondence at work between the anthropological notion of habit [*Gewhonheit*] and the onto-logical notion of immediacy [*Unmittelbarkeit*] in Hegel's philosophy. Nonetheless, I will deliberately not define the specific type of correspondence at work – that is, whether habit and immediacy are *identical* or *equivalent*, or whether habit is a *paradigm* of immediacy. Those questions go beyond the aim of this chapter, which is to clarify the function of immediacy as absolute secondary. I believe this enables us to grasp the speculative nature of the relation between being and thought, and understand the *spiral* structure of spirit [*Geist*] and thus its absolute negativity.

The 'threat of autonomous exteriority'

Hegel's philosophy is shaped by the problem of the identification of being and thought (*SL*, 29). In this respect, it seeks to overcome the 'nothingness of the spectral *thing-in-itself*' left by Kantian critique (SL, 27). According to Hegel, Kant made important progress in the history of philosophy by establishing that the configuration of objectivity is dependent on the subjective forms of receptivity and spontaneity (Kant 1904: 74). The shift of the external notion of the thing-in-itself to the internal notion of phenomenon helped achieve the essential aim of modern philosophy to manifest the subjective structure of objectivity. Nevertheless, in Kantian philosophy, the thing-in-itself characterizes both the unknowable affect of sensory intuition and the hypothetical, albeit necessary object of a non-sensory intuition. Therefore, as Béatrice Longuenesse pointed out, the thing-in-itself simultaneously refers to the regulative idea of knowledge and to the unknowable source of reality (Longuenesse 2007: 22). According to Hegel, this is a theoretical flaw as it maintains an irreducible and unknowable pole of being external to the frame of transcendental subjectivity, thereby preventing it from asserting the full 'assignability' of being to its activity.

In Hegel's philosophy, the problem of the thing-in-itself shifts to the general problem of immediacy. Hegel features immediacy as both the given shape of being (*SL*, 337) – that is, as the primordial and apparently *set* significance of what is – and what 'begins'. Hegel writes: 'Beginnings are in every case data and postulates' (*EI*, §9). As a beginning, immediacy betrays anticipating yet spontaneous mediations, which *appear* to function autonomously. Indeed, any predetermined *method* naturally anticipates the content of knowledge and apprehends a pre-organized *object* that seems to independently stand as such (*PS*, §73). However, by appearing as that which is not mediated, it embodies the risk of an irreducible exteriority for spirit – of absolute otherness. In this respect, immediacy represents what I would call 'the threat of autonomous exteriority', which manifests itself as a potential obstacle for spirit to establish itself as freedom, that is, as being at home with itself in otherness. This entails two important theoretical directions. First, Hegel's main philosophical concern has come to be a refusal of any position of absolute immediacy. Second, this refusal is consubstantial with the positive characterization of spirit as a negative nature.

Justifying and locating the 'given'

In addressing the 'threat of autonomous exteriority', Hegel systematically fulfils the requirement of *justifying* and *locating* the given. This is the essential aim of *essence*. By the end of the *Doctrine of Being*, the immanent determinations of being appear as 'laws'. This appearance of immediate exteriority to itself sublates the resulting 'in-difference' of being and prevents it from being complete (*SL*, 326–335). As a result of this negativity, or infinite relation to itself, being passes into essence in order to reflect itself as negativity. Thus, the reflection of immediacy or of being is not the suppression of the immediateness (conceived as the state of being immediate) but rather the progressive recalling of itself as a conceived and conceiving thing.

In order to circumscribe immediacy to the activity of spirit, and refute its absolute exteriority, Hegel's strategy amounts to operating immediacy as a *logical function* within substance, thereby making it a *moment* of spirit itself. Substance is characterized as the immediacy *of* thought, as the immediacy *for* thought and as the unity of both as *subject* (*PS*, §17). Substance can be described as the reciprocal process by virtue of which subjective immediacy (immediacy *of* thought) and objective immediacy (immediacy *for* thought) mediate one another, thus making it the subject from a speculative standpoint. In logical words, being (as immediacy) is both generated *by* and generating *of* gnosis. Concept [*Begriff*], which is the 'power of substance' (*EI*, §160),[1] is thereby defined as the subjective and productive activity which structures the self-movement of substance, that is to say, as the perpetual process of self-generation of immediacy. In this respect, justifying and locating immediacy entail *assigning* the given to its conceiving origin and acknowledging its function as a conceived thing within the general movement of absolute spirit – absolute spirit being 'the one and universal substance as spiritual' (*EIII*, §554), that is, the speculative and infinite unity of the subjective and objective spirit. On one hand, *justifying* immediacy makes the assignment of reality to its rational and subjective form possible. On the other hand, *locating* immediacy allows asserting the freedom of Concept.

First, *justifying* immediacy is the bringing about of its rational and structuring mediations. In order to achieve this, Hegel uses the device of reflection, which drives the *Doctrine of Essence*. Indeed, Hegel specifies that 'being is, in general, unreflected immediacy' (*EI*, §142 R). Reflection consists in the 'intropassing' of being – that is, the 'recalling' of its essence as negativity. It is the shift from *being* to *shine*, that is, to something that is positedness yet *seems* to be original. However, by defining essence as 'past being' (*SL*, 337), the reflection of being implies that the reflective agent does not differ from the reflected patient, but rather introspects what constituted itself as such. So, reflection is the progressive clarification of the internal and underlying rational determinations of immediacy, thereby producing various levels of intelligibility or forms of what is immediate – existence, phenomenon, effectiveness – which all gradually narrow down the gap between the objective being and its origin. Ultimately, in 'effectual reality' (*Wirklichkeit*), which is fully rationalized reality, being is shown to be identical to thought (*EI*, §142 A).

Secondly, *locating* immediacy does not mean suppressing its authority, but rather acknowledging its function within the general movement of the idea – which is rational reality or the unity of concept and objectivity (*EI*, §213). In order to locate immediacy, Hegel thematizes rationality's spontaneous efficiency within being, thereby clarifying that being is the *inertial positivity of thought*. Indeed, immediacy presupposes a movement that shows its derivation from the free and *autonomous* activity of concept (*EI*, §§157–159). In fact, the idea 'resolves to let [...] the immediate idea, as its reflected image, go forth freely as Nature' (*EI*, §244). In other words, the status of immediacy shifts to what Hegel refers to as a 'second immediacy' (*SL*, 746). In this respect, the main thesis of the *Logic* consists in asserting that immediacy is subjectively conceived yet appears as objective and that a beginning or immediacy is a result. Hegel summarizes this process as follows:

> In passing over into essence, *being* became [...] a *positedness*, and *becoming* or the passing over into an *other* became a *positing*; conversely, the *positing* or the reflection of essence sublated itself and restored itself to a *non-posited*, an *original* being. (*SL*, 530)

Immediacy is indeed thematized as both a necessary objective actuality – which *appears* as a *law* for consciousness – and the result of any potential subjective or conceptual act of conceiving. The various 'forms' of being that are analysed in the *Logic* are not 'ontologically' different, but vary 'onto-logically' alongside the gradually enhanced capacity for rationality to acknowledge its own active presence within it. In the preface of the *Outlines of the Philosophy of Rights*, Hegel recapitulates this general requirement in practical terms:

> After all, the truth about Right, Ethics, and the state is as old as its public recognition and formulation in the law of the land, in the morality of everyday life, and in religion. What more does this truth require – since the thinking mind is not content to possess it in this ready fashion? It requires to be grasped in thought as well; the content which is already rational in principle must win the *form* of rationality and so appear well-founded to untrammelled thinking. Such thinking does not remain stationary at the given [...]. On the contrary, thought which is free starts out from itself and thereupon claims to know itself as united in its innermost being with the truth. (*OPR*, 3)

In other words, the immediacy that characterizes the mind's relation to the truth as reality – its 'simplicity' and 'oldness' – requires to be negated, that is, turned into an appearance, analysed and rationally justified, in order for free thought to acknowledge its own presence within it, and thus claim *ownership* over it (*PS*, §32). The locating and justifying of immediacy are thus the turning of the *acquired* yet beginning immediacy into a *conquered* immediacy that is apprehended as the result of a rational elaboration.

This general critique of immediacy manifests itself within the system as the dialectic of immediacy and mediation. Yet, this implies two things. Firstly, it demands an ascending dialectical dimension through which thought reflects immediacy and returns to its positing authority. Therein lies the essential movement of the *Phenomenology of Spirit*. Consciousness gradually acquires knowledge of itself within what is given. Yet in Hegel's philosophy, the absolute knowledge is not the condition of possibility of immediacy. On the contrary, as Jean-François Kervégan argued, the ascending dialectic cannot be disassociated from a descending dialectic which 'brings the absolute knowledge back to the sensory certainty, and the absolute idea back to pure being, and the absolute mediation back to pure immediacy' (Kervégan 2011: n.p.; *my translation*). Therefore, secondly, the critique entails a certain *validation* of the given. Only in virtue of this double process can immediacy be effectively identified with reason and apprehended as an appearance of being which derives from the free and autonomous conceptual activity. In other words, 'second immediacy' is the truth of immediacy.

Absolute secondarity and second nature

It is patent that Hegel operates this notion of 'absolute secondarity' in order to suppress any form of definitive and natural given foundation for thought – be it objective or subjective – while at the same time containing any possible disjunction between being and thought. By manifesting the temporal trace and spiral structure from which it proceeds, Hegel establishes that immediacy is comprised of a process through which all mediations simplify into the spontaneous appearance of the given.[2] Moreover, in Hegel's *Philosophy of Spirit*, immediacy operates as a second nature. For this reason, it seems that immediacy harnesses the mechanisms of habit.

However, the notion of habit seems to imply an intuitive empiricist-based philosophical understanding. Scottish empiricism has indeed had the merit of attributing a determining function to habit in its genetic apprehension of immediate reality. In the *Enquiry concerning Human Understanding*, Hume established that the causal scope of our knowledge of reality is not a rationally consistent one, but rather the result of habit. Hume states that 'all inferences from experience [...] are effects of custom, not of reasoning' (Hume 2000: 38). Nonetheless, Hume's philosophy tends to clear habit from its spiritual content and falls short of fully appreciating that the intellectual modalities of the reception of the given participate in the nature of what is received. Indeed, this empiricist-based approach of habit fails to overcome the separation between the given and thought.

Conversely, Hegel operates this notion in its spiritual understanding. Such an understanding can be found within the French spiritualist tradition. Ravaisson in particular thematized habit not as the result of empirical associations but rather as what we earlier referred to as the 'inertial positivity of the activity of spirit'. In *Of Habit*, he characterizes habit as the general and stabilized way of being, which results from change, yet is also the beginning of any other virtual change (Ravaisson 2008: 25). However, habit is never outside the realm of intelligence. First, it cannot derive from what is unintelligent since the mediations in virtue of which habit is possible presuppose intelligence itself.[3] Second, habits themselves are never unintelligent; in fact, habitual thoughts and wills are still structured by the end that reflection and will initially set out for in the form of an inclination. Indeed, the process of habituation consists in the progressive reduction of the gap between the end (the idea of the will or reflection) and the movement. The idea and the inclination soon become one thing. Therefore, habit is the gradual substantialization of the idea (Ravaisson 2008: 55–57). Getting used to something *realizes* the activity of thought, whether it be the active production of ideas or the passive reception of any external movement. Habit allows for the establishing of the coincidence between what is a given and the resulting effect of an intellectual activity. It overcomes any possible dualism between nature and thought insofar as it considers substantial reality as fully spiritual.

For a practical instance, the habit of handwriting is comprised of the acquisition of a natural gesture. Yet, the principle-effort and the mediations of the handwriting gradually vanish into the acquired autonomy of handwriting itself; the effortful and conscious hand soon subjects itself to a spontaneous and autonomous *law* of movement and to an effortless conduct. In turn, habit thus becomes the pace that pre-scribes the effort. In other words, being is seen to be a resulting intelligence, that is, a 'spontaneous thoughtlessness', which at the same time anticipates and succeeds the activity of spirit. Reflecting the habitual thus entails gaining consciousness of the spiritual *historicity* of being.

The theoretical virtue of the notion of habit as a 'second nature' lies in its utterly speculative nature. According to Hegel, speculation essentially consists in considering that the posited-being is a presupposed-being (*EI*, §238) and that the beginning, or being, is a result (*PS*, §12). Speculation overcomes hard oppositions. In this respect, habit embodies the same function as the Hegelian notion of immediacy; it is both posited and non-posited, both the condition of the heteronomy of the given and the appearance of its autonomy. Habit appears as an immediate immediacy, yet it is a structured and structuring immediacy. Also, the reflection of the habitual involves both an ascending and descending dialectical process: reflecting habit corresponds to the gradual recalling of its spiritual origin, yet this presupposes that the activity of intelligence has declined into a spontaneous and heteronomous form. Thus habit is also the a priori form or beginning of any activity; it is the prescribing shape of the positing.

By acknowledging the absolute secondarity of immediacy, inasmuch as it functions *as* habit, Hegel establishes a circular dynamic where being is seen to derive from the free activity of thought. On this basis, it has become clear that this groundless opening is the speculative condition of a reflective philosophy which overcomes, on the one hand, the irreducibility of a given, independent and autonomous being, and on the other, the unilateral oppositions between subjectivity and objectivity. In this respect, my view is that the notion of habit is an essential resource within Hegel's philosophy of spirit, insofar as it functions as a speculative hinge. Indeed, the general notion of habit seems to enable the logical approach of spirit through its moments, as it enables all its functional immediacies, which spontaneously operate as an immediate and mediating given, yet shows traces of the activity which posited them. Inasmuch as those fixed instances are the inertial positivity of spirit, they are a 'proper otherness'. In this sense, it can at least be claimed that habit *functions* as immediacy.

The function of habit within the philosophy of spirit

Hegel generally operates a vague yet most significant notion of habit in order to characterize various 'self-evident' and 'normal' types of knowing. In his prefaces, introductions, as well as remarks and additions, he frequently refers to the 'habitual way of considering' things.[4] In this respect, habit refers to a thoughtless and compelling dogmatism that naturalizes things. It corresponds to the *unexamined immediacy of thought*. For instance, the 'well-known' is a type of knowledge made of familiar representations concerning existence. It refers to a self-evident starting and stopping standpoint that compels knowledge and requires to be analysed in order to gain access to science (*PS*, §§31–32). However, although these forms of habitual thinking are deceptive, they have an epistemological function. By establishing that there is a convergence between a *natural* starting point and a *historical* result – i.e. a natural and immediate truth and a conceived second nature – Hegel indeed manifests the historically determined position of *any* type of reasoning. Yet, insofar as science itself is described as an *unusual* position for natural consciousness (*PS*, §26), the systematic reference to the *habitual* way of thinking functions as the conditioning twin of the speculative. Habit is not excluded from the spirit's dynamic at all. On the contrary, familiar representations are a necessary moment of its development.

Moreover, Hegel's use of the notion of habit is most fundamental in the life of spirit. Spirit is defined as the *absolute* (*EIII*, §384 R). Yet, what is striking as Hegel examines the 'concept of spirit' (*EIII*, §§381–386) is that it is not conceived for itself, but rather *in regards to nature* – as the sublating of nature. Nature is the idea 'shaped as otherness' and present under the form of 'withdrawal' (*EII*, §247); it is the logical negativity of spirit. And insofar as 'spirit is the truth of nature', the shift from nature to spirit corresponds to the shift from rationality as an external thing to a rational dynamic of *recovering* what is. In this respect, spirit can be described as a 'return out of nature' (*EIII*, §381): it seeks to recall itself as the source of naturality and acknowledges itself as the productive structure of *second nature*. The philosophy of spirit is indeed the reflective movement by which the withdrawal of the immediate idea and its absolute otherness is suppressed and turned into a circumscribed otherness as a second immediacy; its main thesis amounts to saying that spirit weaves its own second nature. On this basis, Hegel is able to ascertain the absolute freedom of spirit. Spirit is thus a *redoubled* and *redoubling* nature, an activity that both presupposes and results in nature. It is a spiral dynamic that both produces and is produced by its own immediacy.

Generally speaking, spirit also corresponds to *substance* (*PS*, §25), which is, as we have seen, subjective and objective immediacy mediating one another as subject and so absolute *negativity*. Thus, my view is that habit is not only the condition of the self-weaving of spirit but also the onto-logical condition for spirit to be absolute substance.

I will now examine how Hegel operates the notion of habit in the philosophy of spirit in order to further hone this correspondence and indicate the possibility of understanding substance from the standpoint of habit. I identify three distinct, yet absolutely dependant, types of functional occurrences.

Habit within anthropology

The notion of habit first occurs in the 'Anthropology' of subjective spirit. The foremost aim of subjective spirit is to develop itself within its ideality, that is, to 'be together with itself' (*EIII*, §385). In this respect, the anthropology seeks to ascertain that spirit is capable of enduring otherness. Spirit must be capable of *referring* to itself while both *differentiating* itself from the other and *remaining* itself. However, as the soul, or the immediate natural spirit, *feels* the external world – as it faces otherness – comes a permanent threat of *derangement*. The soul can either become incapable of facing exteriority and thus fully retreat into self (idiocy) or become unable to remain oneself as it feels and thus scatter (folly) (*EIII*, §408 A). By assuming the 'mechanism of self-feeling' of the soul, habit remedies the various *diseases* of inadequacy to the universal. Indeed, through habituation, the soul can internalize the external without losing itself in the other. In this respect, habit is the essential condition for spirit to endure radical otherness while remaining itself (*EIII*, §410 R): it is the condition of the *negativity* of spirit.

Also, in virtue of habit, the soul is 'potentially anything' (*EIII*, §389). The expression 'second nature' entails two things. First, it means that habit is a *moulded* existence, a *posited* concrete being. Thus, it has no predetermined content or form: it is always a *result*. Yet, it simultaneously corresponds to a *nature*, thus constituting the 'concrete immediacy' of the subject; it is the condition of its *possible materiality* (*EIII*, §410 R). Second, not only is habit a resulting immediacy of the soul, it is also the incorporation of *purpose* into its material body and as such it is a liberation from its naturality. Through habits, the mind generates ends within concrete existence. Dexterity, for instance, is an embodied aim. It is the result of the *simplification* of mediations – the resulting easiness which comes from repeated practising (*E III*, §410 R). Thus, habit allows spirit to develop into various shapes while always remaining itself: it is the general condition of its *plasticity*.

Generally speaking, habit is both the *pure indetermination of potentiality* and the *perfect determination of actuality* of spirit. This means that it is both the *effective* and *possible* 'home' of spirit. Indeed, in virtue of their *familiarity*, habits establish an element of validity for spirit. They operate as a landmark. As a matter of fact, Hegel specifies that 'thinking, too, though wholly free, and active in the pure element of itself, likewise requires habit and familiarity' (*E III*, §410 R). Therefore, habit is not only a resulting immediacy but also a mediating immediacy. As a subjective element, habit assigns the legitimate realms of what is thinkable and doable; it is the *condition* of the processual immediacy of spirit: the 'immediacy *of* knowledge'.

Recollection and memory

The function of habit oversteps its anthropological assignment within subjective spirit: 'Habit is a form that embraces all kinds and stages of mind's activity' (*E III*, §410 R).[5] Yet, Hegel draws a distinction between the mechanism of self-feeling that is habit and the mechanism of intelligence that is memory while stating that 'when *developed*, and *at work* in the mind as such, habit is recollection and memory' (*E III*, §410 R; *my emphasis*). On one hand, habit is indeed distinct from memory and recollection. Both these faculties operate within the theoretical moment of 'psychology', as spirit is apprehended as *intelligence*; and whereas 'self-feeling' assumed the toleration of otherness as an embodied soul, intelligence is the active process of 'remov[ing] [...] unknowingness' (*EIII*, §445 A). On the other hand, however, not only is *passive habit* an essential *condition* for intelligence's weaving process of itself as a knowing structure,[6] but *habit at work* is also the essence of recollection and memory.

In order to become 'knowing intelligence', intelligence *weaves* itself: it generates its own faculties while it gradually enhances its cognition – that is, the intelligibility of its objects.[7] First, the mind intuits something (it posits a feeling as an immediate exteriority); then, it negates this intuition by interiorizing it and turning it into an image; finally, it externalizes it by uttering a word, which is the truth of things and the truth of thought (*EIII*, §462, A). Yet, although recollection [*Erinnerung*] indeed corresponds to the mere *interiorizing* and *recalling* of intuition – that is, its sublating – recollection represents the general process through which intelligence weaves itself (*EIII*, §461).

Moreover, habit is essential to this process. First, recollection corresponds to a 'developed' habit because its element is solely spiritual, whereas mere habit was solely *bodily*. Second, it is habit 'at work' insofar as it consists in both an active *simplification* (i.e. the universalization of the intuition as an image) and an *unconscious preservation* of this universal as the *property* of the mind (*EIII*, §453, R). So, as an *active* habit, recollection turns effective presence into virtual possibility, determines spirit's familiar element and shapes its immediate being. Indeed, it is through recollection that spirit becomes cultivated and requires no exteriority to think (*EIII*, §454 A). As Borges portrayed in his *Ficciones*' 'Funes el memorioso', recollection is not a *passive* memory of details incompatible with thought; rather, it is the *active* motion of generalization, simplification and acquisition which sublates differences. Third, recollection is also habit 'at work' insofar as it turns into a withdrawing *externalization* as objective *memory* (*EIII*, §460). Memory is indeed a *reverse*, active habit: it *recalls* the internalized spiritual content of the 'nocturnal pit in which is stored a world of [...] representations' that is intelligence (*EIII*, §453 R) and *exteriorizes* it as its own. Through this linguistic inhabitation of the world it generates (*EIII*, §462), recollection spiritualizes the world: it *incorporates* its own interiority within objectivity.

Thus, recollection is not only the *recovery* of spirit itself; it also *generates* its *conceiving*. In sum, not only is habit the anthropological *condition* of subjective spirit; it also corresponds to the *active* dimension of the immediacy of knowledge.

Objective spirit as second nature

The third type of occurrence of the notion of habit corresponds to the general characterization of the objective spirit as 'second nature'. The rationality of the objective being corresponds to the world as an institutionalized realm, or spirit as an externalized system: 'the world of mind [is] brought forth out of itself like a second nature' (*OPR*, §4).

It is characterized as such for at least two reasons. First, the objective spirit is in fact the result of the *simplification* of the externalized determinations proceeding from the subjective spirit. This entails apprehending the whole of the world as a spiritually posited being that has turned into an immediate, non-posited, nature, thereby refuting any dualism. These simplified mediations correspond to the world as an objective second nature. Second, the world *appears* as an immediate and stable nature: 'the ethical substance is […] infinitely more firmly established than the being of nature' (*OPR*, §146); it retroactively functions as the *source* of subjectivity. Indeed, in ethical life, the ethical substance is positedness and a non-positedness, as well as a positing and a non-positing instance; it is a conceived objective home – a *resulting* 'immediacy *for* knowledge'. Humans grow *accustomed* to universal forms of the institutions of objective world (family, corporations, the state) and they develop 'customs' (*OPR*, §151). In this respect, the objective spirit is the home of the subjective spirit, its element of validity, as well as its *material*.

Moreover, this effectiveness manifests the reciprocal dynamic that is at work between subjectivity and objectivity. Hegel writes: 'Freedom, shaped into the actuality of a world, acquires the form of necessity, whose substantial interconnection is the system of the determinations of freedom, and its apparent interconnection is power, recognition, i.e. its validity in consciousness' (*EIII*, §484). In this paragraph, Hegel states that both subjective and objective second natures are not distinct, rather they presuppose one another: the validity of the institutions is dependant on its recognition within consciousness, and inversely, the content of objective laws shapes subjectivity by producing its 'general mode of conduct' (*OPR*, §151). Indeed, the ethical element has a double existence, an objective one as 'the concept of freedom developed into the existing world and the nature of self-consciousness' and a subjective one as 'nature of self-consciousness' (*OPR*, §142), that is, as the habit of this objective second nature. Thus, as a second nature, the objective spirit is 'a world produced and to be produced' (*EIII*, §385); it proceeds from the shaping of itself.

In conclusion, the notion of habit functions as a *speculative hinge* in Hegel's philosophy. It combines beginning and result, self and otherness, freedom and necessity, subjectivity and objectivity. It temporalizes being by manifesting its conceiving origin; yet as inertia, it allows being to *appear* as otherness, thus enabling the absolute negativity of spirit.

Moreover, insofar as habit is the immediacy *for* thought (the world as a second nature) as well as the immediacy *of* thought (as feelings, representations, customs), it enables the reciprocal and dynamic shaping of subjectivity and objectivity. In this respect, the reflection or recollection[8] of the *habitual* is spirit acknowledging itself as 'the one and universal substance as spiritual' (*EIII*, §554), that is, absolute spirit. The knowledge of spirit as this subjective and objective self-producing is indeed the absolute knowledge of substance as self-movement. My view is that in corresponding to the absolute secondarity of immediacy – and in virtue of its plasticity, actuality and potentiality – habit seems to assume the theoretical and ontological conditions for substance to produce itself. On this basis, everything is a *disposition* shaped by spirit. Thus, in virtue of this extended notion of habit corresponding to immediacy as absolute secondarity, Hegel interlocks epistemology and history while referring to truth as a process identical to the *activity* through which spirit acquires knowledge of itself. In this respect, the structure of Hegelian philosophy is *spiral* rather than circular.

Notes

1 Wallace translates *Begriff* as 'notion'. However, for the sake of consistency, here and elsewhere I will translate *Begriff* as 'concept'.
2 As Catherine Malabou pointed out, this is the essential meaning of the *Aufhebung* (Malabou 2012: part II, Ch 3).
3 According to Ravaisson, habit is inconceivable within the realm of homogeneity and immediacy. The mediations which make empirical associations possible necessarily imply the activity of intelligence (Ravaisson 2008: I, 1–4).
4 For the thematization of those ways of thinking, see *PS*, §§58–60 and §§67–68.
5 Wallace translates *Geist* as 'mind'. However, for the sake of consistency, here and elsewhere I will translate *Geist* as 'spirit'.

6 In fact, the material that intelligence is to itself calls on its capacity as a *feeling soul*, that is, as a soul capable of habit (*EIII*, §446).
7 Cognition is not 'mere knowledge', it is the knowledge of what the 'susbstantial nature' of the object consists of (*EIII*, §445 A).
8 In the *Logic*, the general movement of the essence corresponds to the 'intropassing' of being as inwardization and recollection of its rational content. Yet this process is not innocuous, as essence returns to what posited being, it rationally *structures* being. In other words, essence is an absolute component of Concept, and recollection is an absolute component of conceiving. Thus, recollection is not only the recovery of spirit itself, as a *reflection*, it is a 'positive moment of the absolute' (*PS*, §21).

References

Hume, D (2000), *An Enquiry concerning Human Understanding* [1748], Oxford: Oxford University Press.

Kant, I. (1904), 'Kritik der reinen Vernunft [1787]', in *Kants gesammelte Schriften*, Königliche Preussichen Akademie der Wissenschaften, Berlin: Walter De Gruyter & Co.

Kervégan, J. F. (March 2011), 'Sortir du "donné"?' Quelques remarques autour d'une observation de Sellars. Viewed 1 November 2014, http://www.implications-philosophiques.org/semaines-thematiques/actualite-de-hegel/sortir-du-«-donne-»/.

Longuenesse, B. (2007), *Hegel's Critique of Metaphysics* [1981], trans. Nicole J. Simek, New York: Cambridge University Press.

Malabou, C. (2012), *L'Avenir de Hegel*, Paris: Vrin.

Ravaisson, F. (2008), *Of Habit* [1838], trans. Clare Carlisle and Mark Sinclair, London: Continuum.

6

Singularity of the Concept – Singularity of the Will: The Logical Ground of Hegel's *Philosophy of Right*

Antonios Kalatzis

Necessity without method. The paradox of Hegel's philosophy of right

In terms of philosophical claims, Hegel's *Outlines of the Philosophy of Right* (published 1820, dated 1821) represents a great paradox. On the one hand, it is nothing but another compendium of the central concepts encountered in every classical modern philosophy of right in the form of a handbook.[1] On the other hand, though, it distances itself from everything of the sort on the basis of the specific Hegelian method.[2] Up to this point we could actually speak about an original but not a paradoxical philosophy of right. Yet, the paradox begins with the Hegelian claim that the *Outlines* is a systematic and necessary exposition of these concepts *not* on the basis of an immanent method, to wit, of a method that would be exposed, justified and used in this work but on the basis of a method that is only *presupposed*. In Hegel's words:

> The primary difference between this manual and an ordinary compendium certainly lies in the method, which constitutes its guiding principle. But in this book I presuppose that philosophy's mode of progression from one topic to another and its mode of scientific proof – this whole speculative way of knowing – is essentially distinct from any other way of knowing. (*OPR*, 4)

Consequently, the reader of Hegel's philosophy of right, and furthermore the reader who has not dealt with the *Science of Logic*, finds herself in a peculiar position. Hegel invites her to read the *Outlines* as a philosophical and, hence, systematic and necessary development of the central concepts of a philosophy of right, but what she actually gets to read is only the *outcome* of this method. In a word, Hegel invites us to regard the conceptual expositions and transitions of the *Outlines* as necessary without, however, actually providing this necessity.

Thus, if someone would actually want to acknowledge the *Outlines* as something particular, original and, most of all, true, she should either accept uncritically Hegel's claim or turn to the *Science of Logic*, where, as Hegel informs us, his method is exposed and justified in an immanent manner. Only by doing the latter someone could relate the fully developed Hegelian method on the contents of the *Outlines* in order to detect the actual, and not only *presupposed*, necessity of the logical development of the *Outlines*. Furthermore, she should have to turn to the *Logic* in order to comprehend crucial parts of the work, which remain – without this application – incomprehensible.

The principle of the 'Science of Right' as its beginning

One, if not the most, crucial part of the *Outlines*, which, in my opinion, remains in terms of argumentation and necessity impossible to follow without reference to the *Logic* are §§5–7 of the *Outlines*. They deal with the concept of universal, particular and singular will respectively, that is, the 'basis' (*OPR*, §4) of the Hegelian philosophy of right.[3] 'Basis' in the double sense of the term, as beginning and as organizing principle of the whole book, which, as we will see, at the same time dictates the ultimate goal of the work. As we can read in the recently published critical edition of Hegel's students' notes: 'The Science of Right has the free will as principle and as beginning' (*GW*, XXVI,1: 8; my translation).[4] Hence, my main goal here is to provide the missing argumentative transparency regarding the overall goal of the *Outlines* and the Hegelian understanding of freedom by relating §§5–7 of the *Outlines* to the relevant subchapters of universal, particular and singular concept from the *Logic*. In addition to this, I will be stressing, to my knowledge for the first time, the importance of what Hegel calls in the *Logic* the 'judgment of the concept' (*SL*, 546–557) for the understanding of the further development and completion of his philosophy of right.

To begin with, what we already encounter in §5 of the *Outlines* is the definition of the universal will, which consists in nothing else than 'pure indeterminacy or [in] that pure reflection of the I into itself which involves the dissolution of every restriction and every content either immediately presented by nature, by needs, desires, and impulses, or given and determined by any means whatever' (*OPR*, §5).

This concept of universal will as such, though, cannot be the proper foundation for a philosophy of right, which aims to have a positive content, rather than just delivering a mere negative conception of freedom,[5] which would lead, according to Hegel's reading, at the dissolution of every particularity and organized reality: 'Consequently, whatever negative freedom means to will can never be anything in itself but an abstract idea, and giving effect to this idea can only be the fury of destruction' (*OPR*, §5 R).

In other words, since the concept of universal will amounts to a universal dissolution of every volitional content, we are forced, according to the *Outlines*, to move to the next attempt to conceptualize will in a consistent manner, this time as particular will, yet, even if the argument seems plausible, it remains an external one. That is an argument that presupposes (the need for) a fully developed philosophy of right, without, though, providing an immanent argument for the need to proceed to further types of will and, ultimately, to a fully developed philosophy of right. What is, in other words, the reason that makes this transition *necessary*? Why, as Schopenhauer did in his *World as Will and Representation*, are we not entitled to accept this concept of universal, negative and destructive will as the only one? Only in vain somebody will search in the *Outlines* for a proper argument, which would prove the inconsistency of the – exclusively – universal will and the need for the transition to the particular will.

Thus, from the very beginning of the *Outlines* we encounter the hermeneutical need to turn to the *Science of Logic* and in particular to the chapter that deals with the concept of universality in general (*SL*, 530–534). There we learn that the logical content of a totally abstract universal, to wit, of a universal, that is semantically isolated from every particularity and, thus, dissolves it shows itself to be in truth a particular, it is a particular since it does not entail all possible logical contents as it should on the grounds of its semantic claim to be universal: if the logical content of universality is exclusively itself, it excludes the logical content of particularity. Thus, it shows itself to be particular (*SL*, 531).

Hence, the methodological presupposition of §5 on universal will, the systematic exposition of the concept of universality in the *Logic*, renders explicit the argumentative ground upon which the concept of universal will shows itself as self-defeating and inconsistent. It reveals also the reason why we are forced to move to the particular will. The concept of an abstract universal will is unstable. While it claims to be universal it is only a particular logical content and the only way to stabilize it appears to be its grasping as – exclusively – particular will:

> Through this positing of itself as something determinate [i.e. particular], the I [i.e. the universal-abstract will] steps into determinate existence [*Dasein*] in general. This is the absolute moment of the finitude or particularization of the I [i.e. of the universal will]. (*OPR*, §6)

It is only now that Hegel's account of the universal will, as 'defective' and 'finite', makes full sense and, indeed, only when related to the chapter on the concept from the *Logic*:

> The first moment – namely as it is for itself – is not true infinity or concrete universality, not the concept, but only something determinate, one-sided; i.e., being abstraction from all determinacy, it is itself not without determinacy; and to be something abstract and one-sided constitutes its determinacy, its defectiveness, and its finitude. (*OPR*, §6 R)

In contrast to the exposition of the universal will, where we encounter some hints regarding the close analogy between universal concept from the *Logic* and universal will from the *Outlines*, we do not encounter in the exposition of the particular will in §6 the slightest indication for an argument for its aporetic character and, thus, for the necessity of the transition to the next type of will, the singular will.

Once again we have to turn to the *Logic* in order to comprehend the need for the transition from particularity to singularity in general. There we come across the following argument: if everything is particular, the concept of particularity is not a particular but a universal concept. Hence, the logical concept of mere particularity shows itself to be logically unstable and inconsistent. Again, as the concept of universality earlier, the *mere* particular will show itself to be the opposite of itself:

> Now the determinateness is indeed an abstraction, as against the other determinateness; but the other determinateness is only universality itself, and this too is therefore abstract universality; and the determinateness of the concept, or particularity, is again nothing more than determinate universality. (*SL*, 537)

This argument from the critical exposition of the logical content of the particular concept from the *Logic* has, though, a further twofold implication for the concept of will in the *Outlines*. As we could not think a purely universal will, since willing everything amounts to willing nothing, we cannot think a purely particular will, that is, a will that wills directly one single object instead of a will that decides for a particular object *over* other particular objects. This insight is a twofold one because it is highly relevant, as we are about to see, in two intrinsically related cases. The first case refers to the understanding of the particular as the will of a particular agent, and it would mean that the particular will cannot be thought in abstraction from the will of other particular agents. The second case refers to the understanding of the particular will as the particular volitional object of one individual agent's will. Both are interconnected, since the particular volitional content of an agent constitutes the individuality of this agent in juxtaposition to the individuality of other agents. Then the argument for the inconsistency of the particular will implies that an agent never has one single volitional object but many particular objects that has to prioritize and that an individual agent can only be grasped within a totality of multiple agents.

Be that as it may, since we cannot think the will either as merely universal or as merely particular we are forced to shift to the next and final type of will, the singular will of §7, which is being introduced in order to overcome the problems of the two latter conceptions of will, the universal and the particular. The singular will is exactly the will that does not exclude particularity, or universality, but rather includes both in an explicit way, exactly as the 'singularity of the concept' in the *Logic* did (*SL*, 546–549). In other words, the singular will contains explicitly the unity of the manifoldness of particular volitional contents and the universal totality of them – their coexistence. It is actually the grasping of the unity of the universal and particular will that allows us to think the particularity of the will as particular: if the particular volitional contents could be grasped in isolation from each other, they wouldn't be particular at all. They would be able to stand outside their relation, that is, outside their totality, which is the universal. Thus, they can only be grasped as real in the double sense that was mentioned earlier: in juxtaposition to each other *and* as one totality they constitute the singular will. This type of will is not the will of an individual, but the will that explicitly contains the universal and the particular will as two sides of one, single type of will. And this is why Hegel calls it 'singular':

> Still, both these moments [i.e. the universal and the particular] are only abstractions; what is concrete and true (and everything true is concrete) is the universality which has the particular as its opposite, but the particular which by its reflection into itself has been equalized with the universal. This unity is singularity, not individuality in its immediacy as a unit, our first idea of individuality, but singularity in accordance with its concept; indeed, singularity in this sense is precisely the concept itself. (*OPR*, §7 R, *translation adjusted*)

Yet, once again, only when we refer to the *Logic* we can reconstruct the arguments for this development in the *Outlines* that simply claim that the transition to the singular will is consistent and necessary: the logical instability of the concepts of universality and of particularity, to wit, the explication that if we actually isolate them from their logical counterpart they show themselves to be this counterpart, leads to a richer logical content, which contains both of them and is nothing else than the argumentation followed for the transition from the particular concept to the singularity of the concept (*SL*, 546–547 and *OPR*, §7 R).[6]

Consequently the true and non-aporetic concept of will is either deprived of particular contents or deprived of universality as their totality. It is the singular will as the unity of both and as the answer to the dualistic and, according to Hegel, problematic gap between universal will and the particular desires and inclinations that the philosophies of Kant and Fichte expose (*OPR*, §6 R).

By means of the reference to the relevant parts in the *Logic* we reach not only a higher level of argumentative transparency, but we are also able to pinpoint the systematic cornerstone, the 'principle', of Hegel's philosophy of right. According to Hegel the particular will, under which he understands individual desires and inclinations, is *not* in an antagonistic relationship to the universal will, as in the Kantian moral and political philosophy (at least to Hegel's understanding).[7] And this insight is intrinsically connected to Hegel's claim that the true concept of will is the singular will. It remains only to see how these two claims are connected in more detail and what sort of implications this connection has for the whole work.

The beginning of the 'Science of Right' as its principle

As we read in §6 of the *Outlines*, the particular will *apparently* receives its contents from two sources: either as 'apparently given by nature [to wit, as raw natural desire] or engendered by the concept of spirit [to wit, as a mental representation of an object to be obtained or of a state of affairs to be achieved]' (*OPR*, §6, *translation adjusted*). But what is the reason for Hegel to distance himself from this account by writing 'apparently given' instead of 'given'? The answer, once again nowhere to be found in the *Outlines*, goes back to the *Logic*.

There, despite the lower degree of inconsistency of the concept of singularity, compared to the concepts of universality and particularity, the transition from the singular concept to the judgement of the concept, or simply to judgement, in the *Logic* (*SL*, 549) is not the achievement of a final stage in the unfolding of the categories but simultaneously the explication of a *new problem*. As we have seen, the singularity of the concept is the explicit unity of the universal and the particular and consequently the explicit coexistence of various particular contents. This exposed necessity of the unity of the particular contents, though, does not say anything about *the way* that these particular contents are regulated, i.e. how they are related to each other, because, in fact, they are *not*. In other words, instead of encountering here the ultimate solution regarding the unity of the universal and the particular it is in this place exactly where the problem of the proper articulation of the Hegelian monism only begins. The necessity of the unity of the particular logical contents, the 'concrete universal', and the simultaneous demonstration that on this level of conceptual development we are still far away from comprehending how this particular contents relate to each other are the two elements that force us to move further from the 'concept of the concept' and pass to 'judgement'. This is the reason why 'judgement' is to be understood as 'primordial division' (*ursprüngliche Teilung*) (*SL*, 552) or the 'loss' of the (unifying) concept (*SL*, 548), i.e. as the explication of the isolation of the particular contents *within* their unity, this time. In short, the only thing achieved with the singularity of the concept is the certainty that universal and particular *must* be thought into a comprehensive unity. The final conceptualization of this unity though still lies far ahead.

On this stage of conceptual development the volitional counterpart of this still abstract particularity, the particular will as part of the singular will, is the will that despite its necessary connection to universality remains external to it in a different fashion. As we have seen, a particular logical content that would remain isolated from the rest particular contents would lose its meaning *as particular*. Hence, even within the unity of universality, an absolutely particular content of volition would show itself as isolated from the other particular contents and, hence, from the universal, as nonsensical and self-destructive. It is the concept of the will not anymore implicitly, as the particular will, but explicitly grasped in a contradictory way – the will as 'arbitrariness':

> This natural will is arbitrariness, the will in the sphere of desires (*Begierden*), of instincts and inclinations. This kind of will has an internally or externally given, and consequently, finite content, that at anytime can be abandoned […] But the other content that is introduced in the place of first one is equally a determined [i.e. particular] one. The will can thus dissolve endlessly this kind of contents, without though being able to overcome this sort of finitude. (*GW* XXVI, 1: 10; my translation)

Arbitrariness, in other words, is the will that decides for a particular volitional object over other particular objects as if there was only one volitional content that ought to materialize. As in the case of the judgement of the concept with the particular(s) as such, arbitrariness deals with the multiple volitional contents as if they were totally disconnected to each other, despite the posited necessity of their coexistence. The dialectic of the particular within the unity of the universal, i.e. within the singularity of the concept and, thus, within the scope of the singular will, forces us to accept and comprehend that every particular volitional content can be conceived and sustained on the basis of an explicit and concrete relation to other particular contents, and not within a necessary but nonetheless abstract and external universal unity (see OPR, §§14–18).

Conversely, universality shows itself as something that ought to be something more than the abstract necessity of the coexistence of the particulars. It has to be conceptualized not as the external but as the immanent and *concrete* relation between particulars. In this way the particular, natural or mental, desires and inclinations that are explicitly integrated in their unity or in their universality cannot be understood as strictly irrational and isolated desires that should be repressed by a universal will à la Kant (always according to Hegel's reading of Kant, see OPR, §29 R), but rather as desires that can only exist within a rational coordination within their unity or universality. Furthermore, because their coordination presupposes them as *particular* volitional contents, all the desires and inclinations that would objectively or subjectively deprive the will from the ability to decide over a particular content over another one turn out to be self-defeating themselves. Since they cancel the ability of the will to coordinate and, thus, decide a particular volitional content over another, they are inconsistent types of volitional contents: they cancel the particularity that they themselves were supposed to be.[8]

Hence the Hegelian 'basis' of right, the singular will, provides ultimately not only an argument for the abstract unison of universal and particular will but the far-reaching normative standard, according to which particular desires and their particular agents are to be grasped in coordination and respect to each other. Hegel translates the problem of the 'loss of the concept' from the *Logic* in the need to think the proper coordination of particular desires and agents in the *Outlines* (OPR, §11 R). Through this dialectic the singularity of the will forces us to move further and conceive adequately the universal will as coordination of our natural, to wit particular inclinations and desires. The will to the solely particular content, the arbitrariness, does *not* show its self to be the necessary 'other' of the free will or the independent source of volitional contents that makes our volitional contents appear as 'given' to us, but something logical *impossible*: 'Instead of being the will in its truth, arbitrariness is rather the will as contradiction' (OPR, §15 R).

In this way the concrete universal will, i.e. the free will that coordinates the particular desires, is not something being *applied* externally to given and, thus, merely particular desires and inclinations, but the immanent normative framework that enables them to coexist. Then, without this framework they would simply exclude and, consequently, annihilate each other. It is on this basis that in the aforementioned passage from §6 that Hegel distances himself from an external, independent source of volitional content, i.e. from the idea of 'given' desires and inclinations. These would not have been possible in first place without a sort of active mediation, to wit of organization and coordination, without which they could not exist *at all* (*OPR*, §21 R).[9]

Consequently, by referring to the exposition of the singular concept and of its own ultimate inadequacy, we understand that what we actually encounter in the singular will is not only the insight that the universal and the particular will should be grasped together. By referring further to the unfolding of the reasons that lead from the singular concept to the judgement of the concept that occurs in the *Logic* and which applies to the singular will as well, in its development as arbitrariness, we understand something further. The singular will, by rendering explicit both the necessity to think universal and particular will together and the resulting inadequacy of the articulation of this thought on the basis of its abstractness, provides the monistic, normative drive that shapes the Hegelian philosophy of right as a whole.

According to this monistic claim, the *Outlines* do not intend to be a theory that is being externally applied to reality and to particular desires and inclinations. On the contrary the *Outlines* are to be seen as a model of a self-regulation of the realm of Spirit (*OPR*, §27) and, ultimately, of the Political[10]: 'The Will has to be a will for something, has to have a content, but this something is not an *Other*.'[11]

In this way we achieve a certain clarification regarding the complex relation between logic and speculation in the case of freedom according to Hegel. Freedom does not mean liberation from particular desires and inclinations but their rational coordination on the basis of their preservation and respect (*OPR*, §22 R). It means further the coordination of the particular subjects of those desires within a scope that does not supress but respect their particularity as agents as well:

> In the demand for the purification of impulses there lies the general notion that they should be freed both from their form as immediate and natural determinations, and also from the subjectivity and contingency of their content, and so brought back to their substantial essence. The truth behind this vague demand is that the impulses should become the rational system of the will's volitions. To grasp them like that, proceeding out of the concept of the will, is the content of the philosophical science of right. (*OPR*, §19)[12]

Thus, the normative standard set in the chapter on singular will in the *Outlines*, along with its logical counterpart, the singularity of the concept in the *Logic*, show themselves to be the leading thread, the driving force and the ultimate goal of all further development of the Hegelian philosophy of right. Hegel's *Outlines* will continue to unfold until an adequate conceptualization is logically and historically achieved, within which the particularities, these being inclinations and desires of the individual as such, of the particular individuals, of the particular members of the family, of the citizens and of the institutions within a state (here of course I refer to all the main parts of the *Outlines*) reach a level of balance[13] within a universality that integrates them instead of annihilating or supressing them.[14]

In this way we can also comprehend how and why the foundation of the philosophy of right, the singular will, is at the same time its ultimate goal,[15] as the grasping of a realized and not transcendent and otherworldly freedom (*OPR*, §22 R). It is anything else than by luck that Hegel himself in the preface of the *Outlines* defines philosophy as the 'the comprehension of the present and the actual, not the setting up of a beyond, supposed to exist, God knows where' (*OPR*, 13).

At the place of the Kantian highest Good and of the question concerning individual happiness and ethical conduct we find in the Hegelian philosophy of right the institutions, the state and the historical development as variations and transformations of this concrete universal of the singular will that preserves and contains these particular contents and volitions. And exactly at this point becomes transparent the Hegelian ideal as opposed to the Kantian one: instead of an other-worldly hope for an absolute fulfilment of our desires, a this-worldly reconciliation with the limits of our happiness and finitude.

Notes

1   See Houlgate 2008: vii ff.
2   *Ibid.*, pp. xviii ff. Houlgate claims correctly, in an earlier book, that the lack of proper understanding of the Hegelian method led so many Hegel interpreters to a series of grave misunderstandings regarding his (in-)famous political philosophy. See Houlgate 2005: 182. See also Pippin 1997: 34ff. Oddly, even if Pippin makes this claim, he hardly discusses Hegel's method in his paper.
3   Usually the crucial question regarding the subject of will that Hegel is referring to is being bypassed by the relevant scholarship or is being uncritically identified with the will of an individual. Yet, under universal, particular and singular will

Hegel does not understand the individual will – even what is being developed here has consequences for the proper grasping and the systematic deduction of the individual will –, but the capacity of Spirit to establish a totality of self-determined individual spirits, which amounts to the only structure adequate to itself and not to the contingency and unfreedom of nature. As Hegel writes, *OPR*, §4 A, the references to self-consciousness are made here 'additionally'. In concrete the individual will, i.e. the will of an individual, emerges only after the 'deduction' of the singular will as arbitrariness (*Willkühr*). This is the place where the will is being 'posited' for the first time as 'the will of one concrete individual', since the will becomes an individual will, when it comes to the decision of one particular volitional content over another, by means of which it discerns itself from another individual, as explicitly stated by Hegel, *OPR*, §13. Yet, the individual will as arbitrariness is being introduced only in order to vanish again in the transition from arbitrariness to 'free will' in *OPR* §21. There, the primacy of individualistic, i.e. of completely arbitrary elements of the will, is overcome. For Hegel's critique of the dominant Kant- and Rousseau-inspired trends in the philosophy of right that take as their foundation the will(s) of the individual(s) without reaching the speculative standpoint, see *OPR*, §29 R; cf. *OPR*, §8.

4   For Hegel's idea of political philosophy as science, see Neuhouser 2011.
5   For an original critique of the dominant distinction between negative and positive freedom, see Sloterdijk 2011: 47ff.
6   For a further elaboration on this point in the *Logic*, see Kalatzis 2016.
7   For an excellent account of Hegel's critique of Kant's ethical theory, see Sedgwick 2011.
8   The free will as mere coordination of the desires and inclinations – happiness – and not simultaneously as exclusion of what could endanger the ability to follow particular desires and inclinations in general is, according to Hegel, another inadequate conceptualization of free will. See *OPR*, §20.
9   As Franz Rosenzweig excellently puts it, this argument is a 'tremendous intensification of the natural law theory'. See Rosenzweig 2010: 380–381. Hegel is explicitly implying that this is the case in *OPR*, §3.
10 For a critical, yet insightful account of Hegel's political philosophy, see Wood 2011.
11 *GW*, XXVI,1, 13; my translation. Cf. 'The abstract concept of the Idea of the will [as the rational system of the spirit] is in general the free will which wills the free will' *OPR*, §27.
12 As Pippin puts it: 'The idea, then, is not to act in way exempt from inclinations, in the service of some view of the good, my own perfectibility or the moral law. The idea of freedom is to be understood in terms *of the way I take up and attempt to execute my inclinations*' (Pippin 1997: 50; cf. 52).
13 According to Hegel, this balance is possible to be achieved within a state, but never within states. See *OPR*, §30 R, §§341–360.

14 See McCumber 2014: 168. As Sebastian Rand in his review of McCumber's book writes: 'The goal of Hegelian practical philosophy is thus very similar, on McCumber's view, to the goal of theoretical idealism: ethical theory seeks to take our desires, motivations, and needs as they are, reducing them to moments in a larger whole, and reappropriating them for the project of freedom through their systematization' (Rand 2014).

15 As Pippin puts it: 'Most importantly and more explicitly, everything claimed henceforth about the true realization of the norm, *Recht*, will depend on the understanding the "basis" (*Boden*) of that norm, spirit (*Geist*), particularly as manifest in a "free will", and so *verwirklicht* in the "system of right"' (Pippin 1997: 33).

References

Houlgate, S. [1991] (2005), *An Introduction to Hegel. Freedom, Truth and History*, Oxford: Blackwell.

Houlgate, S. (2008), 'Introduction', in G.W.F. Hegel (ed.), *Outlines of the Philosophy of Right*, trans. T.M. Knox, revised, edited and introduced by S. Houlgate, vii–xxxiii, Oxford: Oxford University Press.

Houlgate, S. and M. Baur, eds. (2011), *A Companion to Hegel*, Sussex: Wiley-Blackwell.

Kalatzis, A. (2016), 'Macht und Ohnmacht der Mannigfaltigkeit. Hegelscher Begriff vs. Kantische Synthesis', in A. Arndt, Br. Bowman, M. Gerhard and J. Zovko (eds), *Hegel-Jahrbuch*, Volume 2016, Issue 1, 120–124, Berlin: De Gruyter.

McCumber, J. (2014), *Understanding Hegel's Mature Critique of Kant*, Bloomington, Indiana: Stanford University Press.

Neuhouser, Fr. (2011), 'The Idea of a Hegelian "Science" of Society', in St. Houlgate and M. Baur (eds) (2011), *A Companion to Hegel*, 281–296, Sussex: Wiley-Blackwell.

Pippin, R. (1997), 'Hegel, Freedom, The Will. The Philosophy of Right (§§1-33)', in L. Siep (ed.), *G.W.F. Hegel, Grundlinien der Philosophie des Rechts*, 31–53, Berlin: Akademie Verlag.

Rand, S. (2014), review John McCumber (2014), *Understanding Hegel's Mature Critique of Kant*, Bloomington, Indiana: Stanford University Press, in Notre Dame Philosophical Reviews, https://ndpr.nd.edu/news/understanding-hegel-s-mature-critique-of-kant/, retrieved at 23.02.2018.

Rosenzweig, F. [1920] (2010), *Hegel und der Staat*, Frankfurt a.M.: Suhrkamp.

Sedgwick, S. (2011), 'Hegel on the Empty Formalism of Kant's Categorical Imperative', in St. Houlgate and M. Baur (eds), *A Companion to Hegel*, 265–280, Sussex: Wiley-Blackwell.

Sloterdijk, P. (2011), *Stress und Freiheit*, Berlin: Suhrkamp.

Wood, A. (2011), 'Hegel's Political Philosophy', in St. Houlgate and M. Baur (eds), *A Companion to Hegel*, 297–311, Sussex: Wiley-Blackwell.

7

Subverting Practical Philosophy

Myriam Bienenstock

Hegel's mature encyclopaedic system seems resolutely turned towards 'science' (*Wissenschaft*): *The Science of Logic*, the sciences included in the *Philosophy of Nature* – mechanics, organics – and the 'science of spirit' (*Wissenschaft des Geistes*, or *Geisteswissenschaft*). These latter terms are still in use, in many German universities. The denomination spread during the second half of the nineteenth century, but it dates back to Hegel, and to that 'science of spirit' which seems to take the place of practical philosophy in his system. How is one to understand the relation between that 'science of spirit' and the practical philosophy inherited from the past? Does the 'science of spirit' replace classical practical philosophy – and what would such a replacement mean?

It is tempting to insert Hegel's 'science of spirit' in the tidal wave that led throughout the nineteenth century to what was often pejoratively called 'positivism' or 'scientism'. A move of that kind has been suggested by Manfred Riedel (1935–2009), a much celebrated Hegel-specialist who did not merely track back, in carefully documented studies, the formation and development of the notion of 'objective spirit' (*objektiver Geist*) in Hegel's writings (Riedel 1984: 3–30), but also thought it possible to conclude that Hegel's philosophy of spirit had been nothing less than the last step in a process of 'destruction' of traditional practical philosophy (Riedel 1984: 30), thereby arguing that Hegel's dialectical method had succeeded in completing what had still been left undone by the geometrical method of Hobbes and the rational approach of Wolff: the 'dissolution' (*Auflösung*) of the tradition (Riedel 1984: 8f.). The role played by these studies in the 1960s has been important, the more so because Riedel, while still writing on Hegel, had also engaged in a much broader task, which became known under the title of 'rehabilitation of practical philosophy'.[1] He condemned the 'scientistic orientation' and the correlated 'ethicist misunderstanding' weighing in on the evolution of the discipline (Riedel 1972–1974: I, 10), calling for the rehabilitation of a *classical* conception of practical philosophy which prevailed before the emergence of the empirical, 'positive' sciences. His call was echoed by many similar requests, more particularly in Germany, and the 'rehabilitation of practical philosophy', which developed in the following years, happened under the powerful motto of a return to Aristotle – but also to a very large extent against Hegel, and against the author then often considered as his heir, namely Karl Marx.

Is this the way in which the Hegelian philosophy of objective spirit must be understood? Does Hegel's system really amount to a scientistic 'dissolution' of classical practical philosophy, and is it right to say that there is no more practical philosophy in it, in the traditional sense of such a term? Times have changed since Riedel's publications, and few experts would be ready today to acquiesce to the thesis that Hegel 'destructed' the very foundations of practical philosophy. Quite an opposite trend is now taking place, which aims at 'rehabilitating' Hegel's practical philosophy as such, as a practical philosophy, some experts even going as far as turning the Hegelian philosophy of spirit as a whole into a form of practical philosophy. This was one of the achievements of Charles Taylor who, coming from an English-speaking philosophical context, chose nonetheless to turn to Hegel's philosophy of mind in order to elaborate a philosophy of action, which he perceived as opposed to the causal explanation of behaviour predominant in the English-speaking world, but in line with the Aristotelian heritage. Taylor explained that Hegel, inspired by Herder and also by German romanticism, had turned to an interpretative approach, grounded upon an 'expressivist' paradigm, and considered human action as one 'expressive' not just of thoughts or ideas, but also – mainly – of a subjectivity, a self, thereby making himself the advocate of claims as important to our time as already to his own: the claim to autonomy, understood as self-determination; the aspiration of human beings to be recognized as individuals, but also in their collective identity; in other terms, the all-important search for recognition (Taylor 1983: 1–18). The rehabilitation of an Aristotelian line in Hegel's philosophy of mind is even stronger in the work of Robert Pippin, who also thinks it possible, just like Charles Taylor, to identify in Hegel's philosophy of mind a practical philosophy, one grounded upon 'the possibility of a practical rationality, and therewith practical autonomy or self-legislation' (Pippin 1997: 8).

It is certainly correct, and also very fruitful, to adopt such a line of interpretation as a basis in the endeavour to reformulate Hegel's philosophy of spirit in modern terms. However, the question to be asked is whether or not this endeavour does full justice to Hegel's conception of 'objective spirit'. Following a line convincingly developed by the German scholar Nicolai Hartmann (1882–1950), I shall try to show here that this part of Hegel's philosophy of spirit – its second part, which comes after the doctrine of 'subjective spirit' and before the doctrine of 'absolute spirit' – contains one of Hegel's greatest discoveries, in the proper sense of the word 'discovery': the discovery of an 'objective spirit'. This discovery accounts for the difficulties we have in classifying Hegel's work on this matter according to already given categories, but also shows how this work can be, for that very reason, the more fruitful: Hegel's conception of 'objective spirit' *subverts*, i.e. undermines the authority of classical practical philosophy, but thereby enables it to better fulfil the critical, normative role it had heralded in the tradition. In this chapter, after having recalled the reasons for which Pippin's and Taylor's rehabilitation of Hegel's practical philosophy do remain essential to our understanding of this author, I shall present Hegel's 'discovery' of 'objective spirit', and try to bring out its meaning and the importance it could have today.

The 'subjective' side of practical morality

In his endeavour to rehabilitate Hegel's practical philosophy in the eyes of modern readers, Robert Pippin rightly underlines the importance of the sentences in the Preface to the *Principles of the Philosophy of Right* by means of which Hegel had argued not just that modern ethical life and modern social and political institutions *are* rational, but also 'that we cannot be content to stop at what is merely *given* as public law and public morality [...] The task is rather to grasp what is "rational" in such institutions, so that it may also gain a rational form and thereby appear justified to free thinking' (*OPR*, 5; Pippin 1997: 421).

In an Addition to the same Preface, Hegel had explained that 'in right, the human being must encounter his own reason' (*Seine Vernunft muss dem Menschen im Rechte entgegenkommen*) (*OPR*, 7; *TWA* VII, 17).[2] Dealing with 'the subjective will' in the *Philosophy of Right*, he had also said that 'the right of giving recognition only to what my insight sees as rational is the highest right of the subject' (*PR*, §132 R; *GW* XIV, 1: 115). Pippin, who links these sentences to the well-known, resounding thesis of the 1821 Preface to the *Philosophy of Right* on the 'actuality' of the rational, explains what they mean: it is not tradition, sentiment or religion, but 'reason' – i.e. the human being's *own reason* – which has 'power and mastery' in the modern world, in other terms the power to motivate to action (Pippin 1997: 423). Hegel accounts for human action by means of *reasons to act*, and these reasons always presuppose norms. But these norms only count as such, as norms, when it is *for me* that they count as reasons to act; and they count for me as reasons to act only when they are *self-imposed*. A free action, of the kind Hegel wants to elucidate, is not an arbitrary one or an action without motives, but an action under the norms I do impose to myself. Acting freely thus means not being subjected to diverse motivating forces, but being the *subject* of one's own acts (Pippin 1997: 428).

It is the *subjective* side of practical rationality that Pippin emphasizes in this reconstruction. He says – rightly so – that this side has been much too neglected in Hegelian studies. But he also wants to account thereby for its *objective* side, i.e. for the 'objective' sphere of ethics, which according to Hegel constitutes the 'living good' for human beings.[3] He reconstructs Hegel's famous identity-thesis between the rational and the actual as a thesis that involves

> [a denial] that rational, normative principles could be considered norms apart from any demonstration of how and why they could be actual reasons for persons to act [...] To say that the rational is actual is just to say that some reasons *could not but be motivating*; that no person could be presumed to be 'actually' indifferent to what they require. (Pippin 1997: 440)

Pippin explicitly draws here upon an argument that had been put forward by Bernard Williams in an article entitled 'Internal and External Reasons' (Williams 1981: 101–113). The article nowhere deals with Hegel, but is pertinently applied to him by Pippin. Taking over Bernard Williams's distinction between 'internal reasons' statements, which spell out our reasons to act, and 'external reasons statements', which 'can be true independently of the agent's motivations', Pippin argues that Hegel did not hold an 'externalist' view of norms; that he rather stood on the other side, that of 'internalism'.[4]

One of the questions which remains open in such a reconstruction is that of determining whether or not it is possible to hold an 'internalist' conception of norms, and at the same time remain an 'ethical rationalist' of the kind Hegel most certainly was. If one cannot talk about norms or reasons to act which are true independently of the agent's motivations, if one can only refer to self-imposed norms, how will it be possible to avoid relativism? Bernard Williams himself did seem to have accepted a form of relativism (Williams 1972: 20, 1974–5: 226), which, however, would certainly not have been consistent with Hegel's ethical rationalism. Pippin himself, who is very aware of that question, does acknowledge that a 'general metaphysics of the person' would be required in order to convincingly reconstruct Hegel's position according to 'internal', yet non-relativist norms – but also that such a metaphysics does appear as very controversial (Pippin 1997: 424f., 442).

It is interesting to note that Charles Taylor, too, has been critical of 'the bad model of practical reasoning, rooted in an epistemological tradition' which he called 'external': one 'which wants us to look for "criteria" to decide the issue, i.e., some considerations which could be established even outside the perspective in dispute and which would nevertheless be decisive' (Taylor 1989: 73). Charles Taylor denies that there are such 'criteria', thereby defending a line which may well be called, with Bernard Williams, an 'internalist' model of practical reason. According to Charles Taylor, this form of argument rather has its source in a 'biographical narrative'. It consists in rationally convincing one another and ourselves by means of a 'reasoning in transitions', one which aims

> to establish, not that some position is correct absolutely, but rather that some position is superior to some other. It is concerned, covertly or openly, implicitly or explicitly, with comparative propositions. We show one of these comparative claims to be well founded when we can show that the *move* from A to B constitutes a gain epistemically. This is something we do when we show, for instance, that we get from A to B by identifying and resolving a contradiction in A or a confusion which A relied on, or by acknowledging the importance of some factor which A screened out, or something of the sort. The argument fixes on the nature of the transition from A to B. The nerve of the rational proof consists in showing that this transition is an error-reducing one. The argument turns on rival interpretations of possible transitions from A to B, or B to A. (Taylor 1989: 72)

Although Charles Taylor does not explicitly and systematically refer to Hegel in his more recent work, Hegel is most certainly one of the authors who remain at the basis of his conception of practical reason. It is pertinent to ask, if only for this reason, whether or not his reconstruction of practical reasoning matches the Hegelian conception – and in that case how and up to what point did Hegel also want us to convince one another, or to convince ourselves, by means of a 'reasoning in transitions', one which was always 'internal' to a certain perspective, never external?

Although Charles Taylor's and Robert Pippin's argumentations are different from one another and indeed lead to quite different reconstructions of Hegel's system, they do bear similar features, one of them being the rejection of 'external reasons statements', which 'can be true independently of the agent's motivations', and the adoption of an 'internalist' claim. This trend of research is undoubtedly most welcome in the Hegel scholarship of our days, if only because there are, to this day, scholars who persist in turning Hegel into an ethical 'positivist', one who would have assimilated that which is 'rational', viz., 'actual', to that which is simply *given*. Putting emphasis upon the *subjective* side of morality is certainly right. Explaining that when Hegel had referred to the *actuality* of the rational, he had also wanted to show how we are motivated to rationality, and how our whole behaviour, in our political as well as ethical life, does express such a motivation to rationality, is certainly right. Still, however important it is to straighten a long distorted line of interpretation, this should not mislead us into another distortion: overlooking the 'objective' side of practical philosophy.

Hegel's discovery of an 'objective spirit'

The phenomenon which had awoken the astonishment of Hegel, and which subsequently led him to his 'discovery' of an 'objective spirit', had rather pointed to an opposite direction. Hegel had found that there are norms, or systems of norms, which do not *motivate* us any more, whereas they do remain as such, as norms. This was the fact which led, after many years, to his 'discovery' of an 'objective Spirit'.

The formulation, and the thesis, is Nicolai Hartmann's: a German philosopher famous in his days, who fell afterwards in the shadow of Martin Heidegger's fame and seems almost forgotten today – unfairly, though, when one pays attention to his many outstanding works.[5] In one of them, a two-volume work on the philosophy of German idealism (Hartmann 1923–1929), Hartmann, examining Hegel's thought, had argued that in it

> [the concept of 'objective spirit'] is not an implication of the system, it is not a product of his dialectical way of thinking – and certainly not a speculative doctrine, but a plain descriptive concept, the philosophical formulation of a basic phenomenon, which may be shown and described any time, independently of one's viewpoint. Briefly said, this is a discovery originally seen by Hegel, one which is entirely self-supporting. (Hartmann 1929, II, 298f.)

Further, Hartmann insisted, with much force, that 'it is not the system which led to the discovery; it is the discovery which led to the system' (Hartmann 1929, II: 299).

Hartmann did give examples of the way in which the philosopher had resorted to the notion in his system, but it is clear that he was not so much interested in them or, for that matter, in the history of the formation of Hegel's system, as in bringing out the singular nature of that being, the 'objective spirit', discovered by Hegel. Hegel, Hartmann wrote, had been from the very start a philosopher of spirit, not of 'consciousness' like Fichte, for example; and 'spirit' has another mode of being than that of 'consciousness'. Although the reality of the objective spirit only exists in and through our consciousness, it is not that of a 'consciousness', whether individual or collective, or general:

> What is remarkable about the objective Spirit is that it is indeed a general spirit (*ein geistig Allgemeines*), but no general consciousness (*aber nicht allgemeines Bewusstsein*). This is quite paradoxical, considering that a spiritual being cannot exist at all without a consciousness. It is indeed a creation of consciousness. But what is astonishing here is that this being, which has been created in spirit, outgrows its creator, develops a life of its own, takes power over it – without itself having a consciousness outside it.
>
> The community (*Gemeinwesen*), for example, is a creation of the human being, of the conscious, subjective spirit; but it itself has no consciousness. The same can be said of right, morality, customs. Indeed, there is a consciousness of the state, of law, of ethics, but only in the singular subjects, yet such a consciousness is not adequate to it. (Hartmann 1929: II, 301f.)

Hegel fully grasped the remarkable, paradoxical feature of that which he called in his mature work 'objective spirit': the formations this expression designates have an existence which may be said 'objective' – in the state and its institutions, for example – but their existence is not that of consciousness, even if they only occur in and through the consciousness of individuals. Only the individual may be said conscious, and held responsible for his or her acts, but the 'objective spirit' may nevertheless be said 'real'. Hartmann gives credit to Hegel for having acknowledged this reality, without however having given in to the temptation of turning it into a 'subject'. Indeed, it was precisely because Hegel wanted to point out that such a spirit is an 'object' *and not at the same time a 'subject'* – the subject of that object – that he coined the notion of 'objective spirit':

> It may be considered as a high merit of Hegel, that on this fundamental point he does not resort to auxiliary, metaphysical constructions, and introduces no supra-human intellect – the example of the rationalists is well-known –; that he does not escape towards a 'general I' (*zu einem 'allgemeinen Ich'*) or a transcendental subject. All this would seem natural, and provide an easy solution to the contradiction. But Hegel does not let himself be seduced. He lets the phenomenon strictly prevail, as he finds it, and registers the contradiction without minimizing it. (Hartmann 1929, II, 302)

It is also this same question that Hartmann takes over in one of his later works, 'The Problem of Spiritual Being' (*Das Problem des geistigen Seins*): a work which was published in 1933 and subtitled 'Inquiries into the foundation of the philosophy of history and the sciences of Spirit'. Contrary to what he had done in his 1929 work, Hartmann now distances himself from Hegel, thereby criticizing the 'optimism' which had induced Hegel to substantialize objective spirit, and to elaborate a complete 'metaphysics of Spirit'.[6]

Hartmann also engages in an elaborate description of different 'forms of spiritual being' (*Formen des geistigen Seins*), thereby distinguishing between an 'objective spirit' and that which he calls 'Objectified Spirit' (*objektivierter Geist*),[7] a term he most certainly took over from Wilhelm Dilthey (1833–1911), who had introduced it some fifty years earlier in the German *Geisteswissenschaften*, also in the scholarship on Hegel[8] – but then reworked, to fit into his own ontology.[9] The distinction is not merely revelatory of some of Hartmann's own concerns at the time, it also is particularly apt at clarifying the meaning of Hegel's basic concept – and certainly deserves more attention than the one it was given in contemporary research on Hegel. I shall try to briefly present it here.

Dilthey's main purpose in coining the notion of 'objectified spirit' was to clean Hegel's conception from a metaphysical garb he had judged inappropriate to the positivist spirit of his age, a finishing nineteenth century, which he deemed more 'scientific'. 'Hegel constructs metaphysically; we analyse the given,'[10] writes Dilthey in *The Formation of the Historical World in the Human Sciences* (1910), a work in which he had also explained how his own notion of 'objectified spirit' could according to him advantageously encompass both Hegel's sphere of 'objective' spirit and the sphere of 'absolute spirit' – and thus be much better suited than Hegel's distinction to an understanding of the 'historical':

> Only through the idea of the objectification of life do we gain insight into the nature of the historical. Everything here derives from acts of human spirit and bears the hallmark of historicity. As a product of history, everything gets interwoven with the world of sense. The distribution of trees in a park, the arrangement of houses in a street, the handy tool of the artisan, and the sentence propounded in the courtroom are everyday examples of how we are constantly surrounded by what has become historical. What the human spirit is today projecting into some manifestation will tomorrow, when it stands before us, be history. Through the passage of time we become surrounded by Roman ruins, cathedrals, and the country palaces of autocrats. History is not something separated from life or remote from the present. (Dilthey 1985–2010, vol. 3: 169)

Hartmann, who remained, on the face of it, quite laudatory of Dilthey, actually disagreed with the latter's attempt at bringing back the life of spirit as a whole to an 'objectification' of human activities. He argued that one cannot analyse those productions which in Hegel's system belong to the 'absolute spirit' – i.e. art, or for that matter religion – in the same manner as social and political phenomena, as if they all were the 'objectification' of a human activity, whether individual or collective. He found the notion of 'objectified spirit' appropriate for describing those works which in Hegel's system belong to the 'absolute spirit': religion and its products, also the works of art. But he upheld the Hegelian term of 'objective spirit' in order to characterize the formations of the historical world proper (Hartmann 1933: 384), one which had been deemed by Hegel himself an essentially political one.

Insisting – with Hegel, but against Dilthey – upon the difference between the two realms does appear as pertinent, not just because of ontological, metaphysical reasons, but also because the assimilation of the one to the other makes it impossible for us to correctly distinguish between past and present. Dilthey's fundamental presupposition being that 'history is not something separated from life or remote from the present' (*Geschichte ist nichts vom Leben getrenntes, nichts von der Gegenwart durch ihre Zeitferne Gesondertes*), his 'objectified spirit' seems inapt at achieving that aim, which had been fundamental to Hegel from the start. If we presuppose with Dilthey that every state of affairs we can empirically observe in the world which surrounds us is to be considered as an 'objectification', how will it be possible for us to distinguish between the 'living' and the 'dead', between those phenomena which still are 'actual', and those which already belong to the past? How will it be possible for us to distinguish between a cathedral we visit as tourists, or consider as a work of art, and a cathedral that still has a function, a social role in our society?

Hegel's 'discovery' of an 'objective spirit', as reconstructed by Nicolai Hartmann, also aims at providing this distinction. It seems quite close in that sense to some fundamental theses of the French sociologist Emile Durkheim (1858–1917), and in the first place to his famous definition of a 'social fact' in his *Rules of the Sociological Method*, as being 'manners of acting, thinking and feeling external to the individual, which are invested with a coercive power by virtue of which they exercise control over him' (Durkheim 1895: 52). In that part of his system he had devoted to the 'objective spirit', Hegel, behaving like a sociologist *avant la lettre*, seems indeed to have wanted to study the very institutions that were typical of the society of his time.[11]

Another famous rule of Durkheim ought to be mentioned here: 'to consider social facts as things' (Durkheim 1895: 60). Just like Durkheim almost one century after him, Hegel had been, in the terminology of Bernard Williams, an 'externalist': he had wanted to deal with the social facts in the very same way in which the natural sciences specialists commonly account for the phenomena they want to study: by means of empirical observation, causal explanation and laws. Suffice it to mention here the way in which Hegel had paid tribute, precisely for that reason, to the school of political economy which developed in Scotland precisely at that time: quoting Smith, Say and Ricardo, he had said that their science

> is a credit to thought because it finds laws for a mass of accidents [...] The most remarkable thing here is this mutual interlocking of particulars, which is what one would least expect because at first sight everything seems to be given over to the arbitrariness of the individual, and it has a parallel in the solar system which displays to the eye only irregular movements, though its laws may none the less be ascertained. (*OPR*, §189, A; *TWA* VII, 346ff.)[12]

Does this lead him to 'scientism', and to the unavoidable destruction of the critical, normative claims traditionally linked to classical practical philosophy, as Manfred Riedel had believed it possible to argue?

Subverting practical philosophy

Conversely, my contention is that the three 'conditions' under which, according to Manfred Riedel, Hegel's thinking would have been able to achieve, much better and more thoroughly than his predecessors, the 'dissolution of the tradition' (Riedel 1984: 8f.), may well be adopted as the main guiding lines in an endeavour, fulfilled in the spirit of Hegel, to rehabilitate – or, rather, 'subvert' – contemporary practical philosophy: (1) taking over the Kantian idea of the autonomy of the will, (2) including modern political economy in the design of practical philosophy and (3) connecting practical philosophy to history.

The second condition is crucial to this endeavour. It is interesting to note that Riedel, who had explicitly acknowledged Nicolai Hartmann's criticism of the 'equivocations' of the concept of 'objective spirit' (Riedel 1984: 3), nevertheless decided to follow Dilthey's reconstruction of the Hegelian concept, rather than Hartmann's. This becomes obvious when one considers his reconstruction of Hegel's conception of labour. Riedel, who had devoted many studies to Hegel's reception of the new science of political economy, argued that Hegel had defined labour as the 'self-objectification of consciousness' (*sich-zum-Dinge-machen des Bewusstseins*) and thereby abolished the ancient distinction between 'production' (*poiesis*) and 'activity' (*praxis*): he had turned labour into the practical activity par excellence, and considered practical activity itself as an activity productive of a 'work' (*Werk*), like the Greek *poiesis* (Riedel 1984: 20). Riedel's criticism had been directed, in its gist, against Marx: it was Marx's criticism, in his Theses on Feuerbach, of the hitherto 'purely scholastic' discussions on the distinction between theory and practice (Marx 1994: 116f.) which he castigated, in his endeavour to rehabilitate practical philosophy in an Aristotelian form (Riedel 1972, I: 78). But Marx himself, however important the notion of 'alienation' and its distinction from that of 'externalization' had been in his work, had already perfectly understood that Hegel had considered labour and also, in his system, the division of labour and economic life as a whole as objects which needed to be submitted to a strictly *theoretical* study, one answering the same logical and conceptual criteria as those used in any other science. Long before the manuscripts of the young Hegel relevant to this field were discovered, Marx had the prescience that the philosopher had endeavoured to include the modern science of political economy into his own consideration of history.[13]

However, it was not only to his acute understanding of the division of labour in a modern economy that Hegel owed his discovery of 'objective spirit'. There were other historical phenomena that led him to it, among them the question of determining how to distinguish between 'positive' and 'natural' law, and how to 'codify' customary law. Elaborating a legal code was one of the tasks on the political agenda of that time. To perform this task, and thereby fulfil the third condition mentioned by Riedel, Hegel had made use of Montesquieu's 1748 *Spirit of the Laws* he had pointed out, already in his 1802–3 article 'On the Scientific Ways of Treating Natural Law, on Its Place in Practical Philosophy and Its Relation to the Positive Sciences of Right' (*PW*, 102–180), that Montesquieu's very aim had been to conceive the 'present' and to that end 'to distinguish correctly between what is dead and devoid of truth and what is still alive' (*PW*, 177; *GW*, IV, 482); and then emphasized:

> The effect of a purely historical explanation of laws and institutions does not extend beyond this specific end of [attaining] knowledge [*Erkenntnis*]; it will go beyond its function [*Bestimmung*] and truth if it is supposed to justify in the present a law which has truth only in a life which is past. On the contrary, this historical knowledge of the law, which can discover the basis of the law only in bygone customs and in a now departed life, proves precisely that, in the living present, the law lacks any sense or significance. (*PW*, 177; *GW*, IV, 482.)

Hegel, who was not the only one to resort to Montesquieu in order to further that task,[14] also made use of the research developed in Göttingen by a school of new historians, among them J. G. Gatterer (1727–99), who had already endeavoured to bring out, in conformity with Montesquieu's heritage, the 'spirit of the events': the 'connection' which turned them into a 'system' (cf. Waszek 1998: 21f.). Following other historians – more particularly A. L. Schlözer (1735–

1809) – Hegel also wanted to include in his historical research the study of 'material culture' itself: of 'facts' like 'the invention of fire, bread, alcohol', and not just that of 'culture' in the sense of the word used today – i.e. of the higher culture found in art, literature, religion and philosophy (Waszek 1998, *21.*). This is one of the reasons for which Hegel's study of history was path breaking: he wanted to include all these other factors – climatic ones, but also plain material considerations, and economic factors – in his systematic study of history. When, at the very beginning of the *Philosophy of Right*, he writes that the 'true historical view', the 'genuinely philosophical position' is one according to which

> legislation both in general and in its particular provisions is to be treated not as something isolated and abstract but rather as a subordinate moment in a whole, interconnected with all the other features which make up the character of a nation and an epoch. It is in being so connected that the various laws acquire their true meaning and therewith their justification. (*OPR*, §3, R, 16)

He gives credit to Montesquieu, praising him for having known how to reach beyond the narrow framework chosen by all those who, in writing the history of law, would rather limit themselves to considerations of right, as if the evolution of their discipline could be accounted for solely by the evolution of law regulations. Such a conception of history has nothing in common with 'historicism' or for that matter 'scientism', a denomination that Karl Popper once aptly described as meaning nothing more than 'the aping of what is widely mistaken for the method of science'.[15]

It is rather apt to transform the Kantian conception of moral autonomy into a practical philosophy endowed with full normative, critical powers. To this end, one may well follow the line of interpretation indicated by Robert Pippin at the end of his *Idealism as modernism* when, replacing Hegel's ethical rationalism in the succession of Kant's conception of practical rationality, he insists that for Hegel as for Kant, being a free agent means becoming autonomous (Pippin 1997: 417–450). The term 'autonomous', which according to its Greek etymology meant 'having its own laws', may indeed indicate the direction in which Hegel had wanted to move forward, in order to further Kant's practical philosophy. This term should not be taken as having the same meaning as 'self-determination' (*Selbstbestimmung*: see on this Bienenstock 2007), if only because it contains the notion of law as *nomos*. Hegel's lifelong endeavour in his practical philosophy had been to determine how to 'codify' customary law: he refused to merely accept the 'positive' stipulations inherited from the past but also insisted, against some of his pre-romantic adversaries, that not any and every 'determination' of the self may count as an expression of freedom. He rather placed his hopes in the institution of a political constitution. His fights and his hopes are still actual today.

Notes

1. The move had already been initiated by several Hegel-experts, among them Karl-Heinz Ilting (Ilting 1963–1964), but owed much of its fame to Riedel's *Rehabilitierung der praktischen Philosophie*, published in 2 volumes in 1972–4.
2. Cp. Pippin 1997: 423.
3. Pippin 1997: 420; *OPR*, §144 and A; see also Pippin 1997: 428.
4. Cp. Williams 1981: 107 with Pippin 1997: 432, n.34.
5. On Hartmann cf., for example, the good introductory article by Poli (2017), online.
6. Hartmann 1933: 290f. These points were already mentioned, but without the criticism, in his 1929 *Die Philosophie des deutschen Idealismus*, II, 350ff.
7. Cf. for example Hartmann 1933: 169 s. – and the third part of the book as a whole, 348–482: *Der objektivierte Geist*.
8. Cf. here Dilthey 1985–2010, more particularly vol. I: *Einleitung in die Geisteswissenschaften* (1883) and vol. III: *Aufbau der geschichtlichen Welt in den Geisteswissenschaften* (1910). It is no accident that Charles Taylor regularly names Dilthey for having been at the source of his own understanding of the human sciences: see here Taylor 1985: 1, 45; 2, 15. On the difference between Hegel's understanding of an 'objective spirit' and Dilthey's 'objectified spirit', see also Bienenstock (2001), 103–126.
9. On this see, for example, Bollnow (1982) and Bienenstock (2001).
10. Dilthey 1985–2010: vol. 3, 172. *Hegel konstruiert metaphysisch; wir analysieren das Gegebene*: Dilthey 1970: 183.
11. Cf. Durkheim's definition of the notion of *institution*, in the Preface to the 2nd edition of the *Rules of the sociological method* (op. cit., 45): 'One may term an institution all the beliefs and modes of behaviour instituted by the collectivity; sociology can then be defined as the science of institutions, their genesis and their functioning.' The comparison with Durkheim's work would certainly deserve to be further elaborated: on this see again Bienenstock 2001: 113f.
12. On Hegel's reception of the Scottish political economy, see more particularly Waszek 1988.
13. See also on these points Bienenstock (1993). It is certainly no accident that G. Lukacs, one of Dilthey's fiercest opponents on the Marxist side, showed himself especially interested in Nicolai Hartmann's reading of Hegel. See on this interesting but seldom studied filiation Nicolas Tertulian (2003).

14 The reference to Montesquieu's work seems to even have played a significant role in the elaboration of the *Allgemeines Landrecht für die preussischen Staaten*, the new Prussian code of 1794: see here Wieacker (1967), 328, 330, 333.

15 In his *Objective Knowledge*, Karl Popper, who rightly distinguishes between 'scientism', 'the aping of what is widely mistaken for the method of science' (Popper 1972: 185 & n.), and 'positivism' – a term which has many meanings (*op. cit.*, 321), also quite correctly ascribes to him the thesis according to which the same method ought to be used in the natural sciences and the humanities. His reading of Hegel on 'Objective Spirit' is, however, much less pertinent that Hartmann's, as is his earlier ascription to Hegel of that which he called 'historicism' position (Popper 1957).

References

Bienenstock, M. (1993), 'On Marx's "Hegelian' Practice of Abstraction"', *International Studies in Philosophy*, 25 (3): 87–91.

Bienenstock, M. (2001), 'Qu'est-ce que l'esprit objectif selon Hegel ?' in N. Waszek (ed.), *Hegel: droit, histoire, société* [*Revue germanique internationale*, 15], 103–126, Paris: PUF.

Bienenstock, M. (2007), 'Selbstbestimmung bei Hegel', in von R. Bubner und G. Hindrichs hrsg, *Von der Logik zur Sprache. Stuttgarter Hegel-Kongress 2005*, 519–533, Stuttgart: Klett-Cotta.

Bollnow, O.F. (1982), '*Lebendige Vergangenheit. Zum Begriff des objektivierten Geistes bei Nicolai Hartmann*', in von A. J. Buch hrsg, *Nicolai Hartmann 1882–1982*, 70–84, Bonn: Bouvier.

Dilthey, W. (1970), *Der Aufbau der geschichtlichen Welt in den Geisteswissenschaften*. Einleitung von Manfred Riedel, Frankfurt: Suhrkamp.

Dilthey, W. (1985–2010), *Selected Works*, ed. R.A. Makkreel and F. Rodi, Princeton, NJ: U.P. Vol. I: *Introduction to the Human Sciences*, Volume I (1883); Vol. 3: *The Formation of the Historical World in the Human Sciences* (1910).

Durkheim, E. (1895), *The Rules of Sociological Method*, trans. W.D. Halls, ed. (1982) with an Introduction by S. Lukes, New York: Free Press.

Hartmann, N. (1923–1929), *Die Philosophie des deutschen Idealismus*, I. Teil: *Fichte, Schelling und die Romantik* (1923), II. Teil: *Hegel* (1929), Berlin and Leipzig: De Gruyter.

Hartmann, N. (1933), *Das Problem des geistigen Seins. Untersuchungen zur Grundlegung der Geschichtsphilosophie und der Geisteswissenschaften*, Berlin and Leipzig: De Gruyter.

Ilting, K.-H. (1963–1964), 'Hegels Auseinandersetzung mit der aristotelischen Politik', *Philosophisches Jahrbuch* 71 (71): 38–58.

Marx, K. (1994), *Early Political Writings*, ed. J.O'Malley, Cambridge: Cambridge University Press.

Pippin, R. (1989), *Hegel's Idealism: The Satisfaction of Self-Consciousness*, Cambridge: Cambridge University Press.

Pippin, R. (1997), *Idealism as Modernism: Hegelian Variations*, Cambridge: Cambridge University Press.

Poli, R. (2017), 'Nicolai Hartmann', *The Stanford Encyclopedia of Philosophy*, E.N. Zalta (ed.), (Winter 2017 Edition) URL = <https://plato.stanford.edu/archives/win2017/entries/nicolai-hartmann/>.

Popper, K. (1957), *The Poverty of Historicism*, London: Routledge.

Popper, K. (1972), *Objective Knowledge. An Evolutionary Approach*, Revised Edition, Oxford: Clarendon.

Riedel, M. (1972–1974), *Rehabilitierung der praktischen Philosophie*. Vol. 1 : *Geschichte, Probleme, Aufgaben*, Freiburg: Rombach (1972). Vol. 2: *Rezeption, Argumentation, Diskussion*, Freiburg: Rombach (1974).

Riedel, M. (1984), *Between Tradition & Revolution. The Hegelian Transformation of Political Philosophy* (*Studien zu Hegels Rechtsphilosophie*, 1969), trans. W. Wright, Cambridge: Cambridge University Press.

Taylor, C. (1964), *The Explanation of Behaviour*, London: Routledge & Kegan.

Taylor, C. (1983), 'Hegel and the Philosophy of Action', in L.S. Stepelevich and D. Lamb (eds), *Hegel's Philosophy of Action*, 1–18, Atlantic Highlands: Humanities Press.

Taylor, C. (1985), *Philosophical Papers*. Vol. 1: *Human Agency and Language*. Vol. 2: *Philosophy and the Human Sciences*, Cambridge: Cambridge University Press.

Taylor, C. (1989), *Sources of the Self. The Making of the Modern Identity*, Cambridge: Cambridge University Press.

Tertulian, N. (2003), 'Nicolai Hartmann et Georg Lukács. Une alliance féconde', *Archives de Philosophie*, 66 (4): 663–698.

Waszek, N. (1988), *The Scottish Enlightenment and Hegel's Account of 'Civil Society'*, Dordrecht: Kluwer.

Waszek, N. (1998), 'Histoire pragmatique – histoire culturelle : de l'historiographie de l'Aufklärung à Hegel et son école', in M. Espagne (ed.), *Histoire culturelle* [*Revue germanique internationale*, 10], 11–40, Paris: PUF.

Wieacker, F. (1967), *Privatrechtsgeschichte der Neuzeit*, 1st edn. 1952, Göttingen: Vandenhoek & Ruprecht.

Williams, B. (1972), *Morality: An Introduction to Ethics*, New York: Harper.

Williams, B. (1974–5), 'The Truth in Relativism', *Proceedings of the Aristotelian Society* 78 (78): 215–228.

Williams, B. (1981), 'Internal and External Reasons', *Moral Luck*, Cambridge: Cambridge University Press, 101–113.

8

Work and Need, Particular and Universal

Campbell Jones

Work and need animate Hegel's thought. They appear in his early study of liberal political philosophy in Tübingen and his encounter with eighteenth-century Scottish political economy in Bern. These resulted in the lost manuscript on James Steuart's *Principles of Political Economy* and in the Jena *Realphilosophie* lectures on the philosophy of spirit. Work and need are pivotal in the *Phenomenology of Spirit* (1807) and the *Philosophy of Right* (1821) and are key supports for the development of his logic and his speculative philosophy more generally. The early reception of Hegel tended to treat his analysis of work and need superficially, to dismiss it, or to take it on often silently without acknowledging or analysing its significance. In the twentieth century, the intervention of Georg Lukács (1975, also 1978, 1980) and the meticulous scholarly work of Paul Chamley (1963, 1965a), Norbert Waszek (1988) along with many others, have made clear the importance of work, need and political economy in Hegel's thought (see Plant 1977, 1980; Dickey 1987; Waszek 1988; Schmidt am Busch 2002; Renault 2016).

Perceptive commentators such as Domenico Losurdo (2004) have emphasized that work is not one theme among others but ultimately grounds Hegel's insistence that a properly scientific philosophy involves the 'strenuous effort of the concept' (*PS*, §58, *translation modified*). Hegel's thought developed out of his engagement with political economy, alongside his engagement with ancient and modern philosophy. This helps to clarify some of the reasons why his logic has in turn been so valuable for comprehending the capitalist political economy (Uchida 1988; Moseley and Smith 2015). Foundational elements of Hegel's logic, such as plasticity and the relation between the particular and the universal, develop out of Hegel's conception of work and need. The present chapter takes up Hegel's logic, and specifically the concept of plasticity and the interplay between the particular and the universal. The goal is to demonstrate the importance of his analysis of work and need in the development of his logic, and moreover the importance of Hegel's logic for his analysis of work and need. Beyond this, I seek to demonstrate the importance of his logic for any thinking of the future of work and need.

The chapter is divided into three sections. The first section documents Hegel's account of the changeability or 'plasticity' of work and need, and beyond this the plasticity of the worker and the human animal as such. These themes develop in his engagement with eighteenth-century Scottish political economy and ground both his political economy and his logic. The second section turns to the transition Hegel sketches from simple immediate labour to what he calls 'universal labour', which turns on the mediation of the activity of each particular individual worker by the work of others, and further, the connection between the needs of each and the needs of all. Together, the plasticity of work and need, the interplay between particular and universal labour, and between particular and universal need, are vitally important aspects of Hegel's conception of work and need.

The plasticity of work and need

Work, for Hegel, is the transformation or 'mediation' of an object by a subject. In this process the object is given form; at the same time this forming forms and transforms the worker. Work, in short, is change. The history of work clearly demonstrates the radically variable nature of what work is and what appears as work (see, for example, Applebaum 1992; Thomas 1999; Komlosy 2018). The results of work and its imprint on the social and physical environment are of course palpably concrete, as is the experience of grindingly hard work. Work at the same time is fundamentally malleable, transformative and in transformation. Work is both hard and hardening; at the same time it is constantly subject to loosening, variation and change.

Catherine Malabou's book *The Future of Hegel* advances a powerful interpretive reading of Hegel by elaborating from his work the motif of 'plasticity'. For Malabou, plasticity refers to the united but distinct capacities of forming and being formed, the capacities of producing and receiving form (1996: 9). This is a crucial dynamic in, for example, the contemporary neurosciences, in which the concept of neuroplasticity expresses the capacity of the brain to form and, in its repeated action of forming, to be formed (Malabou 2004, 2009). Malabou ingeniously develops Hegel's thinking of plasticity; an active forming that is formed and constantly transformed in its activity. Malabou's considerations on the future of Hegel open themselves concretely to elaboration regarding the nature and indeed the future of work. Further, it should be stressed that the origin and pivot of Hegel's thinking of plasticity is *work*. Beyond the development of the theme of plasticity from his aesthetics and philosophy of spirit to his logic, the primary activity and meaning of the forming of subject and object is work.

Hegel learned from the world and from James Steuart the importance of grasping the historical transformations of work and also the importance of the rise of new needs. Desires do not have the objectivity of either the worker or the tool and are forever arising and vanishing. This led Hegel to emphasize the enduring form of the worker and the instruments of production and the passing nature of consumption and enjoyment: 'The *tool* lasts while the immediate enjoyments pass away and are forgotten' (*SL*, 663).

Work stands between subject and object and must be constantly repeated. Work also mediates between the subjects who work together, and between those who work and those who consume. Hegel therefore advances his classic definition of work, as activity that puts off the immediacy of enjoyment in order to transform matter into something more useful.In a situation in which desire is manifest immediately in consumption:

> Desire has reserved to itself the pure negating of the object and thereby its unalloyed feeling of self. But that is the reason why this satisfaction is itself only a fleeting one, for it lacks the side of objectivity and permanence. Work, on the other hand, is desire held in check, fleetingness staved off. (*PS*, §195)

For Hegel, work has an intimate but complex relationship with need, and work in the modern world brings an increasingly complex chain of mediations between the worker and the object of work. Political economy proper comes onto the scene in light of the mediation of need by work and the interconnection of the work of each with the needs of all. Hegel situates political economy within what he calls 'the system of needs' (*OPR*, §§189–208) which concerns itself with 'the mediation of need and the satisfaction of the individual through his work and through the work and satisfaction of the needs of all the others' (*OPR*, §188).

While Hegel may seem to support an undifferentiated or static sense of universal human need when he stresses that 'there are certain universal needs, such as food, drink, clothing, etc.' (*OPR*, §189A), at the same time he stresses the plastic nature of need. From the eighteenth-century Scottish political economists and from his contemporaries (on this relation see Oz-Salzberger 1995; Waszek 1988) Hegel developed the recognition that human beings have more than simply material needs. James Steuart had explicitly emphasized the multiplication of needs as a concrete strategy for inducing rural populations to enter the cycle of capitalist production (see Steuart 1767: 31–36). Adam Ferguson had stressed that human needs go beyond the merely animal and develop in relation to the needs of other people. For Ferguson, desire is imitative and human beings learn from the desires of other people (see Ferguson 1767: 13 *et passim*). This is a crucial theme in Hegel's own account of desire and the transformation of desire. In Hegel this multiplication of needs is far from politically neutral: 'A need is therefore created not so much by those who immediately experience it, but by those who hope to make a profit from its creation' (*OPR*, §191A).

In the *Philosophy of Right* Hegel defines work as 'the mediation whereby appropriate and *particularized* means are acquired and prepared for similar *particularized* needs' (*OPR*, §196; translation modified). In many ways this definition is quite conventional, following the Aristotelian idea of purposive action or *poiesis* as intentional forming of matter. It is also more or less consistent with the way Marx presents work 'first of all' as a process of mediating the relation to nature in order to make nature more amenable to human needs. On this conception, work is a process by which a human being 'acts on external nature and changes it', such that in working the human being 'sets in motion the natural forces which belong to his own body, his arms, legs, head and hands, in order to appropriate the materials of nature in a form adapted to his own needs' (Marx 1976: 283).

Hegel emphasizes the diversity of the objects and processes of work in the satisfaction of diverse needs: 'Through work the raw material directly supplied by nature is specifically adapted to these numerous ends by all sorts of diverse processes' (*OPR*, §196). This is a thoroughly materialist conception of work in the sense that it stresses the concrete and diverse nature of needs and the concrete and diverse processes of work to satisfy needs.

This conception of work is also materialist in the emphasis it places on concrete human labour in the constitution of value. Here Hegel takes up the labour theory of property from John Locke, who had presented the value of commodities in terms of the labour that is added to or 'mixed' with the products of nature (Locke 1690: §27). For Hegel the value of goods arises from a social relation to the work of others. Further, in consuming the products of others one has a complex and mediated relation to the work of others:

> This formative change confers value on means and gives them their utility, and hence human beings in what they consume are mainly concerned with the products of human beings. It is the products of human effort which human beings consume. (*OPR*, §196)

In the *Philosophy of Right* Hegel very briefly sketches 'the universal and objective aspect in work' and 'the process of *abstraction* which effects the subdivision of needs and means' (*OPR*, §198). He takes this to involve a historical transformation from work done for the satisfaction of one's own needs to work done in order to produce goods for others. Abstraction and universality enter the world of work, for Hegel, with the division of labour and the capitalist market. Such a vision of an original state of working for oneself, which is superseded later by working for others, is of course historically false. It reflects Hegel's uncritical absorption of a political economy that fails entirely to understand the complexity, sociality and socially coordinated nature of pre-capitalist forms of production. Such a conception rests on an idea of original isolation, which only notices the forms of interconnection that develop after pre-capitalist social bonds have been destroyed by the forcible institution of capitalist relations of production.

Still, Hegel is very attentive to the new social bonds between people that develop under the capital-relation. He therefore takes up from eighteenth-century political economy the notion of an integrative mechanism that unites in spite of the appearance of diversity and separation. This notion was well established in the political economists he read, for example in Mandeville's (1714) image of the 'grumbling hive' of bees that nevertheless produces a positive outcome, Ferguson's idea of effects which are 'the result of human action, but not the execution of any human design' (1767: 119), Steuart's idea that modern society is a complex integrated mechanism akin to a watch (1767: 249–250) and Smith's idea that capitalist society is coordinated by a mysterious integrative 'invisible hand' (1776: 32). At his most optimistic or rather naive, Hegel therefore follows this line of thinking and leaps from potentiality to actuality, marvelling at the idea that 'subjective self-seeking turns into a contribution to the satisfaction of the needs of everyone else' (*OPR*, §199). He claims that this is a necessity of cooperation, for the reason that:

> the complex interdependence of each on all, now presents itself to each individual as the *universal permanent resources* which give each the opportunity, by the exercise of his education and skill, to draw a share from it and be assured of his livelihood, while what he thus earns by means of his work maintains and increases the general resources. (*OPR*, §199)

Whether everyone's needs are satisfied by the work of others is of course far from necessary or automatic. The realities of capitalist production have made it patently clear that fully socialized production can coexist perfectly well with individualized appropriation. Whether or not needs will be satisfied turns on the question of distribution, and results not from economic laws but from class struggle. Hegel's optimism regarding the prospect that massive increases in productive capacity would lead to the satisfaction of the needs of all leads him at moments such as this to underplay the massive human costs of capitalist production. This is perhaps peculiar given that, as we will see, elsewhere he recognizes this very clearly. It is for this reason that at key moments Hegel is quite rightly criticized by Marx (1844: 386) and others for overemphasizing the positive aspect of work in satisfying needs and forming subjects, at the expense of the negative side, in which a few live off the work of the many; and in which work for the overwhelming majority is degrading, deforming and precarious.

In spite of these fatal defects in his own ability to systematically comprehend the realities of work, Hegel draws out from eighteenth-century political economy the incredibly important theme of the interconnected nature of work. He formalizes this in terms of a passing over from the particular to the universal in work. Such a passing over is equally a pivotal theme in his logic. In his political economy this movement between the particular and the universal is sometimes assumed to arise, as has been seen, from trade or the market. Just as often, it appears in changes in the nature of work and in the interconnections produced when working with and for others. While much in Hegel remains mysterious about how this actually functions, and its political consequences are very rarely rigorously considered, it is to his great credit that he emphasized so clearly how the work of any individual rests on the work of others and how the work of others enables and transforms each and all, while also providing radical opportunities for satisfying the ever-expanding needs of each and all.

Particular and universal labour

Hegel sketches a historical trajectory in which 'individual labour' is transformed over time into what he calls 'universal labour' (*JPS*, 119). In individual labour, which Hegel associates with peasant labour, the central productive agent is nature, and thus the soil, seasons and weather govern the rhythms and life of those working on the land. Hegel shows a keen awareness of the historical processes, which he learned from his reading of Hume, Ferguson, Steuart and others, of the 'improvement' of land that unfolded from the late medieval period in England (see Wood 2002).

Hegel is equally aware of the accompanying process of the vastly increasing productivity of labour that took place with the rise of cooperative work, first in agriculture and later in manufactories and then industrial factories. With the increasing productivity of labour, the central productive agent is no longer unimproved land, nor simple unimproved work. As the productivity of labour increases the nature of work changes, and Hegel observed this transformation, even if he was not able to draw out all of the consequences that follow from it. In short, with the application and development of new productive capacities, work is no longer simple, individual or 'concrete' labour but rather, in his terms, work passes over into the abstract and the universal (*JPS*, 164).

In this process, new skills and techniques are adopted across the social whole and new relations with others develop. This is why he maintains that 'labor is of all and for all, and enjoyment is enjoyment by all. Each serves the other and provides help. Only here does the individual have existence, as individual' (*JPS*, 120). These ideas of interconnection in work are refined in the *Phenomenology of Spirit* in what is probably the most precise condensation of Hegel's philosophy of work:

> What the individual does *is* the universal skillfulness [*allgemeine Geschicklichkeit*] and ethos of all. In his actuality, he is entangled with the doings of all insofar as this content completely isolates itself. The individual's *work* for his needs is a satisfaction of the needs of others as much as it is of his own needs, and the satisfaction of his own needs is something he attains only through the work of others. Just as the singular individual in his *singular* labor already *without awareness* performs a *universal* work [*allgemeine Arbeit*], he also achieves the universal as his *consciously known* object. The whole becomes, *as the whole*, his own work, for which he sacrifices himself and through which he gets himself back. (*PS*, §351; translation modified)

In work, then, one loses immediate natural existence and gains access to the whole. This break from immediacy is why, in the *Phenomenology*, work is 'desire held in check' (*PS*, §195). Moreover, at this point Hegel adds a crucial expression, omitted in Miller's translation but restored by Pinkard: 'Work cultivates and educates' (*PS*, §195, *translation modified*). This process of cultivation and education involves undoing natural immediate subjective existence. To learn how to work in abstract universal labour requires not doing what comes naturally but rather involves actively building habits that incorporate the skills and capacities that have been developed by others. Learning and transformation of individuals becomes something dispersed across the social whole, as individuals learn a range of physical, technical and social skills, along with great refinements of language and affect which in many forms of work today have become directly productive forces in their own right. Today, the capacity and desire to be constantly formed and transformed is a key aspect of the most privileged forms of work, just as a willingness to submit oneself to degrading and deforming work is a key feature of less privileged work. Hegel is clear about this much:

> Labor is not an *instinct*, but a rationality that makes itself universal in the people, and is therefore opposed to the singularity of the individual, which must be conquered; and laboring is precisely for this reason not *as an instinct* but in the mode of the spirit, because it *has become something other than the subjective activity of the single agent*; it is a universal routine, and it becomes the skill of the single through this process of learning; through its process of othering itself it returns to itself. (*FPS*, 246)

This circle of externalization and return, which is for Hegel also the nature of spirit, is here used to characterize the material 'externalization' (*Entäusserung*) of self in work, a theme that was importantly drawn out by Lukács (1975). This movement goes both ways, with the individual using universal skills and at the same time creating them at work. Further, abstract universal labour involves not only universal skilfulness but also an individualization in which the universal skill of the age is particularized in each individual person. This is a movement from the particular to the universal, but also a movement back from the universal to the particular. In a fragment of 1803 Hegel writes, in relation to the creativity of the artist:

> Those who are called *geniuses* have acquired a certain type of special skill, by which they make the universal shapes of the people into their work just as others do other things. What they produce is not their discovery, but a discovery by the people *as a whole*. It is the *finding* that the people has found its essence. What belongs to the artist as *this man here* is his formal activity, his particular skill in this mode of exposition, and it is precisely to this that he has been educated in the universal skill. (RR, 255)

Hegel immediately continues with examples of work and of revolution; both of which, he stresses, are fundamentally collective even though the final result might be concretely particularized in what appears to be the work of one single individual. He offers the example of the collective construction of a stone arch, in which one person places the last stone to complete the collective work, and the situation in which, 'when laborers are digging for a spring, the one who happens to take out the last clod has the same work to do as the rest – and for him the spring gushes forth' (RR, 255). Work today clearly expands beyond the digging of springs. While it would be preposterous to suggest that much could be grasped about work today and in the future with Hegel alone, two things remain: first, the plastic nature of work and need; second, the constant interplay between the particular and the universal.

In the Jena lectures, Hegel is clear that the universality of skill does not mean that all become the same or that all participate equally in this universality. Individual capacities to take up the universal, in the absence of universal rights to protection from the vagaries of contingency, result in the singularity of life circumstances. In this context Hegel is very clear about the brutality of the capital-relation:

> In the individual's skill is the possibility of sustaining his existence. This is subject to all the tangled and complex contingency in the whole. Thus a vast number of people are condemned to a labor that is totally stupefying, unhealthy and unsafe – in workshops, factories and mines, etc. – shrinking their skills. And entire branches of industry, which supported a large class of people, go dry all at once because of fashion or a fall in prices due to inventions in other countries, etc. – and this huge population is thrown into helpless poverty. (*JPS*, 139–140)

This constant interchange, in work, between the particular and the universal, is perhaps the best example of the substitutive movement that summarizes the movement of self-consciousness in the *Phenomenology*: "'I' that is 'We' and 'We' that is 'I'" (*PS*, §177). Hegel is clear about the concrete actuality of this leap and its enormous social importance. The substitution of the particular for the universal and the universal for the particular is not a logical or speculative abstraction, but one of the basic realities of social and economic cooperation.

Along with its many costs, a society of work departs from any immediacy of instinctual work. Indeed, modern management is premised precisely on such a transformation and denaturalization of the worker. The Taylor system of so-called scientific management, for example, which is palpable today in its generality, is premised on the idea that the manager is a 'teacher' whose purpose is to eradicate instinctual and conventional 'rules of thumb', in short, to transform and socialize the worker (Taylor 1911). Ideas of cultivation and transformation of the worker in order to construct less instinctual and more productive forms of action are at the heart of what is known as 'human capital theory' and in numerous variants of this in programmes for 'social investment' and 'employability'. All of these share the common idea of the improvability of each and all, and offer targeted intervention in order to bring out and expand the capacities of each individual. This logic of improvement is staple fare of educational programmes at every level and is relentless and never-ending. It seems that one can never stamp out human instinct enough, and that the wilfulness and intransigence of subjects is always a problem for capital. It is not enough to simply throw more human meat under the juggernaut wheels of industry, but in order to get the most out of each and all, it is necessary for capital to forever transform and make human capacities more useful.

While contemporary capitalism involves massive programmes for the transformation of work and the worker, it should be noted that at the same time the capital-relation equally rests on the direct pillaging of what seems to be unmodified nature. This involves the uncompensated extraction of wealth from the land and seas with catastrophic ecological consequences. A process of exploiting what Jason Moore (2015) calls 'cheap nature' remains a key premise of capitalist expansion. Extraction also involves the capture and utilization of the affective capacities of sociability, communication and care, those forms of human social intercourse, which as Marx (1867: 647) notes, developed over thousands of centuries before capitalism and continue to develop outside of capitalist intervention. Notably, those parts of humanity that seem to display only these natural capacities of being human, while they are in fact the result of the plasticity of humans, who have developed over millennia, are today derided as if they were 'unskilled' workers. At the height of human development, then, the vast majority of human beings are claimed to have no particular or distinguishing skills by those who use them and enjoy their labour.

While Hegel's historical portrayal of changes in work is seriously limited, the systematic painfulness of work is not thought through, and the assumption that each benefits equally from the work of all is outright false, his effort to think work is important because of the emphasis that he places on both the plasticity of work and the increasingly mediated, relational and social nature of work and need. For Hegel the human being is fully social, which does not in any way reduce the person to their social situation or erase differences in the possibilities for action. Sociality is for Hegel radically enabling: 'The single individual is incomplete Spirit' (*PS*, §28). This basic sociality, which only increases with modern interconnectivity, is both a result of the rise of 'civil society' and the reality of modern interconnected economies.

This interconnection was further elaborated in Marx's account of the 'increase in the productive power of the individual, by means of cooperation, by the creation of a new productive power, which is intrinsically a collective one' (Marx 1867: 443). In his own discussion of what he also calls the '*systems of needs*' in the *Grundrisse*, Marx speaks of the 'pulling away of the natural ground from the foundation of every industry' and the expansion of luxury; and further the pitting of luxury against necessity in 'antithetical form' with the development of capitalism (Marx 1857–1858: 528). He goes on to outline the development of a 'general productive power' and of the 'general powers of the human head', 'the power of knowledge, objectified' and a 'general social knowledge' (Marx 1857–1858: 705–706). It is only in light of this well-developed theme, which far exceeds the boundaries of his own thought as an individual, that Marx then speaks of 'the general intellect' and 'the powers of social production' (Marx 1857–1858: 706).

The future of work and need

While work and need have always been sites of political struggle, there are signs today that work and need are returning to the centre stage of politics (see Jones 2017). At the most basic, Hegel's idealism emphasizes the way that the future of work and need will be, in important ways, produced by the ideas that people have about them. More specifically, Hegel's discussions of work and need, even when they need radical revision, and his logic as such, hold great relevance for any thoughtful consideration of the future of work and need and of any progressive political programme that might be developed. This can be seen with particular clarity in relation to these themes that have been outlined here, of the plasticity of work and need and the interplay between the particular and the universal.

Often analysis of work and need, and political positions that follow from such analyses, are advanced either as if work and need are purely particular to individuals, or alternatively as if there were tendencies that govern changes of work or need in general and as a whole. In a crucial transition in the categories of his logic, Hegel stresses that 'in Being, everything is immediate; in Essence, by contrast, everything is relational' (*EI*, §111A, translation modified). Following this, we should stress that if there is an immediacy to the being of work and need, the essence of work is determined in relation to other instances of work, and the essence of the need of each is determined by the needs of others.

Hegel places considerable emphasis throughout his work on difference, the multiple and the relation to what is other (Haas 2000). This is philosophically important in the construction of a differential or relational ontology in which the differences and subsequent relations between elements are of more significance than elements in their isolation. What Hegel called 'the understanding' remains with difference, which is already a great achievement: 'The activity of separating is the force and labor of the understanding, the most astonishing and the greatest of all the powers' (*PS*, §32; translation modified). For reason, however, the question is no longer the particular or the universal, in opposition to one another; more so it is the construction of a concept that maintains within it both the particular *and* the universal (*EI*, §163; *SL*, 546). A particular which is only reflected in its distinction from all other particulars is a category of the understanding; at the same time a universal that does not include all of the particulars of which it is composed is nothing but an 'abstract universal'. The demand of Hegel's logic is to think *both* particularity and universality together, in a way that does not erase either (Hyppolite 1946: 238). The promise of such a logic, when it comes to work and need, is to account for the place of both the particular and the universal, and their relation, in the concrete context of work and need.

For all the importance of his ontology, Hegel's philosophy is perhaps most productive in the opening it offers to what can be called a differential political economy, which starts out from the fact of difference and the multiple, and seeks to grasp the relation between the elements of which the economy is composed. It rejects both unmediated particularism and abstract universalism. One of the many reasons why this is important is because of the simultaneously particularizing and universalizing aspects of the capital-relation. At once, the capital-relation bears universal pressures: 'Accumulate, accumulate! That is Moses and the Prophets!' (Marx 1867: 742). But at the same time, accumulation only takes place in relation to the concrete particularities of each and all. What must be stressed is that difference and the multiple are not aberrant defects of a process of general transformation of 'levelling' of differences effected by capital. Rather the relation between particularities, indeed difference as such, is one of the most fundamental and least understood dynamics of the capital-relation. In short, the logic of capital is the logic of difference and the multiple; the logic of capital unites particularity and universality.

Without a clear recognition of difference and multiplicity, the dynamics of exclusion and restriction of movement under capital appear anomalous. Of course capital knocks down walls and breaks through barriers; but it is just as active in building walls. Passage through these material, legal and political barriers is then only available to those who can pay. Capitalist economics of course reflects the universalization of a particular interest, the interest of capital; but at the same time capitalist economics is even more subtly a science of the unequal, a science of differential access, of differential capacities, differential rewards and differential rates of profit. In these ways the world of finance purifies the logic of capital, in which arbitrage effects the pure logic of difference in which the existence of positive terms and indeed the world is incidental to trade on differences (Jones 2016).

Many of the challenges to thinking the future of work are political and ideological; but many are logical and turn on the challenge of thinking difference and the multiple. For many, following the logic of the understanding, work is pure particularity, a matter of honing individual capacities and fitting the individual to the particular job to which their knowledge, skills and abilities are most suited. This is the logic that will help to endlessly foster 'employability' and offer ways of adjusting each and all to the brave new world of work. For others, equally following the logic of the understanding, a generalized process of change is underway in which 'work' as such is undergoing a relatively homogeneous transformation. The 'future of work', it is then imagined, involves a generalized process of automation, precarity and so forth (see Srnicek and Williams 2015).

Pure particularism simply ignores any analysis of general tendencies, or more accurately, surreptitiously flips from decontextualized particulars to implied accounts of the whole. Equally, accounts of the future of work that rest on ideas of undifferentiated universal movements obscure the logic of difference at play within the logic of the capital-relation. Indeed, the differentiating tendencies of valuation under capital mean that the most likely future of work and need, absent direct political intervention, is the rise of ever-sharper divisions. What this means is that there will be, on the one hand, a violently exclusionary guild who take themselves to be the height of human civilization, while on the other hand the remainder of humanity will be reduced to servile human sludge, to be adjusted and forever 'improved', that is, to be made more useful in their service to others.

Of course, gradations within the class of those who work for capital are important, and will become even more so. Capital has already instituted an estate of often highly skilled and refined functionaries, who are rewarded very handsomely for ensuring the extortion of work from the rest. They are differentiated in principle and in fact by a way of life, travel, culture, education and entertainment that is far from rudimentary or 'basic'. Distributing these often costly pleasures to the professional managerial class more than repays its costs. For the rest, the daily struggle is one of maintaining the basics or the constant struggle to escape the estate into which one is thrown.

One major proposal, sometimes but not always arising from generalized predictions regarding the future of work, is a universal basic income. This is an income or grant that is paid to all citizens of a certain age, paid universally and unconditionally, that is, not in relation to work or any other social contribution (see, for example, Standing 2017; Van Parijs and Vanderborght 2017). While advocates claim many benefits, there are obvious criticisms of such proposals. Economists tend to focus on issues such as what level is sustainable, the problem of inflation and questions such as national boundaries; others emphasize how a universal basic income can be used by employers to drive down wages and by landlords to increase rents. While these are all important considerations, the themes that have been drawn from Hegel in this chapter raise fundamental philosophical obstacles to the idea of a universal basic income.

The first obstacle turns on the specific conception of the universal involved in proposals for a universal basic income. While traditionally, welfare benefits and transfer payments are designed to provide a guaranteed minimum income targeted to the particularities of need, a universal basic income provides exactly the same payment to each citizen. Advocates stress that this equality of payment is what makes the universal basic income inherently egalitarian. Following Hegel's analysis of the particular and the universal, though, it should be clear that this appearance of egalitarianism is rather thin; a universal that does not take account of each particular is not a universal but rather an 'abstract universal'. Any universal basic income, then, that does not include within it a structural account of differences of circumstance and need will fall radically short of universality. If the goal is genuinely to address massive and accelerating inequalities of income and wealth and provide social participation, what is required is not a universal basic income but instead thoughtfully targeted intervention and social provision of access to resources that takes into account the situation and needs of each and all. As was noted in the nineteenth century, equality in the genuine sense is possible only in light of a recognition of the reality of the differences of capacity and the differences of need (Proudhon 1840; Marx 1875).

The second and even deeper obstacle for a universal basic income turns on the nature of human need as such. Any particular level of basic income involves profound judgements about what would sufficiently satisfy human needs. Many prominent advocates of a universal basic income propose that such an income should be very modest, providing for only the basic prospects of survival. Guy Standing, for example, stresses that a basic income 'means an amount that would enable someone to survive *in extremis*, in the society in which they live' (Standing 2017: 3). For Standing, this involves neither 'participation in society', an expression he dismisses as 'both unnecessary and too vague'; nor 'basic economic security', which he considers 'neither feasible nor desirable' (Standing 2017: 3–4). There is little to distinguish such versions of a universal basic income from 'poor laws' designed to keep the working population alive, but only just; or from the proposals by, for instance Milton Friedman, 'to set, as it were, a floor under the standard of life of every person in the community' (1962: 191).

Nearly three centuries ago, Montesquieu demanded that the state 'owes all the citizens an assured sustenance, nourishment, suitable clothing, and a kind of life which is not contrary to health' (1748: 455). While he is deeply indebted to Montesquieu in many ways, and makes almost precisely this same demand (*OPR*, §189A), for Hegel the question of need does not end here. For Hegel the human being is at once a finite mortal animal but is at the same time much more than this. With his contemporaries such as Friedrich Schiller (1795), and on this point in continuity with important philosophers today (see, for example, Badiou 2006: 507–514), Hegel emphasized that human beings are more than animals. We have basic physical needs, but are also social animals whose desires and horizons are not fixed but constantly expand to include things that are far from necessary. This follows from Hegel's emphasis on the importance of the escape from the 'state of nature'; but is also anchored in crucially important ways in the motif of the multiplicity and multiplication of wants that was so important for eighteenth-century Scottish political economists such as Ferguson and Steuart, in the idea that need and desire are not fixed but are plastic, social and relational.

What is important here in relation to questions of work and need is that human beings rightly demand much more than subsistence. The demand for the right to social participation, for Hegel, involves the very real and concrete nature of demands to satisfy the 'spiritual' nature of the human being. Need is plastic, social and relational; work is plastic, social and relational. The work one does rests on the work of others and in turn creates profound possibilities for others; the work of each and all creates the possibility for the satisfaction of the needs of self and others, but does not in any way guarantee this. To think that it does implies at best blind faith and at worst a theodicy that serves to justify massive unnecessary suffering. Nothing in nature directly grounds that expansion of needs. Rather, needs are expressed in real concrete political demands. These demands can never be only for survival, but involve the demand to be and to be counted as fully human, which means to be fully a part of the situation in which one works and lives. So, beyond all of the criticism that can be made of Hegel's account of work and need, there remains a deep sense in his political economy, as in his logic, of human dignity, the dignity of forever becoming what it is possible for a human being to become. This, ultimately, is a dignity that far exceeds the barbarism to which capitalism seeks to reduce us all.

References

Applebaum, H. (1992), *The Concept of Work: Ancient, Medieval and Modern*, New York: State University of New York Press.
Badiou, A. (2006/2009), *Logics of Worlds: Being and Event, 2*, trans. A. Toscano, London: Continuum.
Chamley, P. (1963), *Économie politique et philosophie chez Stuart et Hegel*, Paris: Dalloz.
Chamley, P. (1965a), 'La doctrine economique de Hegel et la conception Hegelienne du travail', *Hegel Studien*, Beiheft, 4: 147–159.
Chamley, P. (1965b), 'Les origines de la pensée économique de Hegel', *Hegel Studien*, 3: 225–261.
Dickey, L. (1987), *Hegel: Religion, Economics and the Politics of Spirit 1770–1807*, Cambridge: Cambridge University Press.
Ferguson, A. (1767/1995), *An Essay on the History of Civil Society*, ed. F. Oz-Salzberger, Cambridge: Cambridge University Press.
Friedman, M. (1962), *Capitalism and Freedom*, Chicago, IL: University of Chicago Press.
Haas, A. (2000), *Hegel and the Problem of Multiplicity*, Evanston, IL: Northwestern University Press.
Hyppolite, J. (1946/1974), *Genesis and Structure of Hegel's* Phenomenology of Spirit, trans. S. Cherniak and J. Heckman, Evanston, IL: Northwestern University Press.
Jones, C. (2016), 'The World of Finance', *diacritics*, 44 (3): 30–54.
Jones, C. (2017), 'The Value of Work and the Future of the Left', *Counterfutures: Left Thought and Practice Aotearoa*, 4: 137–165.
Komlosy, A. (2018), *Work: The Last 1,000 Years*, trans. J.K. Watson, London: Verso.
Locke, J. (1690/1980), *Second Treatise of Government*, ed. C.B. Macpherson, Indianapolis, IN: Hackett.
Losurdo, D. (2004), *Hegel and the Freedom of Moderns*, Durham, NC: Duke University Press.
Lukács, G. (1975), *The Young Hegel: Studies in the Relations between Dialectics and Economics*, [1948], trans. R. Livingstone, London: Merlin.
Lukács, G. (1978), *The Ontology of Social Being, 1: Hegel's False and His Genuine Ontology*, trans. D. Fernbach, London: Merlin.

Lukács, G. (1980), *The Ontology of Social Being, 3: Labour*, trans. D. Fernbach, London: Merlin.
Malabou, C. (1996/2005), *The Future of Hegel: Plasticity, Temporality and the Dialectic*, trans. L. During, Oxford: Routledge.
Malabou, C. (2004/2008), *What Should We Do with Our Brain?* trans. S. Rand, New York: Fordham University Press.
Malabou, C. (2009), *La chambre du milieu: De Hegel aux neurosciences*, Paris: Hermann.
Mandeville, B. (1714/1989), *The Fable of the Bees*, ed. P. Harth, London: Penguin.
Marx, K. (1844/1974), 'Economic and Philosophical Manuscripts', in R. Livingtone and G. Benton, trans. *Early Writings*, London: Penguin.
Marx, K. (1857–1858/1993), *Grundrisse: Foundations of the Critique of Political Economy*, trans. M. Nicolaus, London: Penguin.
Marx, K. (1867/1976), *Capital: A Critique of Political Economy, Volume One*, trans. B. Fowkes, London: Penguin.
Marx, K. (1875/2010), 'Critique of the Gotha Programme', in D. Fernbach, trans. *The First International and After: Political Writings, Volume Three*, London: Verso.
Montesquieu (1748/2002), *The Spirit of Laws*, Amherst, NY: Prometheus.
Moore, J.W. (2015), *Capitalism in the Web of Life: Ecology and the Accumulation of Capital*, London: Verso.
Moseley, F. and T. Smith (2015), *Marx's* Capital *and Hegel's* Logic: *A Reexamination*, London: Haymarket.
Oz-Salzberger, F. (1995), *Translating the Enlightenment: Scottish Civic Discourse in Eighteenth-Century Germany*, Oxford: Oxford University Press.
Plant, R. (1977), 'Hegel and Political Economy', *New Left Review*, 103 (May-June): 79–92 and (July-August): 103–113.
Plant, R. (1980), 'Economic and Social Integration in Hegel's Political Philosophy', in D.P. Verene (ed.), *Hegel's Social and Political Thought*, New Jersey, NJ: Humanities Press.
Proudhon, Pierre-Joseph (1840/1994), *What Is Property?* ed. and trans. Donald Kelley and Bonnie Smith, Cambridge: Cambridge University Press.
Renault, E. (2016), 'Hegel et le paradigme du travail', *Revue internationale de philosophie* 278 (4): 469–490.
Schiller, F. (1795/2016), *On the Aesthetic Education of Man*, trans. K. Tribe, London: Penguin.
Schmidt Am Busch, H.-C. (2002), *Hegels Begriff der Arbeit*, Berlin: Akademie Verlag.
Smith, A. (1776/1999), *The Wealth of Nations, Books IV-V*, ed. A. Skinner, London: Penguin.
Srnicek, N. and A. Williams (2015), *Inventing the Future: Postcapitalism and a World without Work*, London: Verso.
Standing, G. (2017), *Basic Income: And How to Make It Happen*, London: Pelican.
Steuart, J. (1767), *An Inquiry into the Principles of Political Oeconomy, Vol. 1*, London: Millar and Cadell.
Taylor, F.W. (1911), *Principles of Scientific Management*, New York: Norton.

Thomas, K., ed. (1999), *The Oxford Book of Work*, Oxford: Oxford University Press.
Uchida, Hiroshi (1988), *Marx's* Grundrisse *and Hegel's* Logic, ed. T. Carver, London: Routledge.
Van Parijs, P. and Y. Vanderborght (2017), *Basic Income: A Radical Proposal for a Free and Sane Society*, Harvard, MA: Harvard University Press.
Waszek, N. (1988), *The Scottish Enlightenment and Hegel's Account of Civil Society*, Dordrecht: Kluwer.
Wood, E.M. (2002), *The Origin of Capitalism: A Longer View*, London: Verso.

9

Hegel's Conception of Personality and the Tension between Logic and Realphilosophy

Lauri Kallio

Introduction

In this chapter, I discuss four different topics: (1) the role of personality in Hegel's system; his definitions of both (2) logical and (3) realphilosophical personality; and (4) the tension between the two.

One can justifiably say that personality is not a substantial theme for Hegel. He provided a systematic definition of personality only in his *Outlines of Philosophy of Right*, where personality is defined as the elementary legal concept (*OPR*, §35–§36). According to Hegel's definition, 'the will that is abstract or for itself is the person. The highest thing for a human being is to be a person' (*OPR*, §35 A). The fact that Hegel thematized personality only occasionally in his works does not mean that personality has no importance for his philosophy. Quite the opposite: Hegel suggested in the chapter 'The Absolute Idea' at the end of his *Science of Logic* that the category of personality is applicable for the description of the highest stage of the development of spirit. The essence of Hegel's conception of personality is thus logical. Besides the philosophy of right and the logic, the theme of personality is also present in other parts of Hegel's realphilosophy, although he seldom uses the term 'personality'.

In order to clarify the proper content of this chapter, I present two introductory questions. One asks how to conceive the relationship between personality and subjectivity. It is clear that Hegel's concept of subjectivity covers partially the colloquial conception of personality. Hegel also occasionally uses the term 'person' 'in a critical one-sided-sense in which the accidental and arbitrary particularity of the individual's self-consciousness (and will) is stressed at the expense of what is more universal' (Hicks 1990: 54).

Thus, the question is whether Hegel's concept of personality is eventually identical with his concept of subjectivity. My answer is negative. It is clear that Hegel's conception of personality has some affinity with his conception of subjectivity. He discusses the same phenomena with reference to both personality and subjectivity. Yet in this chapter, I argue that this does not imply mere repetition. Personality implies an essentially higher stage of speculation than subjectivity. According to Hegel '"person" is essentially different from "subject", since "subject" is only the possibility of personality; every living thing of any sort is a subject' (*OPR*, §35 A).

Another introductory question concerns the difference between person and personality. Does this difference express something essential? It appears to me that the term 'personality' primarily refers to logic. The term 'person', on the contrary, encompasses reality. Thus it is primarily a realphilosophical category. Yet it would be misleading to describe the difference between personality and person as absolute. I would describe it as a difference in determination: the concept of person contains more determinations than the concept of personality.

Logical personality

As mentioned above, Hegel discusses the category of personality in the last section of his *Science of Logic*. Hegel's logic culminates in the subjective logic or the doctrine of the concept. The concept has three moments: the universal, the particular and the singular. This hierarchy makes it evident that singularity – instead of universality – constitutes the highest stage of the logic: 'Life, spirit, God, as well as the pure concept, are for this reason beyond the grasp of abstraction, for abstraction keeps singularity away from its products, and singularity is the principle of individuality and personality' (*SL*, 547). The singularity implies the principle of personality; the concept is to be characterized as personal.

The idea is further the highest stage of the development of the concept, and according to Hegel the absolute idea is the pure personality (*SL*, 750). The dialectic comes to an end as the pure personality is achieved. The pure personality is, on the other hand, simple as it contains all the previous stages. This simplicity means the return to the beginning.

The three moments of the concept hint to what personality means for Hegel. The highest stage of singularity is achieved through sublating the two other moments – universality and particularity.

> [The singularity] [...] is thus the universal as the positedness (the particular) of the positedness (the universal) [...] The singularity manifests the positedness as being in and for itself, and as the positedness constitutes the different determinations of the concept, it is posited in the singularity that every determination is being in and for itself, totality. (Wagner 1971: 238)

The singularity of the concept expresses the fundamental unity of the concept:

> In singularity, the earlier true relation, the *inseparability* of the determinations of the concept, is *posited*; for as the negation of negation, singularity contains the opposition of those determinations and this opposition itself at its ground or the unity where the determinations have come together, each in the other. (*SL*, 548)

In ordinary usage, the term 'personality' refers to the separation between the 'I' and its other. That is to say that the 'I' is bound with exclusion. The personality in the Hegelian sense does not imply simple exclusion, as the personality contains the universality as sublated. The boundary between singular and universal is thus not absolute. This statement makes sense only under the condition that determinations are not sharply distinct from each other. One asks why the stage of the personality is higher than the preceding stages. The simple answer is that the personality contains more concretion. With concretion Hegel refers to determinacy: as personal the concept has more determinations than as universal or as particular.

Personality in realphilosophy

The theme of the personality is interesting in relation to various parts of Hegel's realphilosophy. I shall address three of them. These realphilosophical spheres correspond to the three contexts of Western philosophy in which personality has been discussed – namely the philosophical-psychological, the theological and the legal contexts (Drüe 1976: 102–103).

The definition of personality in the *Philosophy of Right* is concise and brief, although the subject matter of the work is based on this definition.

> Personality essentially involves the capacity for rights and constitutes the concept and the basis (itself abstract) of the system of abstract and therefore

formal right. Hence the imperative of right is: 'Be a person and respect others as persons'. (*OPR*, §36)

There are, however, good reasons for Hegel's decision not to develop the concept of person within the philosophy of right. The legal person is abstract for a good reason. The abstractness of the legal person expresses universality (*EIII*, §539 R). The legal person is a person who has property, makes contracts and is recognized by other persons. But the legal person is not a concrete individual (Drüe 1976: 105). If the legal person was not universal, the institutions could not be deduced from him (cf. *OPR*, §153). The legal person is also immediate insofar as he or she forms the starting point of the philosophy of right (Amengual 2011: 125). For example, the subject at the beginning of the *Phenomenology* could not take up this role. The personality comes up also in the third part of *Philosophy of Right*. There 'concrete conclusions are drawn, for the most part in the combination of some legal ideas with several psychological-anthropological ideas' (Drüe 1976: 103). The legal definition of personality is based on the definition of concrete personality, which equals human personality in general. The legal person is the result of the mediation, which is presented in the previous part of the philosophy of spirit or the philosophy of subjective spirit. A human being is not a person at birth, but just an individual. Achieving personality requires mediation. The way of mediation is not a straight progression (LaCroix 1971: 51), rather it can be described as a struggle. The freedom of spirit does not exist immediately: the spirit achieves its freedom through its own activity (LaCroix 1971: 53). The realization of personality leads to the transition to the philosophy of right. Thus personality binds the philosophies of subjective and objective spirit or 'it functions at the crucial juncture where the subjective capacities, powers, and dispositions of individual cognitive and volitional agents get expressed externally in objective social, moral, and political structures, institutions, and associations' (Hicks 1990: 4).

The philosophy of subjective spirit covers (although not exclusively) the subject matter of modern psychology. It is thus surprising that Hegel does not use the term 'personality' in his philosophy of subjective spirit. There is, however, evidence indicating that Hegel regarded his philosophy of subjective spirit as incomplete. He stated in the *Philosophy of Right* that he aims to provide a more comprehensive study of the subject in the future.

> There is all the more need for me by so doing to make my contribution to what I hope is the deeper knowledge of the nature of spirit in that [...] scarcely any philosophical science is so neglected and in so bad condition as the theory of spirit which is usually called 'psychology'. (*OPR*, §4)

It seems plausible to me that Hegel had a more profound definition of personality in mind. Hans-Friedrich Fulda argues that it is not clear how the legal expression 'person' comes into play in Hegel's philosophy of right (Fulda 1982: 415). Hegelians paid attention to the absence of the definition of the concrete personality after Hegel's death as well. For example, Carl Ludwig Michelet explicitly addressed the question of personality in his study on Hegel's philosophy of subjective spirit (Michelet 1840).

Hegel's philosophy of subjective spirit is divided into anthropology, phenomenology and psychology (*EIII*, §387). Personality should be discussed in the sphere of psychology, whereas phenomenology discusses subjectivity. I have already indicated that Hegel discusses the same phenomena both in phenomenology and in psychology. There are also evidently parallels between the two disciplines (Fetscher 1970: 136). I argue though that Hegel's psychology is not a mere repetition of his phenomenology. The opposition between subject and object characterizes the latter. This discipline actually addresses the traditional philosophical subject. In the course of the dialectic of subject and object the opposition is sublated. The sublation means achieving the starting point of psychology.

What does this sublation express? In my understanding the different stages of Hegel's philosophy of subjective spirit describe different aspects of the human being. The phenomena within the sphere of phenomenology are not simply left behind, but the person confronts the same phenomena as subject. Everything that is present in phenomenology is activity of the spirit, but in psychology the spirit is present as such in its reality (Fetscher 1970: 137).

As mentioned above, Hegel's statements imply that there is a close relationship between psychological and legal personality. This is evident, as one can actually become a person only in and through a society or 'the real place of the universal' (Fetscher 1970: 219).

As stated before, personality bridges two parts of the system. The essential transition does not take place between the philosophies of subjective and objective spirit, but already in the sphere of the former. Psychology consists of three parts – the theoretical, the practical and the free spirit (*EIII*, §443). The foundation of the philosophy of right is achieved already in the transition to the practical spirit. The practical spirit refers to will, and the free will constitutes the starting point of the philosophy of right. According to Hegel 'right is any existence at all which is the *existence of the free will*' (*OPR*, §29).

I discuss yet another part of Hegel's realphilosophy, namely the philosophy of religion. Hegel famously stated that his philosophy is compatible with

Christianity, which means that the Christian conception of personal God must somehow be present in his philosophy. 'Thus religion and philosophy coincide in one. In fact philosophy is itself the service of God: it *is* religion, because it involves the same renunciation of subjective fancies and opinions in its concern with God' (*LPR* I, 152). Thus for Hegel philosophy is in one sense theology (*LPR* III, 347). Now the question is, how Hegel's concept of spirit relates to the triune Christian conception of God (Huber 1982: 237).

According to Hegel God is to be identified with the absolute spirit (*LPR* III, 66) and Christianity with the absolute religion (*LPR* I, 183). That is to say that in principle the spirit and the Christian God have the same structure. The content of Hegel's logic is the exposition of the eternal essence of God before the Creation (*SL*, 29). The philosophy of religion has, on the contrary, something to do with the presence of spirit, or God (*LPR* I, 119). Hegel clarifies:

> In the philosophy of religion we consider the idea not merely in the way it is determined as idea of pure thought, nor yet in its finite modes of appearance, but as the absolute, or as the logical idea – except that at the same time we also consider it in the way this idea appears and manifests itself. (*LPR* I, 120)

The philosophy of religion requires the logical concept of God. It does not, however, keep to this definition, but concerns the history of the manifestation of the logical determinations of God (Wagner 1971: 204).

On Hegel's account personality is truthfully recognized first with Christianity. Already some pre-Christian religions incorporated the idea of Trinity (*LPR* III, 286), but the Trinity as the first and absolute determination was recognized first in Christianity. The whole pre-Christian history of religions can actually be interpreted as a personification process (Wagner 1971: 212).

So, for Hegel the Christian determination of God as triune marked the turning point in world history. The manifestation of spirit means that the spirit is revealed to another spirit (Theunissen 1970: 61). With the genesis of Christianity the mediation between human and divine personality begins:

> It was Christianity, by the doctrine of the incarnation of God and the presence of the Holy Spirit in the community of believers, that first gave to human consciousness a perfectly free relation to the infinite and thereby made possible the conceptual knowledge of mind in its absolute infinity. (*EIII*, §377 A)

Hegel's philosophy of religion presents the history of the manifestation of God in the religious consciousness. In Hegel's account: 'God is known as personality only as far as a human being also knows him- or herself as personality, and a human being knows him- or herself as personality only as far as God also is known as personality' (Wagner 1971: 208). The religious community is also important for Hegel, since the self-consciousness of God is mediated through the religious community. It is the place where spirit is revealed to another spirit (*LPR* I, 164). The challenge of Hegelian philosophy of religion results from the fact that it does not take the absoluteness of Christianity as granted. The absoluteness is rather the result of the discipline (cf. *EIII*, §573 R). The contemplation of the process of world history shows that the message of Christianity does indeed correspond to speculative philosophy (*LPR* III, 172). However, it is not clear what kind of correspondence there is between the two disciplines. One cannot simply interpret it as a direct correspondence. In my view this correspondence presupposes a certain interpretation of Christianity. Eventually one has to determine the criteria for a Christian doctrine in order to answer the question whether Hegel can establish the correspondence between his philosophy and Christianity. In any case, Hegel does not allow the bifurcation of the category of personality. Personality characterizes the very essence of spirit, and spirit always equals a unity. As spirit embraces both God and human, the personality of God and human must be essentially similar.

The tension between logic and realphilosophy

On the grounds of previous remarks, we can now examine the tension between logic and realphilosophy in relation to personality. In the case of the psychological definition of personality the tension results from Hegel's assertion that the structure of the concept corresponds to the structure of the 'I' (Fetscher 1970: 139). He writes in *Science of Logic*:

> The concept, when it has progressed to a concrete existence which is itself free, is none other than the 'I' or pure self-consciousness. True, I *have* concepts, that is, determinate concepts; but the 'I' is the pure concept itself, the concept that has come into *determinate existence*. (*SL*, 514)

The Hegelian concept and the 'I' can comprehend any object in thinking. The opposition between the concept and its other is not unbridgeable. The 'I' can also – although through struggle – overreach its other. Both the 'I' and the concept are singular, but encompass all the other entities as negative determinations. For example, the concept includes all the other concepts as negative determinations. Both the 'I' and the concept are active. It is also possible to equal the three-part philosophy of subjective spirit and the three-part logic. Then the logic of being corresponds to the anthropology or the spirit as individual, the logic of essence corresponds to the phenomenology or the spirit as subject and the logic of concept corresponds to the psychology or the spirit as person. It is also useful to compare the three sections of the chapter 'The Idea' of the logic of concept (Life – The idea of cognition – The absolute idea) and the entirety of the philosophy of subjective spirit (Fetscher 1970: 246). These comparisons show up that the person constitutes the unity of the two previous stages. The absolute idea or the peak of the logic of concept is the unity of being and cognition. Anthropology depicts the initial, e.g. corporeal, being of the human, whereas phenomenology covers human cognition (consciousness, self-consciousness). Both the absolute idea and the free spirit strive for actualization. The absolute idea manifests itself in nature; the free spirit manifests itself in second nature. As concerns the personality, the idea of the correspondence between the concept and the 'I' is, however, the most important one. The unity of the structures of the 'I' and the concept is based on thinking. Thinking makes the human being eventually divine, as the logic presents God before the Creation. Yet Hegel is not arguing for identification of human being with God. The divine is rather active in human being in a higher, conscious and productive way. The ability to think distinguishes human being from animal. A human being exceeds its singularity in thinking. In thinking human being is universal. In the animal world, species and individuals remain separate. To equate a colony of animals and a human society is incorrect, as in the latter the individual has an inner relationship to the whole (Fetscher 1970: 219). Yet one asks, whether it is contradictory to ground first the development of spirit in thinking and then to define thinking itself?

Psychology covers the systematic exposition of thinking. Karl Rosenkranz discovered this problem and separated the thinking in logic from the thinking in psychology (Rosenkranz 1863: 413). In his view the latter was identified with just the formal logic (Düsing 1979: 213). From the point of view of modern psychology the project of Hegel's psychology seems very ambitious. Hegel criticized the 'faculty psychology' (*Vermögenspsychologie*) of his time, although he did not reject the faculties as objects of philosophical study. He rejected the discussion of faculties detached from the whole of science (Drüe 1976: 11). The object of Hegel's psychology was 'spirit as such':

> *Psychology* accordingly studies the faculties or universal modes of activities of the *mind as such*, intuition [...] etc., desires, etc., disregarding *both* the content, which in *appearance* is found in empirical representation, in thinking also and in desire and will, *and* the forms in which the content occurs, in the soul as a

natural determination, and in consciousness itself as an object of consciousness that is present for itself. (*EIII*, §440 R)

Thus the object of Hegel's psychology is in fact infinite. The finiteness of subjective spirit is – as Michelet puts it – just something relative (Michelet 1840: 11). The crucial question concerns the status of empirical findings. The status of empirical evidence is not problematic in phenomenology or in anthropology, as the opposition between subject and object characterizes these disciplines. The content of these disciplines consists of the mediation between spirit and its other. The opposition between the two is finally sublated in psychology, whose object is infinite and all-encompassing. First at the stage of psychology the tension between logic and realphilosophy becomes crucial, because psychology concerns the spirit as such. As far as the infinity of the object of psychology is concerned, the concept of person appears inapplicable. Ludwig Siep has correctly pointed out that the term 'person' in relation to the infinity is one-sided, which also clarifies why Hegel does not use it in his psychology (Siep 1989: 93).

Concerning the definition of personality of the philosophy of religion, the decisive question is, how the logic is related to the content of the philosophy of religion. The correspondence between the logic and the philosophy of religion is far from straightforward (cf. Wagner 1971: 208–209), yet these two disciplines are inseparably bound to each other. Hegel's claim that his logic makes the truthful understanding of the Christian Trinity possible highlights the importance of logical personality for the philosophy of religion (Theunissen 1970: 254). The truth of Christianity is as such eternal, but the deepest understanding of it became possible first with Hegel's logic. Trinity is central for Hegel's conception of Christianity: the absolute religion is the religion of Trinity.

One could now ask whether the Trinity is to be understood as a collective of three persons. Hegel's answer is negative. The Son, for example, is a person but simultaneously a moment of one God. The moments of God correspond to the moments of concept: the Father corresponds to the moment of universality, the Son to the moment of particularity and the Holy Spirit to the moment of singularity (*LPR* III, 194–5). Nevertheless all the moments are spirit. The unity of God is absolute.

On the one hand, the Trinity is equitable with the simple sentence 'three is one and one is three' (cf. *LPR* III, 192–3). On the other hand, understanding alone cannot truthfully comprehend this sentence. For understanding the separation between one and three is absolute. As concerns understanding and perception, the speculative idea remains a secret (*LPR* III, 280). The sentence 'three is one and one is three' is just pictorial, which expresses within the scope of abstract personality the religion of three gods.

Speculative reason can yet overcome the separation. In the sentence 'three is one and one is three' every person is absolute and rigid being-for-itself. But at the top of the being-for-itself lies the possibility for sublation. Through the logic it becomes apparent that none of the moments is absolutely independent (*LPR* III, 285–6). Every moment is in itself dialectical. The being-for-itself is thus sublated or extended to universality. Hegel describes this sublation as love. In love, I regard my other as identical with myself. Love comprises the identity between something and its other. God or the Holy Spirit is the eternal love (*LPR* III, 276). The above-mentioned inadequateness of the term 'personality' is apparent here, as the term 'love' is more flexible than the term 'personality'. In my view, describing God as love illuminates the linkage between logical and realphilosophical personality. Love means abandonment of the personality in the sense of rigid being-for-itself (*LPR* III, 285–6). I leave my being isolated, but I get it back as more concrete. Or, I give up my abstract personality, yet I gain it back as more concrete. I posit thus the difference between my other and myself. This movement as pure is presented in the logic of concept – as mentioned above, the concept overreaches its other. The structure of the concept mirrors both the structure of the 'I' and the structure of the triune God.

It is noteworthy that the Hegelian concept involves an 'ought' to actualization or manifestation: 'That which is in itself spirit should also become spirit for itself' (Fetscher 1970: 29). The spirit is for Hegel simply 'a self-manifesting, a being for spirit' (*LPR* I, 164). The determinacy of the spirit is further '*manifestation*. The mind is not some one determinacy or content whose expression or externality is only a form distinct from the mind itself. Hence it does not reveal *something*; its determinacy and content is this very revelation' (*EIII*, §383). Personality presupposes the manifestation as well and is to be described rather as striving to manifestation than as a state of tranquillity (cf. LaCroix 1971: 55–56).

This striving characterizes all three spheres of realphilosophy, which we have discussed in this chapter. A human being must become self-conscious and struggle for recognition in order to achieve the true personality. That is: he or she must participate in society (Hicks 1990: 252). Achieving personality is thus dependent not only on particular individuals but also on the era and on the condition of the state. The true freedom of the human individual has become possible first with the modern state (Hicks 1990: 84–85, 228).

> The principle of modern states has prodigious strength and depth because it allows the principle of subjectivity to progress to its culmination in the self-sufficient extreme of personal particularity, and yet at the same time brings it back to the substantial unity and so maintains this unity in the principle of subjectivity itself. (*OPR*, §260)

The prerequisite of manifestation concerns also God or the absolute spirit. Although God is absolutely free, God's self-manifestation or self-revelation is necessary (Bubbio 2014: 139–140; *E III*, §564, R). This is understood in philosophy: 'In philosophy it is more precisely recognised that God's relationship to the world is determined by the determination of God's nature' (*EIII*, §573 R). The revelation is necessary, because God's self-consciousness would remain abstract without it. The transformation of the abstract self-consciousness into the concrete self-consciousness takes place in the sphere of the subjective spirit. The core of Christianity is to be found in this revelation: Christianity alone is the revealed religion.

In conclusion, I want to draw attention to the structural resemblance between the philosophy of religion and the philosophy of subjective spirit. As Fetscher points out, there is a religious thread in Hegel's philosophy of subjective spirit (Fetscher 1970: 230). For Hegel, a human being is always a human being in God. The same applies for personality: human personality is always personality through personal God. On the other hand, God achieves concrete self-consciousness through merging with the world (Theunissen 1970: 69). World history 'is the record of the spirit's efforts to attain *knowledge* of what it is *in inself*' (*LPWH*, 54). The manifestation of God does not mean that God goes outside of Godself: God manifests to another spirit; in God's manifestation God is at home. That is not to say that the divinity of God is dependent on human being (Theunissen 1970: 221; Bubbio 2015: 700). But the personality of God depends – in some sense – on the personality of human being, because the self-manifestation of God is eventually not independent from the social and historical dimension, which determines the relation of human being to God (Bubbio 2015: 701). Freedom and subjectivity characterize the peak of both the path of God towards concrete self-consciousness and the striving of human being for universality. Freedom, subjectivity, universality and concreteness culminate also at the end of Hegel's logic under the category of personality:

> The richest is therefore the most concrete and the *most subjective*, and that which retreats to the simplest depth is the mightiest and the most all-encompassing. The highest and most intense point is the *pure personality* that [...] equally

embraces and holds *everything within itself*, for it makes itself into the supremely free – the simplicity which is the first immediacy and universality. (*SL*, 750)

References

Amengual, G. (2011), 'Natur und Geist in Hegels Begriff der Person', in A. Arndt, P. Cruysberghs and A. Przylebski (eds), *Geist? Zweiter Teil*, 124–128, Berlin: Akademie-Verlag.

Bubbio, P.D. (2014), 'Hegel, the Trinity, and the "I"', *International Journal for Philosophy of Religion*, 76 (2): 129–150.

Bubbio, P.D. (2015), 'Hegel: Death of God and Recognition of the Self', *International Journal of Philosophical Studies*, 23 (5): 689–706.

Drüe, H. (1976), *Psychologie aus dem Begriff. Hegels Persönlichkeitstheorie*, Berlin: de Gruyter.

Düsing, K. (1979), 'Hegels Begriff der Subjektivität in der Logik und in der Philosophie des subjektiven Geistes', in D. Henrich (ed.), *Hegels philosophische Psychologie. Hegel-Tage, Santa Margherita 1973*, 201–214, Bonn: Bouvier.

Fetscher, I. (1970), *Hegels Lehre vom Menschen. Kommentar zu den §§387 bis 482 der Enzyklopädie der Philosophischen Wissenschaften*, Stuttgart-Bad Cannstatt: Frommann.

Fulda, H.-F. (1982), 'Zum Theorietypus der Hegelschen Rechtsphilosophie', in D. Henrich and R. Horstmann (eds), *Hegels Philosophie des Rechts. Die Theorie der Rechtsformen und ihre Logik*, 393–450, Stuttgart: Klett-Cotta.

Hicks, S.V. (1990), *The Concept of the Person in Hegel's System*. PhD Dissertation, Columbia University.

Huber, H. (1982), '"Das Absolute ist der Geist"', in F.W. Graf and F. Wagner (eds), *Die Flucht in den Begriff. Materialen zu Hegels Religionsphilosophie*, 228–246, Stuttgart: Klett-Cotta.

LaCroix, W.L. (1971), 'Hegel's System and Intelligibility of Evil', *Idealistic Studies. An International Philosophical Journal*, 1: 47–64, 102–119.

Michelet, C.L. (1840), *Anthropologie und Psychologie oder die Philosophie des subjectiven Geistes*, Berlin: Verlage der Sander'schen Buchhandlung.

Rosenkranz, K. (1863), *Psychologie oder die Wissenschaft vom subjectiven Geist*, Königsberg: Gebrüder Bornträger.

Siep, L. (1989), 'Person and Law in Kant and Hegel', trans. T. Nenon, in R. Schürmann (ed.), *The Public Realm. Essays on Discursive Types in Political Philosophy*, 82–104, Albany (USA): State University of New York Press.

Theunissen, M. (1970), *Hegels Lehre vom absoluten Geist als theologisch-politischer Traktat*, Berlin: de Gruyter.

Wagner, F. (1971), *Der Gedanke der Persönlichkeit Gottes bei Fichte und Hegel*, Gütersloh: Gerd Mohn.

10

Mind of God, Point of View of Man or Something Not Quite Either?

Some reasons not to be worried about Hegel's critique of the limits Kant placed on human knowledge

Paul Redding

In her illuminating essay 'Point of View of Man or Knowledge of God: Kant and Hegel on Concept, Judgment, and Reason' (2007), Béatrice Longuenesse interprets Hegel's mature metaphysics on the plan of his early transformation of Kant's critical philosophy in the essay from 1802, *Faith and Knowledge*. Importantly, it would be the idea of 'intuitive understanding' alluded to by Kant in the *Critique of Judgment* that would form the template for the 'absolute idea' of Hegel's mature system. But while Kant had utilized the notion to underline the type of knowledge that was *inaccessible* to the 'point of view of man', Hegel would criticize such an abstract opposition between purportedly finite and infinite cognitive capacities. In *Faith and Knowledge* Hegel accused Kant of failing to acknowledge the full implications of his own discovery, as in the process of his reasoning Kant had encountered a type of mental content that gave the lie to his own empiricist assumptions. In the 'Dialectic of Aesthetic Judgment' of the *Critique of Judgment* Kant had broached the idea of the experience of beauty as an indeterminate presentation of the supersensible, implying that what God was capable of knowing was *not* irredeemably denied to human experience. But while Kant had failed to carry through this discovery, Hegel, seeing himself as true to the spirit of Kant's revolutionary philosophy, would aspire to do so.

For Longuenesse, aspects of Hegel's criticisms of Kant in *Faith and Knowledge* were continuous with those of his morally articulated criticisms in earlier works such as *The Spirit of Christianity*, but now they were made without any appeal to the moral role played by 'feeling' nor to the role of the historical Jesus. They had been, we might say, transposed from a moral–religious to a theological–philosophical key. Thus, Hegel now posits the idea of 'a philosophical system that reap[s] the benefits of Kant's Copernican Revolution while unifying what Kant divides: reason and sensibility, thought and being, freedom and necessity' (Longuenesse 2007: 165). That is, Hegel's critique ambitiously tries to reconfigure the complete Kantian system and 'starts with a demand for a new type of moral philosophy [and] goes on with a search for the relevant metaphysics for which Hegel finds the key concepts in Kant's third *Critique*'. This in turn leads to a 'reinterpretation of Kant's *magnum opus*: the *Critique of Pure Reason*' (Longuenesse 2007: 166), such that Hegel challenges the claim from the 'Transcendental Dialectic' that ideas have only *regulative* status and never properly provide *knowledge*. Since for Kant the idea of a divine intuitive intellect is meant to play a predominantly negative role in signaling the limits of the 'point of view of man', the collapse of the regulative–constitutive distinction for Hegel means the restoration of the human aspiration to know the mind of God. And as knowing the mind of God means knowing what God knows, this effectively amounts to coming to know the world as it is *in itself*, rather than as *appearance*.

Longuenesse's treatment of the Hegel–Kant relation in this essay reveals her as, what I will call, a 'qualified' post-Kantian interpreter of Hegel within the ongoing disputes over the commitments of Hegel's philosophy. One of the striking features of Hegel interpretation over the last couple of decades has been the emergence of what might be called *strong* post-Kantian readings of Hegel's philosophy, such as found in the work of Robert Pippin (1989, 2008) and Terry Pinkard (2012). These readings are post-Kantian in the sense of radically challenging the more traditional approaches within which Hegel had been regarded as having endorsed a *pre-Kantian* metaphysics.[1] Like the post-Kantians, Longuenesse sees Hegel as having *accepted* Kant's critique of traditional metaphysics and as having attempted to find a Kantian way beyond the internal problems of Kant's own transcendental idealism. We should, she asserts, 'take Hegel at his word when he claims to have used Kant against Kant, and to have built upon those aspects in Kant's philosophy which pointed the way towards restoring "knowledge of God" over the mere "point of view of man"' (Longuenesse 2007: 167). But while her own *earlier* work had shown a 'striking similarity' to the approach of Pippin (Longuenesse 2007: xiv), this strongly post-Kantian dimension of that earlier interpretation had become qualified in her more recent writings, such as the essay in question here, by a more *Kantian* reluctance to endorse the project at which she sees Hegel as aiming. Hence she seeks a more Kantian way beyond the limits of the historical Kant, suggesting:

Instead of pushing the results of Kant's dialectic, in all three *Critiques*, towards a reconciliation of the 'point of view of man' and the 'knowledge of God', another more defensible option is to retreat once and for all into the Analytic of all three *Critiques* and to further elucidate the 'point of view of man': the nature of the ever more complex ways in which sensibility and discursivity, passivity and activity are entwined in making possible our cognitive and practical access to the world. (Longuenesse 2007: 189)

To this end she seeks to find in Kant's *Critique of Judgment* alternative ways of exploiting those tensions in Kant's own position that Hegel exploits, so that an internal critique of Kant might bypass the reconciliation of 'point of view of man' and 'knowledge of God' that is at the core of Hegel's critique (Longuenesse 2007: 178–179). Here the overall strategy seems to be that the real benefits to be found in Hegel's critique of the Kantian system need to be quarantined against a danger that is internal to Hegel's approach, a danger threatening the genuine insights of Kant's Copernican Revolution that had affirmed the finitude of all human experience and knowledge.

A less qualified endorsement of Hegel's way of challenging the limitations that Kant places on the human point of view is to be found in James Kreines's 'Between the Bounds of Experience and Divine Intellect: Kant's Epistemic Limits and Hegel's Ambitions' (Kreines 2007). In contrast to Longuenesse, Kreines can be thought of as representing a 'revised metaphysical' interpretation of Hegel within the current debate (Redding 2015). Like Hegel's post-Kantian readers, Kreines is critical of those *traditional* metaphysical interpretations, which see Hegel as simply having endorsed the sort of aspiration to metaphysics being criticized by Kant. But for a revised metaphysicalist, post-Kantian readings like that of Pippin go too far in accepting Hegel as continuing Kant's critique of the aspiration to knowledge of the thing in itself. Rather, on Kreines's reading, Hegel was intent on *re-establishing* metaphysics in a revised form by exploiting a sense of thing in itself as knowable, but in a way that such knowledge would *not* be equated with that of a divine intuitive intellect.

According to Kreines, regardless of the commitments expressed in *Faith and Knowledge*, the mature Hegel simply had no need for 'the conception of a divine intuition and of objects knowable only thereby' (Kreines 2007: 312), and yet retained a sense of a 'thing in itself' knowable from the human standpoint. For Hegel, Kant's way of placing limits on human knowledge had failed to account for quite straightforward forms of human knowledge because it ruled out even 'the possibility of strictly or purely empirical knowledge of natural laws governing natural kinds' (Kreines 2007: 317). Such laws and kinds *can be known by us*, according to Hegel, and so in that we can surpass the limits that Kant had placed on human knowledge, we *can know* things in themselves. Indeed, Kreines suggests, the features of the world accessible to thought have *in-itself* status in the stronger sense of being mind-independent *überhaupt*, not just independent of mind in its *Kantian* construal.[2]

One feature that is common to both Longuenesse's and Kreines's readings is their commitments to a normative position that might broadly be called left-Hegelian. Critical of any right-Hegelian tendency to link Hegel's theology to a backward-looking pre-Kantian metaphysics, Longuenesse advocates the adoption of Kant's humanist 'point of view of man'. For his part, Kreines writes as if the mature Hegel had no need of quasi-theological notions like the 'intuitive intellect' at all, and Hegel's theological register drops from sight. That is, both seem implicitly to accept the conceptual link between the theological and pre-critical metaphysical dimensions of Hegel's philosophy that had been endorsed by traditional metaphysical readings. What they differ on is the question of the degree to which these theologico-metaphysical elements were *actually* present in Hegel's mature work. For Longuenesse, they are present and need to be eliminated. For Kreines, they seem not to be present at all.

It is this shared assumption that a philosophically progressive reading of Hegel must be kept free from theological notions that I want to bring into question in this chapter. Concentrating on Longuenesse's account of the Kant–Hegel relation, I suggest that attempts to circumvent the specifically theological dimensions at issue here are misconceived because they risk leaving intact Kant's *own conception* of the 'mind of God'. As Longuenesse makes clear (2007: 181), Hegel was critical of Kant's idea of God, and this must surely extend to Kant's idea of God's *mind*. If we come to understand *better* the shape of Hegel's alternative *idea* of God, at least some of the worries that Longuenesse sees as surrounding Hegel's *reconciliation* of the finite and infinite points of view might be seen to fall away.

In the following section, I start with an anachronism that has been observed in Kant's first *Critique* surrounding his treatment of the mind of God, and then go on to expand on the topic of Kant's specific theological assumptions by relating his idea of God to that of the early church father, Saint Augustine of Hippo. Augustine, of course, had a huge effect on the conception of God in the Christian tradition, but it was not without opposition, and I contrast his conception of God with a very different heterodox one found in Hegel and traceable back through mystics such as Jacob Böhme to *non*-Augustinian ways of inheriting Platonic thought in the early church. With this contrast we are able to see how the polarities meant to be reconciled in Hegel's approach are quite different to those portrayed from a *Kantian* perspective by Longuenesse. I then explore these issues from the perspective of their respective *logico-metaphysical* conceptions. Both tie the idea of God in some way to a particular form of inference structure – the disjunctive syllogism – and this opens up modal issues that, I suggest, separate Kant and Hegel. Specifically Hegel, as a modal *actualist*, is critical of Kant's *possibilism*, and these differences will have important consequences for their respective ideas of God. Finally, I conclude with some general thoughts about how we should regard Hegel's theological views in relation to his metaphysics.

Kant's anachronistic Plato interpretation and the Augustinian conception of God

In his account of Plato's ideas in the first book of the 'Transcendental Dialectic', of the *Critique of Pure Reason*, 'On the Concepts of Pure Reason', Kant, in describing how for Plato ideas were 'archetypes of things themselves', adds that these ideas 'flowed from the highest reason, through which human reason partakes in them' (Kant 1998: A313/B370). Later, in the section of the 'Transcendental Dialectic' treating the 'ideals of pure reason', he notes that an ideal 'was to *Plato*, an *idea in the divine understanding*' (Kant 1998: A568/B596). But the idea of a divine mind as *container* of the ideas was not Plato's and did not appear until the Platonists of the Middle Academy, from whom it 'was later adopted by Platonists as diverse as Philo of Alexandria, Plotinus and St Augustine, and became fundamental to later Christian interpretations of Platonism'.[3]

In the most general terms, it might be said that of the group of late antique Platonists mentioned above by Guyer and Wood in their comment on Kant's anachronism, it is Saint Augustine (354–430AD) who best represents those features of Kant's Platonism to which Hegel was opposed. It could be thought that such an historical comparison is of little relevance for reflecting on the relations between the approaches of Kant and Hegel, but things can look different when Augustine's conception of the mind is examined in relation to similar conceptions in the early modern period. Many have pointed to the structural similarities between Augustine's account of the mind's interiority and the early modern Cartesian view, especially with regard to the role of the will in each (Taylor 1992: Ch 7, Cary 2000; Menn 2002). Augustine, according to John Rist (1996: 403), had come to think of the soul as an immaterial substance – a view 'unusual among western Christians of the age, though long familiar in the East'. When such considerations are taken in relation to the theme of the history of German idealism as involving a *challenge* to the Cartesianism of earlier philosophy, the relevance of the Augustinian model of the mind might be seen in a different light. Moreover, commentators such as John Rawls (2000: 294) and Frederick Beiser (2006: 594) have pointed to what they have taken to be the distinctly Augustinian flavour of Kant's *will-centred* approach to moral philosophy – that voluntarist dimension of Kant's philosophy to which Hegel was particularly opposed.

In fact, the figure of Augustine might be helpful in a further way, given that the voluntaristic features of his thought that reappear in Descartes and Kant seem to have coexisted in an unstable mix with *other* features that might seem closer to the form of Platonism that *for Hegel* best represented the point of transition from ancient thought to Christianity and thence to modernity – the neo-Platonic philosophies of Plotinus and Proclus. The views of the former had fed into Augustine's defence of emerging Christian Trinitarianism, and not surprisingly, the perplexing doctrine of the Trinity had proved particularly contentious during the first centuries of the Christian era and was again to become so for later periods as well. Significantly, during the thirteenth and fourteenth centuries, an interpretative split occurred between the more nominalistic and voluntaristic views of the Franciscans, following Bonaventura, and the more Aristotelian-inflected views of the Dominicans, following Aquinas (Friedman 2010). In very broad terms, it might be said that the voluntarists were happy to leave the Trinity idea as a revealed but incomprehensible mystery, while the opposing movement thought it reconcilable with a philosophical theology. Luther had generally played it down or treated it as a mystery beyond human understanding (Powell 2001: 22), but within the particularly Dominican-influenced *Swabian* variety of Lutheranism within which Hegel was raised, the Trinity doctrine had been highlighted. Moreover, it was subjected to quite heterodox interpretations like that of Jacob Böhme, who took the idea of Christ as son of God as signaling the divinization not only of humankind but of the entire created realm, and Böhme was a figure whom Hegel was to take seriously indeed.[4]

Kant's *Groundwork for the Metaphysics of Morals* commences with a striking statement about the will: 'It is impossible to think of anything at all in the world, or indeed even beyond it, that could be considered good without limitation except a *good will*' (Kant 1997: 7; 4.393).[5] Jerome Schneewind (1998: 512) has described such an equating of the good with that which is 'willed by a will governed by the moral law' as a clear sign of Kant's voluntarist inheritance. 'In his early attempts at theodicy Kant worked with the voluntarist idea that to be good is simply to be what God wills. He gave up on the thought that God creates all possibilities; but he never abandoned the account of goodness inchoately expressed in the early fragments. In the mature theory this point emerges in Kant's identification of practical reason with a free will governed by the moral law.' While it is perhaps to overstate the case to say that Augustine had *invented* the concept of the will, this idea at least captures the extent of Augustine's departure from the moral thought of the Greeks, a departure first and foremost established at the level of theology. As Albrecht Dihle has pointed out, even within the monotheistic pagan theology of later Greek antiquity,

> [God, while having] the desire to create and govern the universe […] does not create *ex nihilo*. He moulds what was without shape, he animates what was without life, he brings to reality what was merely a potential. And, above all, he does not transcend the order which embraces himself as well as his creatures. (Dihle 1982: 4)

This god was more akin to the artificer of Plato's *Timaeus*, who, rather than an absolute originator of the material world, co-exists with and works upon the world. Importantly, the activity of this artificer is informed by, and thereby *constrained* by, 'ideas' external to his own mind. However, as Dihle adds, the biblical cosmology that Augustine was to attempt to synthesize with Platonic thought was 'completely different' (Dihle 1982: 4). The god of the Old Testament had created the world in an act of will, and in Augustine's version, had done so on the basis of ideas *in* the divine mind. Moreover, the Old Testament god within whom Augustine located Plato's ideas was a god whose will was expressed in the form of *laws*, as in the story of the Decalogue. Again, as Remi Brague has pointed out (2007: 22), such an idea of divine law as issuing *from* some act of divine legislation was a notion largely foreign to both Greek philosophy and Greek religion.

Augustine's own voluntaristic *theology*, it is commonly said, was itself bound up with a distinctively new anthropology or psychology, and Augustine's conception of the self is often appealed to as significant for the development of modern subjectivistic concepts of the mind as found in the seventeenth century. As Charles Taylor succinctly puts it (2002: 127): 'On the way from Plato to Descartes stands Augustine.' The context in which this Old Testament voluntaristic theology was linked in this way to a type of subjective experience was

Augustine's *Confessions*, purportedly portraying the experience of an individual struggling against his own bodily and, importantly, sexual inclinations. In this sense, then, in the case of both God *and* man the will came to be conceived as something fundamentally subjective and legislating, to be imposed *on* an external material order grasped as resistant to, but also as able to comply with, such a subjectively projected order. This results in significantly *de-corporealized* conception of the subjective agent.[6]

It is roughly this dimension of Augustine's synthesis, I suggest, that underlies Kant's reading of Plato. Kant seems to have been clearly influenced by the interpretation of Plato given by Johann Jakob Brucker in his widely read *Historia critica philosophiae* (Mollowitz 1935). At the beginning of the 'Transcendental Dialectic', Kant disagrees with Brucker's generally negative assessment of Plato (Kant 1998: A316/B372), but otherwise seems to have followed his interpretation of Plato, and Brucker certainly would have given added weight to Kant's *Augustinian* assumptions about the mind of God. Brucker had consciously tried to separate the views of Plato himself from the neo-Platonistic framework in which Plato had been understood in the Renaissance, and had been entirely hostile to the pagan neo-Platonic 'monism' of Plotinus and Proclus that he saw as a forerunner to Spinoza's atheistic materialism (Franz 2003: 20). Such a negative assessment of Spinoza, however, was to be challenged in the *pantheism dispute* initiated in the mid-1780s by Jacobi. Moreover, by publishing as an appendix to the 1789 edition of his *On the Teaching of Spinoza in Letters to Mr. Moses Mendelssohn*, Giordano Bruno's 'On the Cause, Principle, and the One' (*De la causa, principio e uno*) (Jacobi 2000), Jacobi further associated Bruno's neo-Platonism with Spinoza. During the 1790s, the revival of interest in Platonism reasserted just that neo-Platonic complexion that Brucker had resisted half a century before, with the neo-Platonic Plato being particularly attractive to early Romantics such as Novalis, who saw in Plotinus a type of early version of the transcendental philosophy of Kant and Fichte.

Both Schelling and Hegel were clearly attracted to Plotinian thought as well as that of Spinoza, and especially to the particular role Plotinus had given to the processes of life. In the *Enneads* Plotinus had portrayed life as infused with the processes of intelligence or *nous*, the second member of a triad comprising the one, intelligence and soul (En, nous, psyche).[7] A particularly clear application of the Plotinian processes of egress and regress from 'the one' within the living realm is to be found in Hegel's discussion of life in chapter 4 of the *Phenomenology of Spirit*:

The simple substance of Life is the splitting-up of itself into shapes and at the same time the dissolution of these existent differences; and the dissolution of the splitting-up is just as much a splitting-up and a forming of members. With this, the two sides of the whole movement which before were distinguished, viz. the passive separatedness of the shapes in the general medium of independence, and the process of Life, collapse into one another. (*PS*, §171; *GW* IX, 106)

This process, which in the *Phenomenology* is construed among living beings and linked to a picture of the dynamic biological realm as a struggle for life, is also applied by Hegel in the *Encyclopaedia Logic* at the level of the individual organism in ways that parallel Kant's discussion of the organism in the third *Critique*. Life is the '*immediate* Idea' that, 'in point of its immediacy', is 'this individual living thing' (*EI*, §216). Here, 'the notion' [*der Begriff*] is realized 'as *soul* [...] in a body of whose externality the soul is the immediate self-relating universality'. The *separability* of the soul simply refers to the *mortality* of the living being, rather than any idea of a separable Cartesian substance somehow residing in the body (*EI*, §216). The living being doesn't die because a soul flees it, but 'because it is a contradiction. Implicitly it is the universal or Kind, and yet immediately it exists as an individual only' (*EI*, §221 A). Life, as an indeterminate universal that particularizes itself into determinate living things that inevitably collapse back into it, instantiates the neo-Platonic One.

But the individual soul *also* has a *non*-finite aspect in that it is 'the Individuality of the body as infinite negativity', a 'negative self-asserting unity' (*EI*, §216). Here, the separability of the soul from the body has a different sense – that achieved in *pure thinking*, which is 'capable of grasping the truth of things' (*EII*, §465 A). In the *Phenomenology of Spirit*, Hegel had contextualized this capacity within the process of *reciprocal recognition*, the patterns of which constituted *spirit*, in which again we see an immediate indeterminate unity, a 'we', that splits into 'I's that return as mutually recognizing each other to a mediated 'we' (*PS*, §177; *GW* IX, 108). Here 'self-consciousness exists in and for itself when, and by the fact that, it so exists for another; that is, it exists only in being acknowledged' (*PS*, 178; *GW* IX, 109).

It is this recognitive structure that is again expressed in *theological terms* as Hegel's triune God. While spirit thus conceived is clearly *not* nature, neither is it abstractly *opposed to* nature as some self-sufficient transcendent substance. The developmental processes of spirit are still embodied and located in the processes of nature (itself conceived as 'the idea' in externality) such that 'nous' could now be conceived as distributed across and immanent within the reciprocally recognizing individuals making up the historically developing human community, while dependent on no particular one of them.

It is clear that Hegel's conception of the processes of both life and thought, while starting from abstract universality which is the analogue of the Plotinian One, cannot be understood as grounded in any ego-logical idea of a spiritual self-aware entity in the manner of Augustine's or Descartes's versions of the divine or human minds. Plotinus's 'henologically' conceived One resists any easy characterization,[8] including characterization in terms of what is normally thought of *as a mind*. As the Plotinus scholar E. K. Emilsson puts it: 'The One doesn't even know itself, because self-knowledge requires some distinction between knower and known, and if it were to know itself, it would have to know itself as something non-simple' (Emilsson 2007: 1). Given that 'the One' conceived abstractly is all there is, the ideas must, in some sense, be *in* the one, but not as ideas *in* a mind or properties of some spiritual 'thing'. The ideas can only be portrayed as elements at the level of the second hypostasis, *nous*.[9] Such non-Augustinian readings of the neo-Platonic Trinity were to be found within the tradition of heterodox interpretations of Christianity to which Hegel was drawn (O'Regan 1994).

The synthesis of such neo-Platonic ideas with Old Testament cosmology within the early centuries of Christianity had been a controversy-ridden process. One extreme concerning the compatibility of Greek philosophy with Christianity had been expressed by Tertullian (AD 160–225):

> What indeed has Athens to do with Jerusalem? What has the Academy to do with the Church? What have heretics to do with Christians? Our instruction comes from the porch of Solomon, who had himself taught that the Lord should be sought in simplicity of heart. Away with all attempts to produce a Stoic, Platonic, and dialectic Christianity![10]

But those not as adverse to Athens (or, perhaps, Alexandria) as Tertullian sought in Greek philosophy ways to make coherent the intellectually perplexing idea of three 'persons' in one God, developed in order to make sense of Christ's divinity, one influential move here being that of Marius Victorinus (AD 280–365), the 'Augustine before Augustine' (Harnack 1899: 35). In his transformation of the pagan idea of triunity Victorinus had collapsed the hypostasis of nous *back into* 'the One', personalizing it and, in line with the Old Testament, giving to the *Father* a clear priority *within* the three 'persons' (Rist 1996: 403) and thereby setting off subsequent disputes as how to understand the relations among them (Friedman 2010: ch. 1).

The consequences of this move of personalizing 'the One' can be seen as separating Kant's more Augustinian–Cartesian conception of God from the more *Plotinian* one that Hegel was to embrace, courtesy of Jacob Böhme – for Hegel, a 'barbaric' writer, but profound *thinker*. Böhme's 'principle thought, indeed we can say his sole thought', writes Hegel, 'is the Trinity' (*LHP* 1825–6 III, 96; VGP IV, 80–1),[11] and in Böhme's triune deity, at least as Hegel portrays it in the *Lectures on the History of Philosophy*, God is no prototype of a willing, self-conscious subject inhabiting some beyond: 'You must not think that God stands in heaven or perhaps above the heavens', Hegel quotes Böhme as saying, rather 'you must raise your mind up within spirit and consider the whole of nature, its breadth, depth, height, and so on – all this is the body of God' (*LHP* 1825–6 III, 98; VGP IV 82). In Böhme's Trinity, God the Father consists of 'all the forces' operative in this body, so that 'when we consider nature we see God the Father; we behold in the stars God's strength and wisdom' (*LHP* 1825–6 III, 99; VGP IV, 83). Thus Böhme speaks here of 'the hidden God as we have seen done before by the Neoplatonists' (*LHP* 1825–6 III, 98; VGP IV, 82).

If there is a member of the Trinity that is an identifiable cognitive agent, it is the incarnated *Son* who Böhme calls 'the Separator', an 'I' (*ich*) that is an '*Ichts*' capturing the association of the I with nothingness, 'nichts'. This 'Ichts' or 'Separator' is what instigates and draws *distinctions*, and 'in distinguishing, what has been distinguished posits itself on its own account' (*LHP* 1825–6 III, 101; VGP IV, 85). The I *is* negation in the sense that it is that *for which* the world is presented in cognition rather than being simply *part* of that world and that to be an I is to pass over into nothing. Christ, of course, instantiates the Son, but so does the fallen Lucifer, the 'inborn Son of God and magistrate of nature' who is also 'the origin of evil in God and from God himself'. Hegel continues that 'here we have Jacob Böhme's greatest profundity. The *Ichts*, the self-knowing, the egoity or selfhood, is what forms images of, or imagines, itself within itself; it is the fire that consumes everything inwardly' (*LHP* 1825–6 III, 100–101; VGP IV, 85). Finally, the Spirit represents the unity of these two 'persons'. Hegel quotes Böhme: 'In the entire depths of the Father there is nothing besides the Son, and this unity of Father and Son in the depths is the Spirit – an all-knowing, all-seeing, all-smelling, all-hearing, all-feeling, all-tasting spirit' (*LHP* 1825–6 III, 103; VGP IV, 87). It is far from easy to grasp exactly what Hegel thought it would be to unpack Böhme's barbarisms in *concepts*, but it is relatively easy to see that the idea of God contained here, and, in turn, the idea of his creatures, could not be more different to that found in Kant.

The logic of the idea of God in Kant and Hegel

In 'Point of View of Man or Knowledge of God', Longuenesse considers an objection to her claim that the Absolute of the mature Hegel can be seen as a successor to the 'intuitive understanding' of Kant's third *Critique*. The specific objection she considers comes from Kenneth Westphal (2000: 283–305), who might be considered to be, like Kreines, a revised metaphysicalist. Not surprisingly, the general outlines of Westphal's and Kreines's criticisms here are the same. Hegel may have flirted with the notion of intellectual intuition found in Fichte and Schelling, so this objection goes, but by the time of the *Phenomenology of Spirit* he had abandoned anything like the notion that Kant had discussed in terms of the intuitive understanding.

Longuenesse responds that while Hegel did indeed abandon the notion of intellectual intuition, significantly similar features to his earlier notion of the intuitive intellect are present as mature successor notions such as the absolute idea. Hegel had wanted to separate his early approach from that of Schelling and from any suggestion of some immediate 'given' to consciousness as found in the notion of intellectual intuition. Later notions such as those of absolute knowledge or the absolute idea had to be seen as achieving a determinate content as a *result* of cognitive inquiry; they did not have determinate contents from which inquiry *starts* (Longuenesse 2007: 190). But, she points out, in the *Science of Logic* we still find Hegel 'chastis[ing] Kant for having ignored the standpoint he had himself defined as the only true one: that of intuitive understanding' (Longuenesse 2007: 190) Furthermore, the distinctly theological language of Hegel's 'everrenewed insistence that he means to reinstate metaphysics as knowledge of God' (Longuenesse 2007: 190) runs throughout his mature works.

Longuenesse surely offers a challenge to the *revised metaphysicalists* here to account for this continuing theological imagery in Hegel's mature work. Moreover, it is hard to take this language seriously and still claim that the world, for Hegel, had basic knowable features that were mind-independent (including independent from *any* divine mind) as Kreines, for one, claims. It is precisely this language that had led traditional metaphysical interpreters to the idea that, for Hegel, the world *is* or is the product or expression of the contents of God's mind. Longuenesse thinks that there is an element of truth in the traditional view. It exists as a *threat* within Hegel's overall plan to *follow* Kant in his criticism of traditional metaphysics, and the threat is to be avoided by reinterpreting Hegel's insightful criticisms of Kant back into a more Kantian framework. Nevertheless, Longuenesse's response, I suggest, fails to capture how

Hegel's theological objections to the *idea* of God that Kant presupposes are of a piece with his criticisms of central *logical* features of Kant's thought – that is, the logical framework within which Kant articulates the 'point of view of man'. Fully appreciating Hegel's critique here, I suggest, can allow us to see how Hegel can make good on Kant's ambition to preserve the empirical realism of Kant's account and yet deny that thinking allows us to access a *mind-independent reality*, that is, preserve something of Kant's combination of empirical realism and transcendental *idealism*. Kreines is right that Hegel has no use for the transcendent God's mind presupposed by Kant, but Hegel can relinquish this because he thinks he has a better concept of God available, one without a transcendent mind but nevertheless with a type of divine mindedness distributed over the members of the human genus understood in a way that harks back to the neo-Platonists. Such a conception of the divine mind better fits with Hegel's non-transcendent *actualist* metaphysics. It enables us to understand how, as is stressed by Kreines, there is no limitation of human knowledge to appearances, but how the objects of knowledge are still, in some sense, mind-dependent, as one would expect of an *idealist* metaphysics.

The section 'Transcendental Ideal' in the *Critique of Pure Reason* is particularly significant for understanding Kant's idea of God. There, Kant describes the idea of God as resulting from the *realization, hypostatization* and *personalization* of 'the idea' associated with a particular type of inference pattern, the disjunctive syllogism. In Hegel's *Science of Logic* also, discussion of the disjunctive syllogism is relevant for his conception of the idea of God, as it occupies a crucial role in the transition from the syllogism *subjectively* conceived to *objectivity* – that is, in a process that pictured by religious *Vorstellungen* might be expressed by the idea of God's creation of the world. Comparing Kant's and Hegel's respective views to the logic of these matters might, then, be helpful.

In the *Jäsche Logic*, Kant gives the example of dividing the concept 'learned man' into the subtype of a man who is learned 'historically' on the one hand and the subtype learned 'in matters of reason' on the other, such that these two qualified predicates are understood as exhausting the scope of the superordinate predicate (Kant 1992: 603; 9.107). The peculiar holistic structure of the type of concepts involved here was explored in the early twentieth century by the logician W. E. Johnson with the categories of 'determinable' and 'determinate' (1921: ch. 11). As is the case with Kant's example of *ways of being learned*, being a particular colour amounts to a *way of being coloured*. Johnson argued that this determinable–determinate relation must not be confused with the different genus–species relation. With the determinates of a determinable, the mutually exclusive and exhaustive natures of these subordinate predicates now support an inference. In Kant's example, if one *knows* that this man is learned, and knows that he is not learned *historically*, one thereby knows that he *is* learned in 'matters of reason'.

This inference pattern is a disjunctive syllogism and the regulative idea associated with it will be the notion of that totality of predicates that exhausts the possible states that that thing can be in. In the 'Transcendental Ideal', Kant argues that we cannot possess substantive knowledge of the total range of possible predicates, but that there *is* such a totality must be presupposed. Generalized to judgements concerning *all* the objects in the world, this presupposition results in what Kant calls the 'transcendental ideal', or '*Prototypon transcendentale*' – a representation of the 'whole of possibility', whose parts are all thoroughly determined in terms of the totality of such opposed predicates (Kant 1998: A571–583/B579–611). This idea is meant to capture the content of God's cognitive grip on the world: his omniscience extends beyond every actual state of affairs to the totality of the world's *possible* states of affairs.[12]

Leibniz had, of course, conceived of modal knowledge against the backdrop of an idea of a totality of possible worlds, and it has been revised in our own time (Lewis 1986). An array of possible worlds allows us to understand the claim '*necessarily p*' in terms of the idea of *p* being true in all those possible worlds and understand that of '*possibly p*' in terms of the idea of *p* being true in only some of them. Divine knowledge as the complete knowledge of possibility can then be associated with metaphysical knowledge as traditionally conceived as this had been thought of as knowledge of the necessarily true. While Leibniz had been unclear about why human knowledge necessarily falls short of divine knowledge, Kant after the transcendental turn was exceptionally clear. Conceptual *knowledge* in humans is restricted by the principle that concepts must work in concert with *empirical intuitions*, and this limits the range of determinate knowledge for us to the realm of actuality. Simply knowing that a macroscopic object is extended may be enough to know that it may be thereby *coloured*, but knowing *how* it is coloured requires experience. Nevertheless, non-actual possibilities can, and indeed *must*, according to Kant, enter into our reasoning, as is seen above in the context of the use of disjunctive syllogisms. Reasoning in such ways leads us to the *idea* of a totality of possibility, but it is an idea the content of which we can never *know*.

It is this idea of limitation that invokes the idea of a knower *not* so limited – the idea of God as the idea of a knower of something able to be known but nevertheless denied to us epistemically finite knowers. Consider, for example, that I learn from sensory experience that daffodils are, in fact, yellow. Such a judgement on Kant's classification, being unproblematically synthetic and a posteriori, means that its contradictory can be intelligibly entertained. Daffodils *could have been* coloured otherwise. In the 'Transcendental Ideal', Kant will attempt to accommodate this distinction between a type of non-determinate *thought* about possible states of affairs of which we are capable with a type of godly *exhaustive knowledge* of alternative possibilities by a distinction drawn between two principles: the principles of *determinability* and *thoroughgoing determination*.

The principle of determinability [*Grundsatze der Bestimmbarkeit*] says that a concept 'in regard to what is not contained in it, is indeterminate, and stands under the principle of *determinability*: that of *every two* contradictorily opposed predicates [*kontradiktorisch-entgegengesetzten Prädikaten*] only one can apply to it' (Kant 1998: A571/B599). This 'merely logical principle' 'rests on the principle of contradiction [*Satze des Widerspruchs*]', that is, it holds between an affirmative judgement and its corresponding *negation* – its contradictory. Here negation holds as between the species of a genus. While one species will instantiate some distinguishing property, as with the case of humans being *rational* animals, others will not, as (supposedly) is the case with *cats*. It would seem that the very capacity to use negation and consider the meaning of a negative sentence allows us to entertain *some* abstract thought of, say, daffodils *not* being yellow or cats being rational, but if it is actually the case that daffodils are yellow and cats incapable of reason, this hypothetical thought can become no more determinate.

Kant adds, however, that while every *concept* falls under this principle, every *thing* stands under a *further* principle that he calls the 'principle of *thoroughgoing determination* [*Grundsatze der durchgängigen Bestimmung*]'. According to this distinction, 'among *all possible* predicates of *things* [*Dinge*], insofar as they are compared with their opposites [or contraries, *Gegenteilen*], one must apply to it' (Kant 1998, A571–2/B599–600). Here negation is functioning differently to the way that it functions in the former principle, as here negation is thought of holding between *contrary* predicates – in Johnson's terms, between the determinates of a determinable.

The distinction broadly reflects the difference in traditional logic between Aristotelian term-based and Stoic proposition-based logics. Both logical forms are found in Kant but combined in confusing ways. In his late *pre*-critical writings Kant had employed the distinction to distinguish two forms of judgement utilizing different forms of negation – term and proposition negation – associating the latter with Leibniz.[13] Some of the tasks solved by the distinction among *judgements* in these pre-critical writings had, after the transcendental turn, been taken over by the concept-intuition distinction. For example, Kant uses concepts qua determinates of a determinable to distinguish *directions in space*, a distinction made after the critical turn in terms of the notion of *pure intuition*. In the 'Transcendental Ideal' of the *Critique of Pure Reason*, the principle of determinability employs the external notion of negation of propositional logic and the contrast between *contradictories*, while the principle of thoroughgoing determination employs term negation and the contrast between *contraries*. Here, the main point seems to be that judgements about *actual* things involve the level of determination supplied by empirical intuition; we can think of non-actual *possibilities* only in terms of the *inapplicability* of concepts for which we have matching intuitions. *God*, however, would have fully determinate knowledge of all such non-actual possibilities – he would have the type of knowledge of possibilities that we *would* have only if they were actual.

Hegel's conception of the logic and metaphysics of possibility was, I suggest, crucially different, and this difference must be accompanied by a difference in his idea of God.[14] We might characterize the difference between Kant and Hegel here in terms of the difference between modal *possibilism* and modal *actualism*. Both possibilists and actualists are modal *realists* of some sort – they believe that modal judgements can be true or false – but they conceive of possibility differently. Modal possibilists believe the actual world to be one of a plurality of possible worlds, each of which is *real* in the way the actual world is real. Actualists believe that only the actual world is real and treat possibility as possible alternate states of *it*.[15]

It is clear from his discussion of *Actuality* in both *The Science of Logic* and *the Encyclopaedia Logic* that Hegel is a modal actualist. Thus in his discussion of the concept of actuality in the *Encyclopaedia Logic*, for example, he notes that 'our picture-thought is at first disposed to see in possibility the richer and more comprehensive [...] In real truth, however, if we deal with them as thoughts, actuality is the more comprehensive, because it is the concrtete thought which includes possibility as an abstract element' (*EI*, 143 A). As is well known, Hegel refuses any metaphysical realm beyond the actual, any *'Jenzeits'* – surely the mark of an actualist. Nevertheless, Hegel clearly wants to accommodate modal notions as meaningful and must accommodate possibility *within* the actual.

Hegel's remark can be seen as directed against modal *possibilists* such as Leibniz, with his account of possible worlds, or, Kant, with *his* notion of the a priori knowledge of the possibilities of experience. Kant was, of course, not committed to Leibniz's metaphysics, but he nevertheless seems committed to this underlying possibilist scheme: God's determinate knowledge extends to all possible worlds, whereas *our* knowledge is restricted to just one of them: the actual.

Hegel's modal actualism is further reflected in his account of the Trinity with its lack of the personalistic conception of 'The Father' – the God of Old Testament who could conceive of and create the world ex nihilo. Kant had (Hegel would imply, paradoxically) held to the reality of empirical knowledge, and called himself an empirical *realist*, and yet claimed that our knowledge of the empirical world can be a knowledge of *appearances* only. This is because for Kant the empirical world is relative to what can be known by beings with our cognitive architecture, an empirical world that is deemed partial in relation to a greater reality epistemically accessible only to an omniscient god. But for Hegel there can be nothing *beyond* the actual to limit our knowledge in that way, nor a coherent idea of a radically unobtainable degree of omniscience. Our knowledge of the actual is as fully fledged a type of knowledge as knowledge can be and can't be given the second-hand status of knowledge of appearances. However, there is a sense in which the determinate contents of the actual world are still mind-dependent, as in Kant, in that we *minded-beings* are part of the actual world and our doings contribute to what we know of it. However, the cognitive structures and processes that Kant had bundled into his conception of the human as the finite rational being are now distributed over cognitively evolving populations of actual humans who, in their rational capacity to go beyond their present epistemic limits, have something of the capacity traditionally given to God.

Aristotle had ranked forms of knowledge with philosophy at the top and history at the bottom because philosophy was concerned with the necessary while history was concerned only with the actual. For the actualist, then, it would seem that the status of metaphysics has, in some sense, been downgraded – its sights have been *lowered* to knowing the actual. But this is compensated by the fact that *the actual* is now conceived as having *possibility* internal to it. While for Aristotle, history was concerned with the *mere* facts of what had happened, for Hegel a knowledge of history must be more, and at least incorporate the level of understanding that Aristotle had assigned to the understanding of *drama*, for example, concerned as it was with the exploration of non-actual possibilities. History is a process in which rational agents are able to grasp and make actual those possibilities implicit in the world they inhabit.

Theology and metaphysics in Hegel

According to Longuenesse, Hegel's reorganization of Kant's critical system as a whole had started with the demand for a new type of moral philosophy. This seems right, but Kant's moral philosophy was accompanied (Kant thought necessarily so) by a concept of *God* and for Hegel this appears to signal the need for a new *idea* of God as well.[16] Hegel's new idea of God – a God who *necessarily* comes into the world as a finite man with real but finite powers of self-transcendence – provides us with a new normative image in which we are meant to recognize ourselves.[17] Of course, this is exactly what Kant objects to: Jesus cannot *be* God because were he divine we finite creatures could *not* recognize ourselves *in* him – could not recognize in *his* actions possibilities of our own. And should we not heed Kant's and Longuenesse's warning about the, at the very least, self-deluding idea of humans uniting with the divine – *becoming divine*? Kant's voluntaristic and radically transcendent God at least prevents our falling into such a self-conception. Must not this be a good thing?

There are far too many issues to attempt to take up here, but perhaps a possible approach to an answer might be suggested. One possible Hegelian rejoinder here might be to point to the structure of the concept of 'recognition' that would be presupposed by the notion of *recognizing* our unity with God. Hegel's notion of a 'recognized' unity surely has built into it an irredeemable moment of *difference* between those united by reciprocal recognition – a difference made explicit in the notion of the unity of opposites, for example.[18] To take just one example, for Hegel the modern state cannot be simply modelled on the unity of the family as it was in Aristotle, because Hegel takes family relationships as 'immediate' and one-sidedly recognitive, and so needing to be balanced by the inverse (and equally one-sided) 'mediated' relationships of civil society. In civil society, any 'identity' achieved between members (as rights-bearers, for example) is abstract and attenuated, and not constitutive of some concrete *we*, as in families. In Hegel's political theory, one function of civil society is to prevent the *absorption* of individuals into an unmediated (totalitarian) state by establishing a realm for the operation of abstract rights.[19] Moreover, the recognitive relations constituting the religious community seem to require this same structure for Hegel – hence for him the necessary development of the moment of individual concept-wielding subjectivity within the religious community with modernity, a moment that he identifies with Protestantism and, in particular, Böhme's theology. In turn, we might treat

Böhme's *Vorstellung* of the Trinity as showing how the moment of difference between the Trinitarian God and individual humans is to be maintained.

In Böhme's new image of God, we see the movement characteristic of our *own* rationality, the movement from sensuous immediacy to the concept, but in an inverted or *reversed* way, as in a mirror (Redding 1996: ch. 3). That is, if our characteristic movement is to move *away from* sensuousness to the mediation of concepts, God's characteristic movement starts by moving in the opposite direction: God moves *down* to us, as it were, mirroring our climbing the conceptual tree and *going up* to him. But the next phase of the Trinitarian image has Christ, the anthropologized God, *leaving* us so as to reunite with his transcendent father after death, in order to complete *him*. Consequently, if I am to think of *myself* as something like an inverted instance of this triune God, I should think of *my* characteristic movement as involving, as an essential moment, a return *to* the limited sensuous existence from which I started, and, as a living creature, a return to the universal 'life'. In short, the idea of difference and inversion present in Hegel's concept of recognition works against the effectively *idolatrous* or *fetishistic* idea that reason is going to liberate me *completely* from the finitude of human existence, including the finitude of my epistemic and moral existence. There simply is no *thing* – no I, ego or soul – to *be* liberated from the concrete conditions of its own existence in the way that is pictured here.

Here, as elsewhere, for Hegel the *true religion* will be the enemy of idolatry and false gods. We should resist the lure that conceptual thought will take us to a place free of the limitations of our finite being: the god of *that* conception is dead. But from Hegel's point of view, the idea of such a god still lives on as the defining contrast involved in Kant's conception of the finitude of the point of view of man. The heritage of this can only be a type of scepticism in which humans feel cut off from the world 'in-itself' and limited to appearances, and in this Kant was in the thrall of the voluntarist and nominalist theology of the late medieval period that built on those aspects of Augustine's thought, separating them from his erstwhile Platonism. And as with medieval voluntarism, the downplaying of reason was accompanied by a reassertion of *fideism*, the reassertion of *faith* over *knowledge* as Hegel alleges in his essay of 1802. We might say that, paradoxically, Kant's anthropological thought binds his own Copernican Revolution *to* a religion via an implicit idea of God, and Hegel's alternate theology is meant to free Kant's thought *from* that religion.

If this sketch is at all headed along the right track, then we might regard Longuenesse's move away from her post-Kantian reading of Hegel as unnecessary. When read within the framework of his own idea of God, Hegel's attempt to reconcile the 'point of view of man' with the 'knowledge of God' does not represent a threat to Kant's Copernican Revolution. The condition of this, of course, will be that Hegel's *theology* be not simply read as an expression of any *pre-Kantian* metaphysical stance. I can here give no argument for this other than bringing into question why it *should* be read in the traditional way. Theological language belongs to what Hegel calls 'representation' (*Vorstellung*) and its *philosophical* import only becomes apparent when translated into 'thought'. How we understand the commitments of Hegel's theological language will be dependent on how we understand the commitments of his philosophy *überhaupt*, and, as we have seen, there are many now who read Hegel in opposition to traditional metaphysical interpretations.

There is a separate question, however, as to whether humans can, on Hegel's account, be constituted as finite reasoning subjects *independently* of their participation within the world of *Vorstellungen*. As we have seen, Hegel's idea of God is not that of Kant's, but this in itself should not foreclose the question as to whether Hegel is, like Kant, an *idealist* about God in the sense of God being mind-dependent – that is, dependent on the recognition of his creatures who, of course, are themselves mind-dependent in the sense of dependent on the recognition of each other.[20] Hegel's approach, I suggest, allows us to understand how entities can be mind-dependent in this sense of recognition-dependent, can be *real* without having the in itself mind-independent 'there-anyway' status that revised metaphysicalist Hegelians want to reinstate. We might think of paradigms of such entities as, say, bearers of institutional roles (parents, siblings, spouses, prime ministers, policemen, teachers, etc.) or more abstract normative statuses (rights-bearers, knowers, moral agents, etc.), all of which are in some sense mind-dependent, but in ways that are not dependent on any *individual mind*, either finite or infinite.

Many of the resources for grasping Hegel's thought in ways that challenge the older traditional 'metaphysical' readings are, I suggest, to be found in Hegel's religious thought. Hegel's writings on God should not be discarded, avoided or overlooked in the attempt to rejuvenate his philosophy in ways that are relevant to the present time.[21]

Notes

1 For a good survey of the objections to Pippin's neo-Kantian approach to Hegel, see Stern 2009: Introduction, section I.

2. For Kreines, even what Hegel refers to as *Begriffe* (concepts) are mind-independent. 'So Hegel's *Begriffe*, including initially natural kinds governed by universal laws, are not mind-dependent in the sense we would expect given the term "concept": the reality and the real effective impact of laws governing natural kinds does not depend on their being represented by us. They are not mind-dependent, but they are accessible only to thought.' Kreines 2007: 325. For an elaboration, see Kreines 2015.

3. Paul Guyer and Allen W. Wood, editorial notes to Kant 1998: 746n. 86.

4. In *LHP* 1825–6, Hegel pairs Böhme and Francis Bacon as representing the birth of the modern era in philosophy. Böhme had been rediscovered by the Jena Romantics, Tieck, Novalis and Friedrich Schlegel, in the late 1790s.

5. Here, following pagination (given in margins in the English edition) is to volume and page number of Kant 1968.

6. Thus Stephen Menn (2002: 202–203) argues that it is the doctrine of the incarnation that required Augustine to add a will to Plotinus's God.

7. Friedrich Creuzer, later Hegel's colleague at Heidelberg and correspondent during his Berlin period, in 1805 had translated Plotinus's 'On Nature and On Contemplation and the One', from the *Enneads* book, III. Cf. Beierwaltes 2004: 84.

8. As Dieter Henrich has pointed out (2003: 85–86), Platonism can be contrasted to Aristotelianism in as much as it identifies 'unity' rather than 'being' as the central concept from which all reasoning begins. Platonism is, as he says, a 'henology' (from the Greek '*to hen*', the one) as opposed to an Aristotelian 'ontology'.

9. On the relation of Hegel to ancient neo-Platonism, see Jean-Louis Vieillard-Baron (1979: 267–324) and Beierwaltes (2004 154–187). On the attraction of the Jena romantics to Böhme, see Paola Mayer (1999).

10. Quoted in Stevenson 1987: 167.

11. Here the page numbers following those from the English translation are from the German edition, *VGP IV*.

12. Strictly we can only talk of a whole of possibility *from* the human point of view: from the perspective of the *mind of God*, all modal distinctions would collapse and the 'whole of possibility' would be equally one of actuality and necessity. As Longuenesse points out (2007: 173–174), although Kant introduces the intuitive understanding as 'a merely negative notion, [he] nevertheless gives a vivid account of what the world might be like, as known by such an understanding'. This modal peculiarity is one such feature.

13. See, for example, Immanuel Kant, 'Attempt to introduce the concept of negative magnitudes into philosophy' (first published 1763) and 'Concerning the ultimate ground of the differentiations of directions in space' (first published 1768), in Immanuel Kant 2003. In the former, Kant distinguishes 'logical' from 'real' negation in criticizing Leibniz. Logical negation is essentially the 'external' negation of propositional calculus, while real negation is based on the term negation of Aristotelian logic.

14 With respect to the logic involved, Hegel's position was, I believe, closer to that of Kant's pre-critical essays where a distinction between differently structured *judgements* performed the tasks performed by Kant's later concept – intuition distinction. Hegel's distinction hangs on two types of predication, predication as inherence and predication as subsumption. I explore this further in Redding 2014.

15 Contemporary examples of these respective positions can be found in the work of David Lewis (1986) and Robert Stalnaker (2012).

16 All these considerations, I suggest, can operate in abstraction from the question of *belief* in God. Hegel was an idealist, and we should not be surprised that he could take the *idea* of God to be important in this way.

17 In the *Vorstellungen* of the Christian narrative, Christ comes into the world as if from somewhere beyond it. But this merely reflects the nature of *Vorstellungen*. Philosophically considered, *there is no* 'beyond'.

18 Once more, this testifies to Hegel's neo-Platonic heritage, courtesy of Cusa and Bruno. See Redding 1996: 57–62.

19 I have argued broadly along these lines in 1996: chs 8–11.

20 I am not suggesting that for Hegel these intersubjective patterns could be described *without* a role for the 'god' that is bound up with them; such a view would reduce Hegel's position to a Feuerbachian humanist projectivism (which is in turn closer to Kant). A closer analogue to Hegel, I suggest, would be Nietzsche's late romantic attempt to account for the way humans create themselves in creating their gods, such that we could conceive of no underlying anthropological 'essence' that *could be* projected and personified in some god. The sense in which Hegel's God is dependent on human recognition once more seems to fit with Böhme's theology in which God had been construed as dependent on his creatures as they were on him.

21 Research on this topic was assisted by a Discovery Grant from the Australian Research Council, DP130102346.

References

Beiser, F. C. (2006), 'Moral Faith and the Highest Good', in P. Guyer (ed.), *The Cambridge Companion to Kant and Modern Philosophy*, Cambridge: Cambridge University Press.

Beierwaltes, W. (2004), *Platonismus und Idealismus*, Frankfurt am Main: Vittorio Klostermann.

Brague, R. (2007), *The Law of God: The Philosophical History of an Idea*, trans. Lydia G. Cochrane, Chicago: Chicago University Press.

Cary, P. (2000), *Augustine's Invention of the Inner Self: The Legacy of a Christian Platonist*, Oxford: Oxford University Press.

Dihle, A. (1982), *The Theory of Will in Classical Antiquity*, Berkeley: University of California Press.
Emilsson, E. K. (2007), *Plotinus on Intellect*, Oxford: Oxford University Press.
Franz, M. (2003), 'Der Neuplatonismus in den philosophiehistorische Arbeiten der zweiten Hälfte des 18. Jahrhunderts', in B. Mojsisch and O. F. Summerell (eds), *Platonismus im Idealismus: Die platonishe Tradition in der klassischen deutschen Philosophie*, München: K. G. Saur.
Friedman, R. L. (2010), *Medieval Trinitarian Thought from Aquinas to Ockham*, Cambridge: Cambridge University Press.
Harnack, A. von. (1899), *History of Dogma*, volume V, trans. N. Buchanan, Boston: Little Brown and Co.
Henrich, D. (2003), *Between Kant and Hegel: Lectures on German Idealism*, ed. David S. Pacini, Cambridge, MA: Harvard University Press.
Jacobi, F. H. (2000), *Über die Lehre des Spinoza in Briefen an den Herrn Moses Mendelssohn*, Hamburg: Felix Meiner Verlag, Beilage 1.
Johnson, W. E. (1921), *Logic: Part 1*, Cambridge: Cambridge University Press.
Kant, I. (1968), *Gesammelte Schriften: hrsg von der Preussischen Akademie der Wissenschaften*, Berlin: de Gruyter.
Kant, I. (1992), *Lectures on Logic*, ed. J. M. Young, Cambridge: Cambridge University Press.
Kant, I. (1997), *Groundwork of the Metaphysics of Morals*, ed. M. Gregor, intro. C. M. Korsgaard, Cambridge: Cambridge University Press.
Kant, I. (1998), *Critique of Pure Reason*, ed. and trans. P. Guyer and A. W. Wood, Cambridge: Cambridge University Press.
Kant, I. (2003), *Theoretical Philosophy, 1755-1770*, ed. David Walford, Cambridge: Cambridge University Press.
Kreines, J. (2007), 'Between the Bounds of Experience and Divine Intellect: Kant's Epistemic Limits and Hegel's Ambitions', *Inquiry*, 50 (3): 306-334.
Kreines, J. (2015), *Reason in the World: Hegel's Metaphysics and Its Philosophical Appeal*, Oxford: Oxford University Press.
Lewis, D. K. (1986), *On the Plurality of Worlds*, Oxford: Blackwell.
Longuenesse, B. (2007), 'Point of View of Man or Knowledge of God. Kant and Hegel on Concept, Judgment, and Reason', in *Hegel's Critique of Metaphysics*, Cambridge: Cambridge University Press.
Mayer, P. (1999), *Jena Romanticism and Its Appropriation of Jakob Böhme: Theosophy, Hagiography, Literature*, Montreal: McGill-Queen's University Press.
Menn, S. (2002), *Descartes and Augustine*, Cambridge: Cambridge University Press.
Mollowitz, G. (1935), 'Kants Platoauffassung', *Kant-Studien*, 40: 13-67.
O'Regan, C. (1994), *The Heterodox Hegel*, Albany: State University of New York Press.
Pinkard, T. (2012), *Hegel's Naturalism: Mind, Nature, and the Final Ends of Life*, Oxford: Oxford University Press.

Pippin, R. B. (1989), *Hegel's Idealism: The Satisfactions of Self-Consciousness*, Cambridge: Cambridge University Press.

Pippin, R. B. (2008), *Hegel's Practical Philosophy: Rational Agency as Ethical Life*, Cambridge: Cambridge University Press.

Powell, S. M. (2001), *The Trinity in German Thought*, Cambridge: Cambridge University Press.

Rawls, J. (2000), *Lectures of the History of Moral Philosophy*, Cambridge. MA: Harvard University Press.

Redding, P. (1996), *Hegel's Hermeneutics*, Ithaca: Cornell University Press.

Redding, P. (2014), 'The Role of Logic "Commonly So Called" in Hegel's *Science of Logic*', *British Journal for the History of Philosophy*, 22 (2): 281–301.

Redding, P. (2015), 'Georg Wilhelm Friedrich Hegel', in Edward N. Zalta (ed.), *The Stanford Encyclopedia of Philosophy* (Fall 2015 Edition), URL= <http://plato.stanford.edu/archives/fall2015/entries/hegel/>.

Rist, J. (1996), 'Plotinus and Christian Philosophy', in Lloyd Gerson (ed.), *The Cambridge Companion to Plotinus*, Cambridge: Cambridge University Press.

Schneewind, J. (1998), *The Invention of Autonomy: A History of Modern Moral Philosophy*, Cambridge: Cambridge University Press.

Stalnaker, R. (2012), *Mere Possibilities: Metaphysical Foundations of Modal Semantics*, Princeton: Princeton University Press.

Stern, R. (2009), *Hegelian Metaphysics*, Oxford: Oxford University Press.

Stevenson, J., ed. (1987), *A New Eusebius: Documents: Illustrating the History of the Church to AD 337*, London: SPCK.

Taylor, C. (1992), *Sources of the Self: The Making of Modern Identity*, Cambridge: Cambridge University Press.

Vieillard-Baron, J.-L. (1979), *Platon et L'Idéalism Allemand (1770–1930)*, Paris: Beauchesne.

Westphal, K. R. (2000), 'Kant, Hegel, and the Fate of "the" Intuitive Intellect', in S. Sedgwick (ed.), *The Reception of Kant's Critical Philosophy*, Cambridge: Cambridge University Press.

11

Logic and Theology in Hegel

Roberto Morani

Introduction

Since its inception, within the *Science of Logic* and the *Encyclopaedia*, Hegel's logic has been considered as the conceptual transcription of a religious content. A year after Hegel's death, an authoritative exponent of so-called right Hegelians, Carl Friedrich Göschel, recognized in the absolute idea – the last category of the *Science of Logic* – the speculative structure of the object of religious faith (Göschel 1832: 74). In the same period, this line of interpretation was also supported by an irreducible opponent of Hegel like Schelling, according to whom 'the main intention of the Hegelian Logic, and the one on which it primarily prides itself, is that it should take on in its last result the meaning of speculative theology' (Schelling 1994: 147).

This reading has generally oriented the subsequent development of Hegelian studies, being shared by generations of readers with far different philosophical perspectives. In this regard, the interpretative convergence of two theoretically and politically distant thinkers such as Benedetto Croce and Ernst Bloch is extremely significant. In the monograph *What Is Living and What Is Dead of the Philosophy of Hegel*, published in 1907, Croce recognizes in the triadic organization of the Hegelian system an attempt to overcome the dualism between spirit and nature through the introduction behind them of a transcendent entity, separated from life, from the world, from history, in whose abstract physiognomy reappears 'the dark foundation of the old metaphysic: God, in whom were united the two substances of Descartes, the *substantia sive Deus*, which, in Spinoza, supported the two attributes of thought and of extension' (Croce 1915: 200). In his book *Subjekt-Objekt*, published in 1951, Bloch denounces the abstract, pre-existing and hypostatized character of the categories of Hegel's logic: their status of *universalia ante rem* forms 'the greatest, but also the more monstrous theologization ever discovered by the *a priori*: *in the dialectic of the pure concepts of reason, the human being thinks the fluid [fließenden] concepts of God before the creation of the world*' (Bloch 1962: 161).

The exegesis of Croce and Bloch takes as a privileged reference point the renowned thesis formulated in the *Introduction* of the *Science of Logic*:

> Logic is to be understood as the system of pure reason, as the realm of pure thought. *This realm is truth unveiled, truth as it is in and for itself*. It can therefore be said that this content is *the exposition of God as he is in his eternal essence before the creation of nature and of a finite spirit*. (SL, 29; GW XXI, 34)

This thesis also appears in §17 of the first edition of the *Encyclopaedia* where we read that logic 'achieves the significance of speculative theology [erhält dann die Bedeutung *speculativer Theologie*]' (*GW* XIII, §17 R); in §85 of the Berlin *Encyclopaedia*, where the logical determinations are outlined 'as definitions of the Absolute, or metaphysical Definitions of God' (*EI*, §85); and finally in the *Vorlesung über die Logik* [*Lecture on Logic*] of 1831, when Hegel states that 'in the science of logic, the eternal essence of God is exposited as it still was before the creation of the world [*Erschaffung der Welt*]' (LLO, 79; GW XXIII, 716).

The purpose of this chapter is to show how the theological-metaphysical reading, although it might be supported by some textual evidence and might count authoritative exponents of the *Hegelforschung* among its supporters (Löwith 1962: 117; Bruaire 1964: 16; Düsing 1976: 313; Hogemann 1981: 113; Hösle 1988: 62; Viellard-Baron 2006: 175–176), is ultimately a misunderstanding of Hegel's thought based upon the following assumptions: (1) the identification of the *Denken* with the *reines Denken* thematized by logic and the separation of the content of logic from the *Realphilosophie* domains as an ontologically self-sufficient sphere; (2) the incomprehension of the authentic meaning of the conferment to thought of the predicate of supernaturality; (3) the misunderstanding of the passage on the *Darstellung Gottes* (the representation of God); (4) the transformation into the onto-theological sense of the last category of the *Science of Logic*. My task in the following pages is to show that none of these assumptions do stand up to a rigorous comparison with Hegel's texts.

Thought as structure and forms of thought

Let us begin by examining the first point, which concerns the nature of thought *überhaupt* ('in general'). In §19 of the *Encyclopaedia*, Hegel defines logic as 'the *Science of the pure Idea*; pure, that is, because the Idea is in the abstract medium of Thought' (*EI*, §19). In Hegel's system, philosophy of nature and philosophy of spirit too present themselves as sciences of the idea in the form of exteriority and return to oneself respectively: the specificity of logic depends on its status of science of pure idea, a purity that derives from being thematized in the abstract element of thought. In this lies its peculiar difficulty: unlike other sciences, logic does not deal with objects of perception or, like geometry, with abstract representations of senses but with 'pure abstractions; and because it requires a habit and faculty of abstractions, a firm apprehension of thought *per se*, and a facility of movement among these intangible realities' (*EI*, §19 R). In order to understand the meaning and purpose of logic, we have to investigate the conceptual status of these 'pure abstractions', adequately interpreting the predicate of purity – 'Logic is the study of thought pure and simple, or the immaterial types of thought' (*EI*, §24 A2) – and answering the question whether logical determinations coincide or not with thought *überhaupt*.

Hegel devoted to this subject the introductory paragraphs of the Berlin *Encyclopeadia* (1827 and 1830), where he made a distinction between thought as a *generic structure* and thought as a *specific form* of the understanding of reality. In §2 we read:

> If it be correct to say, that thought makes the distinction between man and the lower animals, then everything human is human, for the sole and simple reason that it is due to the operation of thought. Philosophy, on the other hand, is a *peculiar mode of thinking* – a mode in which thinking becomes knowledge, and knowledge through notions. However great therefore may be the identity and essential unity of the two modes of thought, the philosophic mode gets to be different from the more general thought which acts in all that is human, in all that gives humanity its distinctive character. And this difference connects itself with the fact that the strictly human and thought-induced phenomena of consciousness do not originally appear in the form of a thought, but as a feeling, a perception, or mental image – all of which aspects must be distinguished from the form of thought proper. (*EI*, §2)

For Hegel, thought does not appear at first in the configuration that most corresponds to it; foremost and mostly, it is outside of itself, merged into one with feeling, intuition and representation. Logic and philosophy, the first and the last science of the system, do not identify with the *Denken*, they do not hold its exclusive monopoly; they only represent the most appropriate medium and the most valuable expression of it, the one in which thought as a *generic structure* that manifests itself in every sphere of natural and spiritual reality is reunited with thought as a *distinct form*. The reflective dimension is reached through the speculative operation of the *Nachdenken* (reflective thinking) that separates thought from matter and from the heterogeneous contents in which it was originally immersed: 'Now in any case to think things over is at least to transform feelings, ordinary ideas, etc. into thoughts' (*EI*, §5).

Hegel elaborates this doctrine in order to avoid transforming thought into an exclusive possession of philosophy and reducing religion to the sphere of feeling. Against the reduction of thought to the dry, cold and analytical profile of the understanding, Hegel makes a distinction between philosophical thought and thought in general that permeates all other activities:

> It is one thing to have such feelings and generalized images that have been molded and permeated by thought, and another thing to have thoughts about them. The thoughts, to which after-thought upon those modes of consciousness gives rise, are what is comprised under reflection, general reasoning, and the like, as well as under philosophy itself (*EI*, §2 R).

Thought as a *generic content* and *structure* manifests itself first of all in the *forms* of feeling, intuition, imagination and will, before appearing in that privileged mode of understanding, which is thought as such. For Hegel:

> Feeling, perception, etc., are the *forms* assumed by these contents. The contents remain one and the same, whether they are felt, seen, represented, or willed, and whether they are merely felt, or felt with an admixture of thoughts, or merely and simply thought. (*EI*, §3)

And in the remark we read:

> In our ordinary state of mind the thoughts are clothed upon and made one with the sensuous or spiritual material of the hour; and in reflection, meditation, and general reasoning, we introduce a blend of thoughts into feelings, percepts, and mental images. [...] But it is a very different thing to make the thoughts pure and simple our object. (*EI*, §3 R)

We can find in the addition to a paragraph of the *Encyclopaedia* a clear confirmation of the fact that Hegel conceived thought as a *generic structure* that crosses the domains of nature and spirit: 'for thinking in general is so much inherent in the nature of man that he always thinks, even in sleep. In all forms of mind, in feeling, in intuition, as well as representation, thinking remains the foundation' (*EIII*, §398 A). The *Denken überhaupt* crosses the entire spiritual circle and forms the base (*Grundlage*) that marks its multiple activities. When thinking *qua Nachdenken* (reflective Thinking) 'deals with thoughts as thoughts, and brings them into consciousness' (*EI*, §2 A), then it rises to the logical science and takes the profile of the '*Denken des Denkens* [thinking of thinking]' (*EI*, §19 R). There is a pre-reflective dimension of thought that, only thanks to a work of purification accomplished by the *Nachdenken*, becomes the object of thought in the form of the *reines Denken*. Logic (*die Logik*) deals with the supreme manifestation of thought and shows a deferred genesis, inasmuch as its content (*das Logische*) first manifests itself in the totality of the spheres of spirit and nature: only thanks to an act of abstraction performed by the *Nachdenken*, thought separates itself from otherness and becomes *reines Denken*. Thus we begin to understand that the purity (*rein*) of logical categories has nothing to do with an *ontological priority* over natural and spiritual reality, but derives from the abstractive operation that separates these categories from otherness to fathom its intrinsic meaning and to allow its knowledge.[1]

Logical element as supernatural

Once the difference between the two configurations of thought (*die Logik* and *das Logische*) has been acquired, and the impossibility of understanding the logical scope as an ontologically separated sphere that precedes the *Realphilosophie* domains has been verified, we can proceed further in our investigation and understand the reasons that led Hegel, in the *Preface to Second Edition* of the *Science of Logic*, to give the *Denken* the status of the 'supernatural'.

> So much is logic [*das Logische*] natural to the human being, is indeed his very *nature*. If we however contrast nature as such, as the realm of the physical, with the realm of the spiritual, then we must say that logic [*das Logische*] is the supernatural element that permeates all his natural behavior, his ways of sensing, intuiting, desiring, his needs and impulses; and it thereby makes them into something truly human, even though only formally human – makes them into representations and purposes (*SL*, 12; *GW* XXI, 11)

For Hegel, thought does not coincide with philosophy nor resides in the upper levels of systematic construction, but lives, we might say, in the cellars or basement: it permeates the *Naturverhalten* (natural behavior) of the human being, that is, feeling, intuition, desire; it assumes an unconscious, erotic, incarnate profile. Against all forms of dualism, especially a Cartesian-like dualism that rigidly separates *res cogitans* and *res extensa*, Hegel believes that the logical element pervades the material sphere of the *Leiblichkeit* [bodiliness] and, by virtue of its incisive presence, ensures full spiritual citizenship to the natural determinations of the human beings, assuring that they show themselves within the spirit 'in a radically different way from that in which they are in external nature' (*EIII*, §381 A).

Insofar as it presents a 'reconstruction' of the unconscious thought, Hegel's Logic does not seem to fall within the traditional interpretative framework, which judges it as a form of abstract rationalism: this depends on the fact that interpretations of his work have not always emphasized enough the difference between *das Logische* and *die Logik*, and they have attributed to the carnal, erotic, vital, unconscious dimension of thought the qualities (transparency, circularity, purity) that belong to the *reines Denken* as the object of the systematic exposition. Indeed, the logical element and logic express thought's two different ways of being: the first constitutes its daily and immediate configuration, while the second constitutes the highest configuration of thought (the *denkende Betrachtung*), which thematizes it to itself and purifies it from the extranoetic elements.

The most striking aspect of the passage in the Preface (*Vorrede*) mentioned above is that not logic as a science of the *reines Denken*, but its content, *das Logische*, is defined by Hegel as 'das Übernatürliche' (the supernatural):

> So much is logical element natural to the human being, is indeed his very *nature*. If we however contrast nature as such, as the realm of the physical, with the realm of the spiritual, then we must say that logical element [*das Logische*] is the supernatural element (*SL*, 12; *GW* XXI, 11; translation modified).[2]

At first glance, Hegel seems to assign to *Denken* the predicate that the metaphysical tradition, in the Christian tradition, has attributed to the divine. With the advent of the notion of the *creatio ex nihilo*, a new way of conceiving religious space arises. Such a new way upsets the ancient conceptual framework of Greek metaphysics, which was centred on the theoretical paradigm of stable permanence and which in turn was the rationale for the becoming. The conception of God as creator (ontologically infinite, perfect, self-sufficient) removes the sphere of the divine from the created and finite world. Insofar as, due to its absoluteness, it transcends the realm of nature, the *ens supremum* can be defined as 'supernatural' (*übernatürlich*), thus acknowledging its transcendence as measured by the ontological degrees that articulate the hierarchical order of being. The reference to thought that follows in the text – thought as a generic structure that imprints and permeates the sphere of corporeality, the world of impulses and the sphere of feeling – indicates, however, that it is not in this traditional and ultrametaphysical sense that Hegel conceives the ulteriorness of thought, that is, its being irreducibly *beyond*.

To correctly interpret Hegel's thesis, it is necessary to avoid misinterpreting the relationship of the dialectical logic with the metaphysical tradition. Interpreters often quote the thesis according to which 'the science of logic makes up metaphysics proper or pure speculative philosophy' (*SL*, 9; *GW* XXI, 7), as if the philosophical project of Hegel consisted in conferring to the *reines Denken* the same absoluteness that the metaphysical tradition recognized to the foundation of reality. Actually, the thesis according to which 'logic therefore coincides with Metaphysics, the science of things set and held in thoughts – thoughts accredited able to express the essential reality of things' (*EI*, §24) – shows that logic inherits from the metaphysical perspective only the ambition to understand things through thought and not through the senses (see *EI*, §28). The 'metaphysical' attribute is not used by Hegel to designate the absolute value of thought, but it is deployed for its ability to grasp the deep core of things beyond their phenomenal rind. Despite the resumption of this specific aspect, the traditional metaphysical account is significantly rethought by Hegel, starting from the method of conferring the predicates to the absolute, which in traditional metaphysics presupposes the substrates as positively given according to a dogmatically fixed meaning. After the Kantian transformation of metaphysics into logic (*SL*, 30; *GW* XXI, 35), contemporary thought can no longer renounce the *freedom* of the tribunal of Kantian reason, which calls into judgement the determinations (simplicity, immateriality, etc.) that the old metaphysics assumed as valid for preaching the absolute, even if in the Kantian criticism the examination of logical forms presents the defect of not investigating them in and for themselves, in their intrinsic theoretical content, but only from the perspective that leads them back to the a priori forms of the subject and not to the objective structure of things.

Hegel is aware of the impossibility of *going back* to the substantialist perspective of the old metaphysics and of the necessity to *move forward* along the *critical* path traced by Kant. Going beyond metaphysics means neither ignoring it, nor merely resigning to the impossibility of experiencing and knowing its 'objects' (as Kant does, according to Hegel), but it implies the definitive liberation from the ontological substrates derived from the religious *Vorstellung*, as well as the awareness of the crisis of the substantialist paradigm that justifies its adoption, examining its logical forms in order to grasp the conceptual truth hidden in their representative profile. Investigating the metaphysical *Grundformen*, or basic forms, 'free from substrates' means, methodologically, leaving their existence aside:

> Philosophical thinking in general still deals with concrete subject matters, with God, Nature, Spirit; but logic occupies itself exclusively with these thoughts as thought, in complete abstraction by themselves. (*SL*, 14; *GW* XXI, 13)

Without the conceptual support provided by subjects, those categories change their original features, because they are no longer the predicates to be attributed to a being dogmatically fixed in its traditional meaning. By virtue of this complex philosophical strategy, Hegel transforms the three overall areas of special metaphysics (God, world and the soul) into the dimensions of the logical (*das Logische*), the natural (*das Natürliche*) and the spiritual (*das Geistige*). However, these dimensions, as autonomous parts of the system, are not respectively identical with logic, nature and spirit. The logical element does not indicate a separate sphere in itself, but resides in both nature and spirit, while the natural, characterized by the self-externality (*Außersichsein*), crosses, in different ways, nature and spirit, and assumes a peculiar meaning according to the part of the system in which it is realized. In logic, in the *Naturphilosophie*, and in the *Geistesphilosophie*, the logical, the natural and the spiritual are described in their specific prerogatives and in the different degrees of realization of their conceptual *proprium*, but this does not mean that they exist only in their narrow systematic framework and that they are not intertwined in various ways.

On the grounds of these considerations, we can clarify the meaning of the passage in which Hegel attributes to the logical (*das Logische*) the attribute 'supernatural': on one hand, a predicate of metaphysics is taken over; on the other hand, it is stripped of its original appearance, redefined and resumed in the system with a new speculative coinage. Recognizing the 'supernatural' status of the logical, Hegel emphasizes its *irreducibility* to the determinations of nature and spirit with which it is also originally and inextricably linked; in particular, he aims at preserving its independence from the human being, who neither invents the forms of thought nor has them at her disposal *ad libitum* as his productions, but she finds them in herself, buried and forgotten in her own interiority. Referring to a renowned passage from Aristotle's *Metaphysics* (Met. A 2, 982), Hegel, in the *Vorrede* of the *Science of Logic*, writes that the science of pure thought 'appears not to be a human possession' (*SL*, 14; *GW* XXI, 13): a statement that does not reflect the onto-theo-logical obsession that celebrates the omnipotence of thought and the will to dominate reality, but stems from the opposite preoccupation of not engulfing the *Denken*, of preserving its autonomy from the human being and from her omnivorous tendency to incorporate everything to which she relates. The divine origin of thought does not refer to an ontologically subsistent ultramundane dimension, which carries out the function of foundation and sufficient reason, but implies that 'the logical' is not a heritage, a faculty, a prerogative of the human being.

Logic as exposition of God?

Everything that has been said so far allows us to correctly interpret the famous thesis expressed in the 'Introduction' to the *Science of Logic* mentioned above, which is the locus classicus for the construction of the theological-metaphysical interpretative line. 'Accordingly', Hegel writes:

> Logic is to be understood as the system of pure reason, as the realm of pure thought. *This realm is truth unveiled, truth as it is in and for itself.* It can therefore be said that this content is *the exposition of God as he is in his eternal essence before the creation of nature and of a finite spirit.* (SL, 29; GW XXI, 34)

This thesis was considered scandalous, since it appeared as a wicked attempt to deify human thought, forgetting the limits of human reason. Trendelenburg's complaint is very significant in this regard:

> The one who denies the dialectic must therefore give up that logic which wants to picture the system of pure reason as the realm of pure thought and show God 'as he is in his eternal essence before the creation of nature and of a finite spirit'. (Trendelenburg 1870: 109)

For Trendelenburg, Hegel is the advocate of an immanentist position that forgets the difference between finite and infinite, brings back the absolute to thought and the sphere of the sacred to immanence, denies the horizon of transcendence and breaks down the limits of the finite, tempting an insane and swaggering climb to the heavens. In my view, this reading misunderstands Hegel's philosophical intentions and does not allow us to grasp the authentic sense of the passage quoted above, also because it omits the first part of the sentence, namely the introductory formula 'It can therefore be said [*man kann sich deswegen ausdrücken*]' (SL, 29; GW XXI, 34). This is a decisive omission, because the wording shows that Hegel uses the image of the *Darstellung Gottes* as a simile to facilitate the reader's comprehension and therefore belongs more to the level of representation rather than to the level of the concept. The claim is expressed through 'inadequate and exoteric language' (Doz 1987: 22), namely represents 'a joke – strictly speaking, an analogy; it is certainly not a description or a definition' (Ferrarin 2016: 95). If the image of the *Darstellung Gottes*, against Hegel's intentions, is taken literally and its metaphorical nature is forgotten, then the relation between religion and philosophy is also misunderstood in a way incompatible with Hegel's system: indeed, the two activities of the absolute spirit would not only have the common content (*EI*, §1), but they would be totally identical, since 'if a divine subject, assumed as presupposition, could be attributed to thought, for Hegel it would only be a mere religious representation' (Jaeschke 2016: 233). It is from religion and from the sphere of representation that stem both the image of God as creator and that relation of temporal succession (*before* and *after*) that in the aforementioned passage seems to link logic and *Realphilosophie*. Paradoxically, philosophy and *Begriff* would be deprived of autonomy and they would appear as subordinated to religion and the *Vorstellung*.

As Bloch maintained, the image of the *Darstellung Gottes* contains an implicit reference to a statement by Goethe:

> The similarity of this sentence with Goethe's claim about Bach's music, which would make one hear what it was like in the bosom of God just before the creation of the world, is remarkable. (Bloch 1962: 161)

Thus, for Bloch too the sentence has a metaphorical value that must be kept in mind in the interpretation and cannot be taken literally as an attestation of an a priori theology. Moreover, it should not be forgotten that the god whose manifestation logic should guarantee does not reside in the heavens and is not detached from the world by virtue of god's supreme ontological excellence; rather, god lives in 'the realm of shadows, the world of simple essentialities, freed of all sensuous concretion' (*SL*, 37; *GW* XXI, 42), namely god is a *god of the underworld, of corporeity and of the unconscious*, which very little resembles that 'macrosubject' allergic to every limit or external dependence with which, traditionally, it has been identified. On the other hand, if Hegel really considered the object of logic as a metaphysical entity in itself (omnipotent, self-sufficient and endowed with the onto-theo-logic prerogative of self-causation), why would he be then concerned with the protection of its autonomy from the spheres of the natural and the spiritual with which it is originally and inextricably linked? Moreover, it would be difficult to reconcile the theological-metaphysical reading of logic as the *Darstellung Gottes* with the claim, placed at the end of Hegel's account of the process of development of the categories, that 'this idea is still logical; it is shut up in pure thought, the science only of the divine *concept*' (*SL*, 752; *GW* XII, 253). The adverbs *noch* ('*diese Idee [ist] noch logisch*') and *nur* ('*[sie] ist] die Wissenschaft nur des göttlichen Begriffs*') show a clear restrictive intent, which would be unjustified or barely understandable if referred to the Kingdom of God. How can we reconcile this defective aspect with the feature of the God of the Christian tradition, with the unattainable perfection and integral positivity of the *summum et realissimum ens*, indeed of the *id quo maius cogitari nequit*?

It has been said that categories belong as *realiter* to things, that is, they are abstracted as logical forms only after their primeval 'incarnation', their concrete and original existence *in re*: there is no neo-Platonic or spiritualistic attitude that separates and opposes the sphere of pure thought to life, to corporeality, to matter, to language and to the unconscious. If it is true that the realm of pure thought does not express a temporal anteriority of the content of logic with respect to those of the Philosophy of Nature and the Philosophy of Spirit, how should we interpret the *before (vor)* of '*before the creation of nature and of a finite spirit [vor der Erschaffung der Natur und eines endlichen Geistes]*' (SL, 29; GW XXI, 34), stripping it of its chronological-representative shell? Considered in a purely conceptual sense, the *before* assumes a sense analogous to the *über* of the term *Übernatürlichkeit*, namely it refers to the irreducibility and autonomy of the sphere of thought with respect to the natural and spiritual element with which it is inseparably connected.

Absolute idea and dialectical method

The last point that demonstrates the inconsistency of the theological-metaphysical reading of Hegel's logic concerns the absolute idea. We read in §237 of the *Encyclopaedia*:

> To speak of the absolute idea may suggest the conception that we are at length reaching the right thing and the sum of the whole matter. It is certainly possible to indulge in a vast amount of senseless declamation about the idea absolute. But its true content is only the whole system of which we have been hitherto studying the development. (*EI*, §237)

From this statement, it is clear that the absolute idea does not refer to a logical content among others, that is, a new category that is added to the previous ones and completes them, thanks to its conceptual excellence; rather, it represents the dimension of thought that reconstructs *ex post* the process of generation of the thought determinations [*Denkbestimmungen*] and collects them in a unitary totality, assigning to each its specific systematic meaning and showing the overall sense of the logical path. The absolute idea does not suggest a *primum* of ontological matrix as the last term of the process of thought, that is, a new form of the *óntôs ón* that can be fixed in its isolation from what precedes it.

The impossibility of conceiving the absolute idea as a modern version of the old *ens realissimum*, in continuity with the traditional ontology, has been strongly defended by Angelica Nuzzo, who argues:

> According to the speculative critique of all metaphysics, and given that the absolute idea is nothing but the speculative method of thinking, the 'absolute' of Hegel's idea is neither an entity – i.e. the name for a metaphisical *ens* – nor the hypostatization of an ontological property, but rather a *dialectical* predicate can apply to reason itself only once it has reached the end of a *Logic* and never before. At this stage, the dialectical predicate 'absolute' expresses the epistemological *norm* for all scientific thinking (Nuzzo 1999: 1).

The speculative use of the term 'absolute' is therefore limited to its predicative use as an adjective and excludes the possibility of being valid as a noun, in relation to an *ens absolutus*: only the method can be absolute, not a substantial presence (subtracted from negativity, temporality and death). Nuzzo argued that the absolute idea designates the strength of the method as a radical *self-production*:

> Self-production, however, is possible only when the condition of complete *immanence* is fulfilled – that is, when all external intervention, goal, and standpoint is eliminated. Viewing the end of the *Logic* by recalling, at the same time, its beginning, it is clear that according to Hegel *before and outside the process there is neither something to be produced nor something that produces*. The development that the conclusion of the Logic names 'absolute method' – and that retrospectively encompasses the logical process as a whole – is 'absolute' first of all in a strictly etymological sense: it is *ab-solutus* from all possible presuppositions, assumptions, conditions or even goals. *Method is a law without legislator, a process without subject, an activity without a faculty that exercises it; it is the utterance of the 'original word (ursprüngliches Wort)' without a voice uttering it.* (Nuzzo 2006: 80–81)

Here Nuzzo argues that the absolute idea designates a process without subject and foundation, in which immanence is realized completely through the progressive negation of any external intervention. In my view, this argument allows only a partial understanding of the architecture of Hegel's logic. It is true that in the 'Introduction' to the Nuremberg work, we read: 'the system of concepts is to be to erected – and it has to come to completion in an unstoppable and pure progression that admits of nothing extraneous' (*SL*, 33; *GW* XXI, 38). It is necessary, however, to clarify that logic and the dialectical method possess at least one centre of gravity, a foundation, a normative principle: that is, the concept. In the final pages of the *Science of Logic*, Hegel writes:

What is to be considered as method here is only the movement of the *concept* itself. We already know the nature of this movement, but it now has, *first*, the added significance that the *concept is all*, and that its movement is the *universal absolute activity*, the self-determining and self-realizing movement. (*SL*, 737; *GW* XXI, 238)

Der Begriff ist alles, the concept is all. This thesis undermines the onto-theo-logical tradition not because it frees reason from any foundation but because it recognizes in the logical development the stages of the immanent self-determinating process of the concept:

> Universality is the pure, simple concept, and the method, as the consciousness of this concept, is aware that universality is only a moment and that in it the concept is still not determined in and for itself. [...] But in the absolute method the universal has the value [...] of the objective universal, that is, the universal that is *in itself* the *concrete totality*, but a totality as yet not *posited*, not yet *for itself*. (*SL*, 739; *GW* XXI, 240)

The Concept is the protagonist of the entire categorial movement, the source of origin of the logical forms and the abysmal foundation of the total mass of the noematic contents that appear gradually during the journey. Hegel undermines the substantialist metaphysical paradigm of an always already-given totality, autonomously constituted in its accomplished articulation; in his philosophy the totality (of the concept) is in need of mediation and of process development. The dialectical subversion of the myth of stable and permanent presence makes Hegel's logic refractory to the theoretical coordinates of the theological-metaphysical reading.

Notes

1 'It must be regarded as an infinite step forward that the forms of thought have been freed from the material in which they are submerged in self-conscious intuition, in representation, as well as in our desires and volitions or, more accurately, in ideational desiring and willing [...]; a step forward that these universalities have been brought to light and made the subject of study on their own, as was done by Plato, and after him by Aristotle especially; this step marks the beginning of our knowledge of them' (*SL*, 13–14; *GW* XXI, 12).
2 'So sehr natürlich ist ihm das Logische, oder vielmehr: dasselbige ist seine eigentümliche *Natur* selbst. Stellt man aber die Natur überhaupt, als das Physikalische, dem Geistigen gegenüber, so müßte man sagen, daß das Logische vielmehr das Übernatürliche ist' (*GW* XXI, 11).

References

Bloch, E. (1962), *Subjekt-Objekt: Erläuterungen zu Hegel*, Frankfurt a.M.: Suhrkamp.

Bruaire, C. (1964), *Logique et religion chrétienne dans la philosophie de Hegel*, Paris: Éditions du Seuil.

Croce, B. (1915), *What Is Living and What Is Dead of the Philosophy of Hegel*, trans. D. Ainslie, London: Macmillan and Co.

Doz, A. (1987), *La logique de Hegel et les problèmes traditionelles de l'ontologie*, Paris: Vrin.

Düsing, K. (1976), *Das Problem der Subjektivität in Hegels Logik*, Bonn: Bouvier.

Ferrarin, A. (2016), *Il pensare e l'io. Hegel e la critica di Kant*, Rome: Carocci.

Göschel, C.F. (1832), *Hegel und seine Zeit: mit Rücksicht auf Göthe; zum Unterrichte in der gegenwärtigen Philosophie nach ihren Verhältnissen zur Zeit und nach ihren wesentlichen Grundzügen*, Frankfurt a.M.: Minerva.

Hogemann, F. (1981), 'L'idée absolue dans la "Science de la logique" de Hegel', in AA. VV., *Hegel. L'esprit absolue/The absolute Spirit*. Conference proceedings on the meaning of absolute spirit, University of Ottawa 6–8 November 1981, 109–126, Ottawa: Éditions de l'Université d'Ottawa.

Hösle, V. (1988), *Hegels System. Der Idealismus der Subjektivität und das Problem der Intersubjektivität*, Band I: *Systementwicklung und Logik*, Hamburg: Meiner.

Jaeschke, W. (2016), *Hegel Handbuch. Leben – Werk – Schule*, Stuttgart: Metzler.

Löwith, K. (1962), *Hegels Aufhebung der christlichen Religion*, in Id., *Hegel und die Aufhebung der Philosophie*, Stuttgart: Metzler, 1988.

Nuzzo, A. (1999), 'The Idea of "Method" in Hegel's Science of Logic. A Method for Finite Thinking and Absolute Knowing', *Bulletin of the Hegel Society of Great Britain*, 20 (1/2): 1–18.

Nuzzo, A. (2006), 'The Language of Hegel's Speculative Philosophy', in J. O'Neill Surber (ed.), *Hegel and the Language*, 75–91, Albany: State University of New York.

Schelling F.W.J. (1994), *On the History of Modern Philosophy*, trans. A. Bowie, Introduction and Notes by A. Bowie, Cambridge: Cambridge University Press.

Trendelenburg, F.A. (1870), *Logische Untersuchungen*, dritte vermehrte Auflage, Bd. I, Leipzig: Hirzel.

Vieillard-Baron, J.-L. (2006), *Hegel. Système et structures théologiques*, Paris: Cerf.

12

The Concept of Religion and Its Hermeneutic Function

Maurizio Pagano

The spiritual situation of the period

Each of the four lecture courses Hegel devoted to the philosophy of religion begins with an appraisal of the spiritual situation of his time. This appears to him to be marked by a deep conflict, which radically opposes the autonomy of the subject and the need to do justice to the absolute content – that is, God – which is inherited from tradition. The freedom of the modern subject has developed an autonomous and universal thought that exalts the value of knowledge, but which constrains it to the finite world and in fact excludes religion from the set of arguments that relate to all human beings. Thus, religious consciousness has been expelled from the public sphere; it seeks to keep alive its devotion to God, but it has lost confidence in being able to know God, to give faith a determined and concrete content.

This attitude of renunciation is also expressed in the religious thought of the period: its most authoritative representatives, such as Jacobi and Schleiermacher, likewise assign the relation to God to immediate knowledge or to feeling and essentially deny that knowledge of God is possible. Similarly, contemporary theology gives up considering the fundamental contents of Christianity, reduces dogmas to a minimum and assigns to them a merely historical, peripheral treatment.

In this sense the religious thought of the period shows a profound convergence with the results of the work of Kant. On the one hand, Kant was entirely correct in his critique of traditional metaphysics, including rational theology, and

Translated from Italian by Theodore Ell, revised by Paolo Diego Bubbio

generally in sustaining the reasons of critical and universal thought. Hegel is sympathetic to this approach: his thought is quite distant from the dogmatism of traditional metaphysics; at the same time, he advocates for the universal character of philosophical thought against the esotericism of the romantics (as exemplarily shown by the Preface to the *Phenomenology of Spirit*). On the other hand, Kant denied the possibility of knowing God and generally argued for a thought entirely *of* and *for* the finite, which remains radically separate from the infinite and in the end affirms the positivity of the finite. This perspective was decisively criticized by Hegel in the opening pages of the Introduction to the *Phenomenology*. Therefore, we have to remark that, at least in the field of the philosophy of religion, Kant is for Hegel more an adversary than an ally.

For his part, Hegel intends to consider the meaning of the crisis he finds before him in all its seriousness: once it has arisen, the conflict between insight (*Einsicht*) and religion leads, if unresolved, to despair; however, as Hegel points out, despair is itself a form of conciliation, but one that is realized in a unilateral way: either the (subjective) spirit that experiences this contradiction returns to an ingenuous religious feeling, forcibly rejecting the instance of thought, or it develops indifference towards religion; but the later attitude is merely 'the consistency of shallow souls' (*LPR* I, 108 R; *VPR* I, 26 R). In reality, Christianity contains within itself, in the most elaborate form that representation can offer, both the theme of 'scission' and that of conciliation. Unlike the serene view of paganism and the anthropological optimism of the Enlightenment, Christianity knows that the human being is not naturally good, but inwardly divided and led by his or her egoism to oppose his or her infinite destination; and indeed it is this laceration that grounds the need for conciliation. Furthermore, Christianity contains within itself the two elements that are in conflict: on the one hand, it appeals to the subject, to his or her freedom and his or her subjective certitude; on the other, it contains knowledge, that is, the infinite content: however, it offers the latter as 'filtered' through the scission, in the form of representation.

What Hegel proposes is precisely to fully accept the two elements of this contrast and to reconcile them, while still maintaining their full radical character: on the one hand, the freedom of autonomous and universal thought, and on the other, the infinite content. In this way, the philosophy of religion proposes to offer true conciliation for the modern conscience and at the same time to bridge the gap between religion and philosophy.

The project devised by Hegel must consider the entire religious experience in all its various forms, as well as the entire history of religions. As is well known, the Enlightenment, troubled by the recent experience of the wars between Catholics and Protestants, took little interest in the variety of religious experience. At the dawn of the Romantic age, Schleiermacher had drawn attention to the various religious intuitions of the universe but had not reached the point of conducting a true examination of their various perspectives. Hegel is the first thinker to dare to propose an organic philosophical interpretation of the entire history of religions. In the same period, and in the following years, a similar task was undertaken by Schelling, with his lectures on the philosophy of mythology and revelation; yet his examination focused only on the vicissitudes of the mythological consciousness, whereas Hegel looks further at the concrete and institutional reality of religions.

The question that arises at this point is how such an examination should be conducted. At first sight there are two alternative solutions. The first presupposes that there is only one true religion and therefore seeks to argue that all the others are false or at least inadequate; the second, by contrast, seeks to do justice to all religions, placing them all on the same level and thus concluding that each is relative to its context (as it expresses the society and culture in which it is born), so that in essence none is false but all are relative. Even the theological and philosophical thought of today, which has returned to considering this problem with extreme interest, debates these two alternative solutions of absolutism or relativism. Hegel, for his part, tries to avoid either of these two extreme solutions: in his philosophy he elaborates a concept of religion and conducts his examination on these grounds. This is how Hegel's *Philosophy of Religion* obtains its peculiar structure, articulated in three parts, which remain unchanged in all four series of Hegel's lectures: we begin with the 'concept of religion', then move to 'determinate religion', that is, the history of religions, and we arrive lastly at 'consummate religion', which is Christianity.

Logic and hermeneutics: The concept of religion

'The concept of religion' is the part of the lectures which undergoes the greatest changes in the transition from one series to the next[1]; this is quite understandable, if we consider that it represents the first and fundamental ground on which Hegel's theoretical requirements confront the reality of religion and on which Hegel attempts to find an agreement between the two dimensions. On one side, there are the instances of logic and of the speculative conception of the spirit; on the other, the contents of religion. According to the philosopher's repeated claims, the fundamental intention which guides his work is to demonstrate the truth of religion, its necessity; it is not a matter of presupposing a determined religious conception and of attempting to demonstrate it (this would be an apologetic approach, not a critical one); rather, it is necessary to demonstrate 'the necessity of the content in and for itself' (*LPR* I, 223; *VPR* I, 131); to achieve this, it is important to delineate religious experience in all its essential moments and to bring out its rational structure, which is governed by the rhythm of the concept and therefore refers to logic. In this way, we achieve the authentic presentation (*Darstellung*) of religion, which on the one hand demonstrates its truth and on the other inserts it, as the last and most elevated step, in the encyclopaedic journey of the system. From this perspective we can easily recognize the decisive weight that demonstration bears for Hegel, and we can understand that the philosophy of religion also has a critical significance vis-à-vis religious experience, precisely because at every step it compares religion against the structure of the concept.

At the same time, however, it should be observed that Hegel's main goal, which is to provide the presentation of religion, and the ambitious way in which he fulfils it, by confronting all the various aspects of this experience and its entire history, implies that alongside the task of demonstrating the truth of religion, there is also that of describing all its essential traits. To *demonstrate* and to *describe* are therefore the two great endeavours that guide Hegel in the accomplishment of his work. It is clear already that these two undertakings imply one another. In order to demonstrate the truth of religious experience, it is necessary to expose it through its nodal points, a process which therefore involves individuation and interpretation; the description of these traits on the one hand is guided by logic, while on the other it poses to the concept the task of renewing interpretation each time.

In the initial phase of his work, when he composes the manuscript which will serve as the basis of his 1821 course, Hegel projects a strategy in two phases: first, one must draw the concept from experience, that is, from the sphere of representation; second, one must demonstrate the necessity of that concept. This programme requires that the two tasks that we have singled out as fundamental, namely demonstration and description, be separated and distributed in two distinct steps in the process. In this way, however, the first step, devoted to the description of religion, is, as it were, abandoned to itself: it lacks a criterion and a conceptual guide, and this will motivate Hegel's dissatisfaction with this first solution. Nonetheless, this first draft description allows Hegel to provide a fundamental indication of the orientation of his thought; when we speak of religion, we must always keep in mind that in essence it contains two moments: on the one hand the object, God; on the other the subject, the consciousness of the human being. From here, we can immediately grasp the difference between Hegel's perspective and the competing perspectives: the natural theology of the old metaphysics was concerned only with God and did not grasp the fact that the concept of God as spirit includes the necessity of becoming objective, of realizing itself in the community and in human consciousness, so that it leads necessarily to religion. On the other hand, the prevalent position of Hegel's time, which reduces religion to a solely subjective experience, is equally unilateral and does not grasp the dimension of spiritual objectivity, which remains valid in itself and for itself, and does not depend upon our yearning or upon our projections.

Moving from representation, as described along its essential lines, Hegel then attempts to demonstrate its necessity: this requires that religion be understood as an end result. In accordance with the entire orientation of Hegel's thought, however, that which is understood as an end result must in itself overcome the quality of being a mere result and demonstrate itself as the first truth, in which everything else finds an adequate mediation. Furthermore, it is necessary that this passage be indicated in the content, demonstrating that it contains within itself the passage to such a result.

If that is the case, it is necessary to return to the first phase of the work and add a supplementary description, which prepares the demonstration more adequately. In short, Hegel is forced by the progress of his own work to turn his initial programme in a direction that requires a stricter interconnection of the logical and hermeneutical moments: it is the need for demonstration, in fact, that demands an augmentation and a different structure of interpretation; and this in turn, while it prepares the demonstration, brings to light new aspects of the religious experience.

The supplementary description which Hegel now proposes is in fact already directed by the demands of demonstration: this requires a passage, or better, an elevation towards that end result which is the first truth, and this type of passage and elevation from immediate experience to the sphere of truth can effectively be identified in religion. What is essential in religion resides in *thought* and certainly not in feeling (as the romantics would have it); however, this is not the fully actualized thought of philosophy, but rather a movement towards the universal, *An-dacht* more than *Denken*, that is, devotion and meditation. At the same time this elevation towards the universal in religion coexists with its opposite moment, namely the immediateness of the single individual, which is present here with all the demands and tensions of her subjectivity. The characteristic element of religion is indeed the presence of, and the conflict between, these two moments. These two moments will be unified in philosophy, but here each one of them exerts its full strength, and together they give life to the most dramatic, and in a sense emblematic, sphere of existence (*LPR* I, 213; *VPR* I, 121).

Thanks to this in-depth analysis, Hegel resumes his demonstration, showing that religion is the truth of the entire universe and that, at the same time, it is true in and for itself. Thus philosophy of religion reclaims, and realizes on a spiritual level, the logical thesis of the connection of beginning and result. This demands a change in the demonstrative strategy: if religion is an end result that is true in itself and for itself, the demonstration of its truth requires two moments; first it must be demonstrated that it is an end result; then its truth has to be developed as such. The first step implies an ascent towards the truth, the second an exposition of the truth that has been attained. Therefore, the first phase will no longer be about describing the representation; rather, it will be about showing how the experience of the world rises to religion as its own truth. In this way we obtain a stricter relation between description and demonstration, because this first moment of the ascent is already guided by a conceptual structure. This course of elevation is described by Hegel in a somewhat nervous and not always perspicuous way; on the one hand it refers back to the journey of the *Encyclopaedia*, which shows how, from the level of nature and the subjective spirit, one rises gradually towards the absolute spirit; on the other hand Hegel explicitly recalls the *Phenomenology* and effectively pays particular attention to the opposition between consciousness and object that characterises the finite starting point of the journey. The second step, however, is situated at the level at which the destination has already been reached: it starts with religion, in this case Christian religion, and shows that it includes, within its contents, the meaning of the entire worldly experience.

The 1824 lecture course took place in the moment when Hegel felt most acutely the conflict with contemporary culture, whose various forms and streams seemed all in agreement when it came to opposing the fundamental instance of the *Religionsphilosophie* – that is, knowing God.

Hegel's concern about this state of affairs drove him to completely revise the structure of the concept of religion, now articulated in two parts, dedicated to 'empirical observation' and to the 'speculative concept' respectively. In the first part Hegel works from the point of view of the culture of the day in order to confute it from within. This point of view, which is indeed one of empirical observation, assumes the experience of finite subjectivity as the site in which it is possible to directly locate the foundation of religion. Hegel's strategy is to observe finite subjectivity from within, together with his intellectual opponents, to show that it is inadequate and that its own nature requires to go beyond the limits of finite consciousness and to rise to the speculative viewpoint. However, Hegel does not entirely succeed in realizing this project, which consists in taking up the method of the *Phenomenology of Spirit* and showing how finite consciousness, precisely because of the tension that animates it, elevates itself to the absolute point of view. The reason for this failure is that Hegel's real adversary here is not so much the common consciousness, which could perhaps accept the elevation to the speculative viewpoint, but the point of view of contemporary culture, that is, the perspective of reflection, which makes finiteness its banner and does not even think about abandoning it. Thus in the end Hegel loses patience, abandons the method of immanent analysis and provides a more direct confutation of his adversaries' point of view, a confutation grounded on the theory of the true infinite elaborated in his logic.

What particularly arouses Hegel's opposition, and even indignation, is the fact that the culture of reflection does not only situate itself in the point of view of the finite, and it does not only affirm that this point of view cannot be abandoned, so that the passage to the infinite is regarded as impossible. There is more: the finite, which apparently presents itself with humility, declaring to be incapable of reaching the infinite, actually affirms itself as the only reality and as an *entirely positive* reality. By this conception, it follows that the human being is good by nature: my morality does not consist in doing what is good in itself and for itself, with reference to laws which transcend me, but in enacting that of which I am convinced in my particular subjectivity.

Hegel opposes this position head-on. The core of his argument is that religion is the overcoming of that opposition, it is the affirmative relation of the consciousness to the truth: on the one hand, the self-sufficiency of the finite must be negated, but on the other hand, it must be acknowledged that the finite is an essential moment of the infinite. To demonstrate in general a particular content, we must start from something else and arrive at it from there: in this way our content, in this case religion, results as necessary. In this form, however, the content is presented as mediated by something else and as dependent upon it. In our case, however, given that we are concerned with the supreme content (the Absolute), a second passage must intervene, in which it is shown that the truth of religion is not only a result, but overcomes within itself the very character of being a result and affirms itself as the first truth. This represents, Hegel claims, the 'counterthrust' (*Gegenstoss*) against that first movement (*LPR* I, 322; *VPR* I, 225); the choice of this word is significant, because it appears at several important points in his published works. The Preface to the *Phenomenology* employs it to indicate the relation of the speculative proposition to the form of judgement

(*PS*, §60; *GW* IX, 43), while the *Science of Logic* uses it to illustrate the difficult passage between positing reflection and presupposing reflection (*SL*, 348; *GW* XI, 252), and then to explain the relation between the concept and the spheres that preceded it, namely being and essence (*SL*, 530; *GW* XII, 33).[2]

Through this journey, the level of spirit, which we have now achieved, is revealed as the first level; as for the external element from which we started, that is, the finite world, it turns out that this is no longer a presupposition, achieved in an immediate way, but something posited by spirit itself. This structure must now be identified within religion itself. In fact, according to Hegel we find this twofold movement even within experience: in the first instance there is a process of elevation, which starts from the finite world and rises towards religion, and thus results as a moment external to religion understood in the strict sense; there follows a second progression, which by contrast is internal to religion and which develops only after it is acknowledged that 'God is strictly the first' (*LPR* I, 323; *VPR* I, 226). In this sense we may conclude that religion is the truth of the world and at the same time it is true in itself.

Thus the movement required and enacted by logic, for which proceeding ahead does not involve a passage into something else but leads to the recognition that that which presents itself as a result is in reality the first (*SL*, 49; *GW* XXI, 57), can also be found in religious experience: this is the point at which, in Hegel's reading, the logic and the hermeneutics of religious experience bind most closely together.

As is well known, for Hegel this movement of elevation is discernible throughout the whole of spiritual experience: at the structural level this journey is described in the *Encyclopaedia*, where it is shown how the spirit rises from the level of nature and arrives at full realization and knowledge of itself; universal history, and the history of religions in particular, then shows how this journey is realized through the stages of the human adventure over time. Religion represents the conclusive moment of this itinerary: in its 'external' phase it displays the last step in the process of elevation; in its 'internal' phase it reveals, in the mode of representation, the awareness of the meaning of this entire journey. If the core of the experience of the spirit consists in returning from the other to the self, religion, as the final juncture of this movement, marks the moment in which spirit arrives at itself from the other, and at the same time shows the overcoming of this other in the end result. In this context Hegel observes that 'the syllogistic outcome of religion, the true religion, is the one which produces the consciousness of itself, the one which has for its object what religion is' (*LPR* I, 317; *VPR* I, 220): the character of completeness, or absoluteness, of Christianity does not consist only in the fact that it realizes the concept of religion but also in the fact that, in its journey from the absolute fracture of the death of God to God's resurrection in the spirit of community, it produces the awareness of what spiritual experience is.

In this religious itinerary, we also witness the development of a profound experience of freedom, which is propaedeutic to philosophy. Religious experience is interlaced with elements which are taken from the outside and accepted as presuppositions and which can therefore assume an authoritative, 'positive' form, but its logic drives it to gradually overcome these external impositions, to reconsider the presupposition as something posited by spirit and which leads, by its very structure, to philosophy; as Hegel claims in the 1831 lectures, 'the ultimate analysis, in which there are no longer any assumed principles, arrives only in the advance to philosophy' (*LPR* I, 449 R; *VPR* I, 338 R).

This deeper analysis of the relation between logic and the content of religious experience leads Hegel to provide a new articulation of the two elements that convey his exposition, that is, the ascent towards the religious point of view and its development. The ascent from the finite to religion finds its true presentation in the system as a whole, and therefore it can be recalled here only in broad terms; as for the development, it no longer refers, as occurred in the manuscript, to the contents of Christian religion, but displays the fundamental moments that are common to all religions and shows how they achieve, through representation and *cultus*, the process of reunification of the finite spirit with God. From this new scheme Hegel derives a completely revised articulation of the two fundamental tasks that we have identified in the concept of religion, namely demonstration and description, which are now more strictly united than in the manuscript.

The lectures of 1827 present the mature form of Hegel's philosophy of religion. It is also the last lecture series that we know in its entirety, because the lecture course of 1831 is known to us only as a synthesis of notes that have since been lost. At this point Hegel turns a more conciliatory glance towards contemporary culture: despite its shortcomings, in its insistence on the principle of immediate knowledge this culture still affirms that consciousness has direct access to God. This thesis can be assumed by Hegel and integrated into his thought, given that for him too, God is present in the world and is revealed to the finite spirit. What he proposes, then, is to set out from the principle of immediate knowledge in order to go beyond it towards the contents: in this way he is able to reinterpret the objective side of the doctrine of religion connecting it to the subjective element (the immediate certainty of consciousness). The result is a more balanced and coherent exposition, which unites the subjective and objective sides within the single dimension of spiritual experience.

Actually, what characterizes this series of lectures is precisely the fact that, thanks to the attempts of previous years and the new, less polemical relationship to contemporary culture, Hegel has attained a deeper awareness of the ground on which his exposition unfolds: this ground is that of the spirit. From this entirely spiritual perspective, the subjective dimension of certainty and the objective dimension of contents attain a more linear and also more intense composition. This allows Hegel to find a more appropriate solution to the problem of the relation with experience external to religion on the one hand, and on the other hand to better connect, in the exposition of religion, the logical structure and the examination of contents.

Regarding the first aspect, in the new context, the need to begin from an external point of view (that of common consciousness or that of contemporary culture) to lead it as far as science becomes less pressing. This allows Hegel to offer a new solution to the problem of the relation between ascent and development. On the question of ascent, certainly it must be demonstrated that religion is the sphere that witnesses the culmination of the entire experience of the world, of which it constitutes the truth; but this demonstration is provided, rigorously, by the entire encyclopaedic journey, which begins from the lowest levels and arrives at religion in its last step before the philosophical conclusion. Thus, philosophy of religion does not need to provide this demonstration *again*, but can point to the disciplines that precede it in the system, and thus focus on the development of the religious truth that has been reached.

As for the second aspect, the exposition is focused on the illustration of the universal contents of religious experience by ordering them according to the ascending movement of the concept, which is the rhythm that articulates the entire life of the spirit. In this way Hegel provides a new, and definitive, solution to the problem of the relation between the two tasks which have governed his entire undertaking: description is brought decisively within demonstration and this plays the role of interpreter of religious experience.

The structure of this experience, as it is exposed in the concept of religion, is now articulated in three moments: the first is the still generic and partly implicit concept of the divine, whereas in the second moment the consciousness detaches from this substantial unity and develops a more objective and thematic knowledge of God; the third moment is *cultus*, in which the unification of the human subject and the divine object is realized. This process, too, has the character of an ascent, which this time, however, is realized not outside but within the terrain of the already accomplished truth. In the second moment, having illustrated the journey that leads from immediate knowledge and from feeling to representation and thought, Hegel includes a discussion of the proofs of the existence of God: these are presented as a critical transcription, in conceptual terms, of that process of elevation that constitutes the entire of religious experience.

This twofold purpose, which appeals simultaneously to the universal aspect of spiritual experience and to its concrete and singular dimension, endeavouring to unite them, is also to be found in the concluding section dealing with cultus. If the entire religious experience consists of an ascending progression towards unity with God, cultus is the concluding phase of that itinerary: here the subject undergoes the scission that separates it from the absolute and then overcomes it to eventually join with the divine. This practical journey requires that the individual subject negates and cancels out the egoistic dimension of its subjective particularity; this occurs through sacrifice[3] and repentance, thanks to which my singularity becomes purified and can unite with the universal without disappearing. The culmination of cultus is therefore ethical life (*Sittlichkeit*); it is accompanied by the knowledge of truth, which is accomplished in philosophy; the latter, then, is 'continual cultus' (*LPR* I, 446; *VPR* I, 334). Philosophy, which is 'integrally speculative' activity capable of identifying itself in its contents, therefore requires as its premise the resolution of the relation between singularity and universality and the full composition of the relation between the practical moment and the theoretical moment of existence.

The journey of religions in history

The tripartite scheme that is revealed in the 1827 version of 'the concept of religion' effectively guides the analyses that unfold in the second part of the work even in the preceding versions: for each historical religion, Hegel respectively examines the general concept of God, representation and cultus.[4] The role of this part consists in the effective development of the concept: in this sphere, in fact, the concept 'posits itself', it renders itself objective for the consciousness and thus it gradually acquires its full reality. Along its general lines, this part too displays a process of elevation, which leads from the natural level to the full revelation of the spirit. The first step is constituted by natural religion, seen as unity of the natural and the spiritual. The second step is that in which the spirit gradually gains an initial consciousness of itself; in this section we find the 'religions of spiritual individuality', that is, Judaism and Greek religion. The final step is represented in all the lecture courses by Roman religion, which fulfils, albeit dramatically, this progression and ushers in true religion.

When Hegel delivers his first philosophy of religion course, he has no access yet to an adequate documentation of different religions (especially Eastern religions). Thus he mainly relies on logic and constructs a scheme in which the partitions of logic correspond to these three stages of religious development. Immediate religion corresponds to the logic of being, and here Hegel treats Eastern religions rather generically. In the second stage we encounter the religions of essence, that is, those that go beyond immediacy, and make an initial experience of the dimension of profundity that characterizes spiritual experience. In the third stage we encounter Roman religion: the logic of the concept, or better, its initial part corresponds to it – given that the manifestation of the idea shall be reserved for Christianity. By 1824 Hegel has at his disposal a vast amount of documentation, especially with regard to China and India, but he is not yet able to systematize this material in a coherent way. In this lecture course, the recourse to logic loses its importance, and the author appeals, if somewhat inconsistently, to methods taken from the *Phenomenology of Spirit*.

The 1827 lectures offer a more linear and convincing exposition also for determinate religion, given that Hegel succeeds in organizing the material according to the governing idea of the spirit and its elevation. To interpret this development Hegel returns to using logic, which is only employed, however, along general lines and also appeals to the philosophy of the subjective spirit, bringing its various stages into correspondence with different religions. In the lectures of 1831, as far as we can judge from the extracts we possess, Hegel is interested above all in the historical dimension, so that the succession of religions closely follows that of the peoples presented in the philosophy of history. Hegel devotes much attention to Eastern religions, neatly separating them from immediate religion and placing them in a second and more advanced section. China in particular receives more attentive and organic treatment: it is no longer depicted as a religion of magic, but is interpreted as the 'religion of measure', which allows Hegel to connect the official religion of the Empire with Taoism and with Confucian ethics.

As we can grasp from this synthetic exposition, Hegel introduces a multiplicity of different elements alongside logic to construct his interpretation; thus from time to time he turns to ideas taken from the *Phenomenology of Spirit*, to considerations of the philosophy of history and even of nature, and especially to the contribution of the philosophy of the subjective spirit. This last aspect, which concerns the lecture course of 1827, is also the most interesting. Here in fact Hegel makes every principal religion correspond to a specific step in the process of formation of the subjective spirit. Thus China corresponds to the purely practical level of *Begierde*, that is, the desire that aims to take possession of external reality, as in the famous pages of the *Phenomenology* which introduce the struggle for recognition. Buddhism signals a suspension of the primitive appetite and thus leads into the dimension of interiority and contemplation that rises above the sphere of need. Indian polytheism corresponds to an initial level of fantasy, which at this stage, however, is still devoid of order and coherence. Egypt attains for the first time the sphere of representation, but has yet to render it intuitable in the form of the symbol; the level of representation is fully elaborated by Greece, where beautiful fantasy gives life to a divine figure in which the natural element is an adequate sign of the spiritual. The spiritual conception of God delineated in Judaism leads into the dimension of thought; Roman religion, too, moves on this plane, but remains at the level of the finite understanding, directed towards external finality.

In short, in his programmatic declarations Hegel always maintains the determining role of logic, but in his effective practice he integrates it with other elements of the system. It must be observed that when he truly seeks to systematize concrete experience according to logical schemes, his attempt often fails, or produces unsatisfactory results, which constrain him to devise new explanations later on. At other times, it is Hegel himself who refutes his own declarations, at least in part: this happens particularly in the case of the explanation of the general structure of the philosophy of religion, which is illustrated in the first lecture course with the positing of the concept in objectivity, followed by the passage towards the idea, while in 1824 Hegel refers to the general scheme of the *Encyclopaedia* (idea–nature–spirit), and in 1827 he talks about the *Urteil* of the concept, that is, the series concept–judgement–syllogism.

In these cases, as in others, Hegel demonstrates a certain careless detachment from his own schemes. What he holds firm without wavering in the least, however, is the general sense of the journey: this is always a path from the general concept to its determination in the history of religions and from there to its realization in consummate religion; as for determinate religion, this is always a passage from a level of immediate unity towards a specification and then an ulterior elaboration, which logically is more elevated, but which historically, with Rome, signals the failure of pre-Christian religions. What really counts for Hegel is that in the religious adventure of humanity there is a certain logic; this logic has real worth along its general lines, which contemplate the constant passage from an immediate and general unity towards a fracturing, or a distancing, thanks to which alone a more mature and articulated unity may arise, in which conciliation is realized. With respect to this basic line of thinking, single schemes have only a secondary and auxiliary function.

This general logical line, then, is effectively the rhythm of spirit itself, as Hegel understands it: the meaning of human experience lies within this realization of the spirit, which is present from the very beginning, but as a *telos* which must be reached it can be attained only through the conscious and painful workings of the subject. The logical scheme that leads from the initial concept towards scission and conciliation formalizes this vision of human experience. In conclusion, we may say that the concept of religion, and logic in general, represents an important instrument in the hermeneutics of religions. This role, however, is entirely rooted in the relation that logical structure has with the spirit. Ever since his youth, Hegel matured his dialectical conception by reflecting on human experience, on the scissions running deeply through it and on the need for conciliation, and he sought to bring the meaning of this experience into the transparency and the universal validity of the concept. It is in this nexus between the concrete foundations of dialectics and its formal and argumentative dimension, a nexus that points to the spirit, that the hermeneutic importance of Hegel's logic has its roots.

Notes

1 For a more detailed analysis of the philosophy of religion, I refer to my own volume: Pagano 1992, and specifically, to the section on the concept of religion (35–106). See also Jaeschke 1986: 218–263 and Hodgson 2005: 75–126.
2 *Gegenstoss* is translated in English as 'counter-repelling' in the first case and as 'self-repulsion' in the second.
3 On the topic of sacrifice, see Bubbio 2014, particularly the chapter on Hegel (61–85).
4 On the subject of determinate religion, refer to Pagano 1995 and Monaldi 1996. See also: Jaeschke 1986: 263–284; Hodgson 2005: 205–243.

References

Bubbio, P. D. (2014), *Sacrifice in the Post-Kantian Tradition*, Albany: SUNY Press.

Hodgson, P. C. (2005), *Hegel and Christian Theology: A Reading of the Lectures on the Philosophy of Religion*, Oxford: Oxford University Press.

Jaeschke, W. (1986), *Die Vernunft in der Religion*, Stuttgart – Bad Cannstatt: Frommann-Holzboog, trans. J. Michael Stewart and Peter C. Hodgson, *Reason in Religion: the Foundations of Hegel's Philosophy of Religion* (1990), Berkeley: University of California Press.

Monaldi, M. (1996), *Storicità e religione in Hegel*, Pisa: ETS.

Pagano, M. (1992), *Hegel: La religione e l'ermeneutica del concetto*, Napoli: E.S.I.

Pagano, M. (1995), 'La storia delle religioni nell'interpretazione di Hegel', *Annuario Filosofico* 10 (1994), 325–373.

13

A Speculative Logic for Images in Hegel's Philosophy

Haris Ch. Papoulias

An iconophilic iconoclasm

Unlike other great philosophers of his generation, Hegel has not yet been the subject of a full study dedicated to the role of the image in his system of knowledge. To consider Hegel as an iconoclast is a *cliché* that has definitely prevailed[1] despite the great influence of his aesthetics, perhaps because the attention to images *notwithstanding* a theory of art is one of the most recent achievements in the scholarly community (Boehm 1994; Mitchell 1994).

The notion of 'image' not only plays an important role in the development of the Hegelian system, but it also concerned Hegel, even in his private life, due to the fact that he has always been very interested in issues which are known today, in the broadest sense, as visual culture studies.[2] Since it would be unrealistic to fill this gap in the scholarship with a short chapter like this one, I will simply expose a couple of points that could help to sketch a basic principle concerning the status of images in the System of Knowledge; elsewhere (Papoulias 2017), I framed this question more extensively, with the paradoxical function of the 'endogenous' iconoclasm of the image, that is, as something completely different from that which 'iconoclasm' historically was. If Hegel was an iconoclast, how can we explain his decision to place art in the highest sphere of the absolute spirit? The frequent reference to the importance of image and representation in many other fields would be even more difficult to account for.[3] In spite of this, scholars who spoke of Hegelian iconoclasm were not entirely wrong, because the image is always destined to disappear. However, to confuse this disappearance with 'iconoclasm' implies an uncritical attitude according to which the 'image' should be conceived as an object, as a permanent being. This implicit and uncritical assumption of thinking about the image as something *vor-handen* (graspable-by-hands) compromises our ability to understand its role in Hegel's thought, even if he actually pointed this out in the beginning of the *Encyclopaedia*.[4] Thus, I prefer to talk about *endogenous* iconoclasm because Hegel did not argue in favour of a *Bildersturm* (iconoclasm) like a new Karlstadt; rather, he was, like Luther, dispassionately aware that idols are to be broken down firstly 'in the heart and not in the churches' (Luther 1525). Given the limited scope of this chapter, and not being able to illustrate the entire movement of image as 'existing appearance of being', I will only focus on some aspects of that movement, namely on the transitional property of images.

A case study of an image 'out of tune'

The term *Bild* appears in many chapters of Hegel's *Lectures on Aesthetics*[5]; however, the place where *Bild* is mentioned as an issue to be addressed is apparently unrelated to any concrete artistic product. This section is known as 'conscious symbolism' and deals with 'metaphor', 'image-as-such' (*Bild*) and 'simile' (*Vergleichung*).[6] Although it has caught scholarly attention for its jarring position, as if it were 'out of tune' (D'Angelo 1989: 162) with the rest of the chapters, very little has been said about its conceptual importance. Indeed, its value goes far beyond the discussion on its editorial setting.

The aforementioned section is often approached with an exclusive reference to the art of speech because the forms of expression presented (allegory, metaphor, simile, etc.) were traditionally objects of rhetoric and poetics. However, it would be preposterous to pretend that those forms are exclusive to poetry even though, in fact, every art has always worked with metaphors, symbols, allegories and so on. Aristotle – to whom we owe the first systematic treatment of the figures of speech – was clearly inspired by the act of *seeing*[7]; and Friedrich Creuzer, one of the most influential scholars and Hegel's friend during the Heidelberg years, dealt with these categories under the notion of *Bildlichkeit, representativeness, figurativeness*, but literally *iconicity*, i.e. the essence of being-image (Creuzer 1819: §27). This was not an arbitrary choice. We can realize why 'image' means much more than 'picture'[8] and how conceptually it is connected to 'simile' if we think of the Greek word εἰκών, which could actually be translated as image, picture, description, and of course icon; these are only specific determinations of a further notion that lays behind these terms ('to be alike': εἴκω, i.e. to present a similitude). When Hegel decides to use the term *Bild*, he follows the concept behind the word.⁹ This observation is necessary in order to understand, for instance, why (as I will argue at the end of this chapter), in the context of the doctrine of essence, *Ab-bild* should not be translated as mere 'copy'.¹⁰ 'Copy' usually refers to something 'less' than the original, whereas for Hegel the ontological truth of the image is not a mimetic issue but a *transitional* one. In other words, for appearance to be such, it should be able to disappear; its being shines in its self-dismissal.

Let us focus on the text. The title given in Hegel's 1826 lecture is the most appropriate way to indicate its real content, i.e. *the liberation of the spiritual and of the sensuous.*¹¹ The first two sections have a clear historical reference (to Judaism and oriental pantheism) and thus they are somehow connected to the rest of the symbolic art (Egypt and the pre-Hellenic eastern cultures). Yet, in the final section, the main title is repeated with the addition that here takes place a *Vollkommenes Freiwerden*, a *complete*, *perfect*, liberation of the spiritual and the sensuous. Thus, the forms of artistic expression have little to do with the pre-Hellenic world of symbolic art.¹² However, and regardless of Hegel's correctness on this point, here I am interested in something more specific, something that Hegelian scholar Paolo D'Angelo remarked as follows:

> The most frequently recurring terms to indicate what happens in the conscious symbolization are *Veranschaulichung* and *Verbildlichung*; at stake here is a *bringing to image*, a *giving visibility* to something that is neither intuitive nor figurative for itself.¹³

D'Angelo grasps a central issue: Hegel conceives the image not as a still object but as an activity. Metaphor, image and simile are not three independent moments, in the way a handbook of poetics could present them; rather, together they constitute the development of the iconic: for 'the iconic as such [*Das Bildliche als solches*] – Hegel claims – is generally a metaphor, image in the proper sense and simile' (*Kehler [1826]*, 103). Shortly thereafter, Hegel adds: 'Metaphors are only interruptions of representation, a passage, a transposition [*Hinübergehen*] towards another field of representation.' Later on, he provides a definition of image: 'the image in general is a metaphor better developed, more detailed, more circumscribed' (*Kehler [1826]*, 105). The meaning is not expressed immediately with the image itself (*ist nicht mitausgesprochen*); rather, the image is opposed to its meaning (*gegenübergestellt*). The metaphor pretends to give the proper meaning through an improper meaning, that is to say, *immediately*. The image goes beyond that immediacy; it articulates a scene in details, it expands the gaze while maintaining the metaphor in its core, ensuring that meaning and image as such are posited as opposites. This is not the mere rationalistic approach of the understanding that 'dissects a living organism'. The analysis helps to capture the *frames* of this process of transition from one notion to the other (metaphor-image-simile, but also image-meaning-representation). However, Hegel reminds us that 'in Thought there is no longer any difference between representations [*Vorstellungen*], images [*oder Bildern*] and their meaning; Thought is what signifies itself and it is given as it is in itself'.[14]

The next paragraph, entitled '*Image*' (*Bild*), introduces a decisive element that takes us out of the silent claim for identity, which is proper to metaphor. Image, Hegel argues, creates a contrast between figure and meaning. It creates *distance*. Goethe's poem *Mahomet's Song* is taken as an example – not for its formal elements but for its particular ability to produce images: it describes a stream that rises from the rocks and becomes a river, which grows more and more powerful until it flows into the ocean. Accordingly, the Prophet's doctrine is poured into the world. But this realization, Hegel claims, is possible only because of the title; without it, it would be nothing but the description of a river.[15] Thus, for Hegel, image is neither merely a still-image nor a description, but the unity of meaning and figure as a result of a development.

Furthermore, Hegel highlights that the determination of an image depends on the context.[16] The fact that meaning must be grasped by the context is very important because it denotes the overcoming of any one-sidedness, figurative or conceptual, historical, mythological, formal or of content. The interdisciplinarity of visual culture studies is essentially rooted in such a prevalence of the context (Baxandall 1972; Alpers 1983). The dialectical constitution of this movement may be observed even better in another term in which all these elements flow together: the *simile*. Unlike the 'image-as-such', the simile is a *developed* image. It is a new and higher identity, expressed with a dynamism that goes beyond the symbolic, static nature of a mere metaphor. The simile assumes an important task precisely because it is the last figure of this triad and thus a *result*.

In these three forms of tension between meaning and figure we should recognize three declensions, or modes of 'image', in a progressively dialectical order: in the 1823 lectures, Hegel significantly maintains that 'simile is a metaphor brought to accomplishment' (*Hotho [1823]*, 147). Therefore, the simile reveals the profound dialectical essence of the iconic (*Bildlich*). The words that follow – if read in the context suggested here and not as marginal aesthetic issues – assume an ontological relevance: 'the interest of dwelling in the object is the source of images and similes'.[17] In Hegel's view, when an object relates to another *through* (*dadurch*) this being-in-relationship, it rises up, sublimates and transfigures itself.

More precisely, 'dwelling through similes' means that the spirit shows itself by deepening in an object; it finds pleasure in it, and its interest becomes *more theoretical than practical*.[18] The object as image of a simile in fantasy (*Phantasie*) is not an object of nostalgia (*Sehnsucht*) or craving (*Schmachten*), i.e. of lack and desire, but it is an item of a theoretical approach to the world, and its picturing is an act of freedom. Later on, Hegel adds: 'A feeling [*Empfindung*] is, on the one hand, the Restlessness in itself [*die Unruhe in sich*], which however, on the other hand, does not want to abandon the object, it becomes intuitive [*Einfälle sich macht*], it creates images and similes.' Creating images and similes, Hegel claims, means to create a sensible dwelling (*sinnliche Verweilen*) – and with this claim he himself uses a very successful simile, because of the double sense of '*dwelling*', which perfectly corresponds to the double direction of the internal movement of the image: a *dwelling* in which the idea gives body and worldly presence to itself, but also a *dwelling* in which the idea could become prisoner and perish.

A keyword that expresses the transitive property of image, the '*dadurch*' is the passage *through* which the meaning is accomplished. Images may begin subjectively from an aniconic state, e.g. from a feeling; however, they become proper images only by making this feeling objective. Conversely, starting from an objective aniconic idea (a given notion, e.g. freedom), they appear in the act of giving body to this idea. In both cases there is a *substitution* of something proper with something improper; therefore, in both cases a metaphorical process is in act. If the simile is used as an unfolded process, it means that a *transition* takes place and that the *medium* – i.e. the image *as such* – should disappear, not always and not necessarily in a material or physical sense, since it is sufficient to become *diaphanous*, acquiring a transparency that allows the gaze to pass through.[19]

This 'mode of image' emerges only if it is conceived not as a 'still-image' but as a frame of an action. In the age of cinema, it may seem quite familiar; but in Hegel's age, the conception of an image as an action had no empirical counterpart (not even the *Zoetrope*, which was invented after his death). Hegel focuses here on poetry because it offers the best approach to a picture-thinking in development. In Hotho's *Aesthetics*, after citing *Mahomet's Song*, Hegel focuses on a *Xenia* by Goethe/Schiller, undertaking an important reflection:

> The content [...] is here a subject who acts, produces things, lives through situations and now, *not* as subject but only in respect of what he does or effects or what meets him, is represented in an image [*verbildlicht wird*]. Whereas as subject, he is himself introduced without an image [*bildlos*] and only his literal actions and affairs acquire the form of a metaphorical expression. Here too, as in the case of the image in general, the *entire* meaning is not severed from its cloak;

on the contrary, the subject alone is revealed explicitly, while his determinate content at once acquires an imaged shape; and thus the subject is represented as if he himself brought into being the objects and actions in this their imaged existence. To the expressly named subject something metaphorical is ascribed. This mixture of the literal and the metaphorical has often been blamed, but the grounds for this blame are weak.[20]

This is a case in which the 'iconic presence' of an 'aniconic subject' is clearly given. A 'shine' becomes effective due to the subject's acts and surely does not regard poetry alone but painting as well.[21] Another 'image' quoted by Hegel in 1823 may better display the extension of this issue. Speaking of the simile, Hegel quotes the well-known Lutheran verse *Ein' feste Burg ist unser Gott* (*Hotho [1823]*, 120).[22] This is for Hegel a simile par excellence in which the meaning (God) is immediately connected to the image (Fortress). Then, he adds: 'in simile, it is quite clear that it is not necessary to recognize validity to the sensuous existence as such' (*Hotho [1823]*, 120). This denial is not a denial of the aesthetic experience; conversely, it theorizes the possibility to express such a denial aesthetically, as long as there are arts that pretend to achieve a full attachment to the sensuous and arts that operate its removal.

The well-known painter Caspar David Friedrich attempted to express the very same denial in his pictures, provoking an important debate on the right of using a landscape for liturgical purposes (i.e. as an *Altarbild*); in Hegelian terms, it was a debate about the right of picturing the aniconic through a *developed* metaphor. In one of his letters, the painter protests against Ramdohr, a famous art-critic of that period, for his failure to understand the distinction – the same distinction drawn by Hegel. Friedrich writes: 'Of course the image has a meaning, even if [Ramdohr] does not understand it [...]. The cross rises on a firm, unyielding rock [*unerschütterlich fest*], like our faith in Jesus Christ' (Grave 2010: 56). Consider Hegel's words again: 'to the sensuous existence as such we must not recognize validity'. In Friedrich's painting, it is not *the flesh* of Christ that shows us the Divine, like in the art of Counter-Reformation, but a rising sun over a firm rock. However, it would not be correct to consider them as symbols. They do not stand in substitution of something else. The crucified *is still there*, but withdrawn in the shadow. All the best romantic paintings similarly display *not the sensuous but its withdrawal*. Hegel's thesis has nothing to do with rationalistic commonplaces. Rather, they concern the unveiling of the essence of the image as such. Friedrich, as well as many of his followers, strives to provide an adequate picture for a meaning; to succeed, he must bring into appearance both the shine of the divine *and* its sensuous disappearance. Johannes Grave, making a reference to the same painting, makes an appropriate remark, and his words could perfectly illustrate Hegel's idea:

> The important thing in Friedrich's *Tetschener Altar* lies not only in the disquieting presentation of the cross. Friedrich translates the indissoluble simultaneity between Revelation and Concealment of God on the cross [*die unauflösliche Gleichzeitigkeit von Offenbarung und Verborgenheit Gottes im Kreuz*], in a radical way, in a representation [*Darstellung*] in which the represented [*das Dargestellte*] makes itself present and at the same time withdrawn [*sowohl vergegenwärtigt als auch entzieht*] (Grave 2010: 55).

Shining in the sinking: Backwards to the essence of (dis-)appearance

The internal withdrawal of the image, as accomplishment of the iconic, is a movement that we can trace every time Hegel addresses *Bild* (image/picture). In the doctrine of *subjective spirit*, the appearance and the disappearance of the image are produced by the faculty of representation (*Vorstellung*) in the most surprising way. *Bild* appears at the beginning of this faculty, as an inward-product of *recollection* (*Erinnerung*) (*EIII*, §452; see also *EIII*, §451 A). It reaches its proper place in imagination (and fantasy, §§455ff.), and through the action of sign (*EIII*, §459), and finally disappears in memory, becoming a *Bildlose Vorstellung*, i.e. an aniconic or image-less representation (*EIII*, §462 R).

Every discipline works in the frame of just one of these stages (e.g. the stage of *Einbildungskraft* has an obvious importance in aesthetics); however, if they are taken separately, they decay to abstract moments of *the one and the same faculty* of representation. Conversely, in Hegelian terms, to represent something properly means to follow the rise and fall of its image in all its extension. If it is true that Hegel takes on the Aristotelian precept according to which 'the soul never thinks without an image' (Aristotle 2016: 431a), it is also likely that he would add: 'but the image, eventually, should disappear', not because it is 'inferior' to thought, or to an empty mnemonic sign, but because this is its own duty: to bring forth something and to retreat in order to actualize the transition. Against 'iconoclasts', he may affirm the necessity of images for rational thinking; against 'iconodules', he may affirm that images should be sublated. The importance of maintaining both actions inside the productive field of representation could be better appreciated in contemporary art.[23]

Against this background, and unsurprisingly, in the 'Anthropology' Hegel considers many 'imagistic phenomena' of the inner psychic life, as pathological cases, as long as they *persist*, pretending an actual existence (*GW* XXV/1, 326ff.). Conversely, a 'true' image would be something like the expressive instant of a gesture, a self-dissolving image of the body, posited to the highest stage of the *actual soul* (*EIII*, §411ff.). Gesture being an *act*, it lives only for an instant. This is undoubtedly the complementary systematic place in which many aesthetic features are rooted. The actual soul produces and dissolves its own images, exactly as *Vorstellung* does at a superior level.

In the same way, but looking backwards, we find in the *Philosophy of Nature* the production and dissolution of the multicoloured world through the action of light, developed in a theory of *Sichtbarkeit*, as a sublation of both mere optics (Newton) and mere theory of colour (Goethe).[24] This constant play of appearance/disappearance, I argue, should not be flattened as if it were a question of taste, but we should consider it as the empirical counterpart of a well-designed theory pointing to the essence of appearance, as an (onto-)logical background that precedes and determines both *Bildlichkeit* and *Sichtbarkeit*. This theory is Hegel's *Doctrine of Essence*, second book of his *Science of Logic*.

The relationship between truth and appearance cannot be founded on Hegel's *taste*; if anything, the opposite is true. Everything I have said so far involves the idea that shine (*Schein*) is not false, but the very first appearance of the truth of being. It is not by chance that Hegel wanted to highlight it not only in his *Science of Logic* but also at the very beginning of his *Lectures on Aesthetics*: 'Shine is not something unessential; on the contrary, it is an essential moment of essence itself' (*Hotho [1823]*, 2). This is a real turning point for Western thought: for the first time after the early Greek thought, shining is not conceived as an illusion, as a veil of being, but as its very essence.[25] The material offered in the *Science of Logic* as logical ground for a Hegelian theory of image is incredibly rich; here we can only focus on the most intimate paradox that belongs to everything that appears in the form of an image, or rather to every self-dismissal of the image, as fullness of being-appearance. How and where does this emerge in this text?

Such a fullness of the appearance of essence is reached only in the last chapter on *Wirklichkeit* (*Effectivity*). The relevance of this chapter for an ontological approach to the visual arts becomes clear if we realize that for Hegel 'effectivity' was a synonym for *manifestation* (Souche-Dagues 1990: 41–74) or – even more faithfully to Hegel's text – '*Revelation*' (*Offenbarung*). 'First, essence *shines within itself* [*scheint*] or is *reflection*; second, it *appears* [*erscheint*]; third, it *reveals* itself [*offenbart es sich*]' (*SL*, 339; *GW* XI, 243; Schmidt 1997: 189). Revelation is thus the effectiveness of shine. When shine reaches this last level, it will be called *Schein als Schein* or simply *das Scheinen*,[26] meaning that it is not an effectiveness of something *other*: it is always the initial and apparently illusionary shine that we address. *Shine* becomes *Shine-as-Shine* by passing through the dissolution of every fixed position, of every autonomous determination, into spheres of relationality, always wider and higher.[27] Revelation is the effectiveness of the appearance, but such an effectiveness takes place only as self-dismissal of the autonomy of every determination in essential *relationships*. Namely not only does an 'effect' follow its 'cause' but the cause is really such *only* in its effect. From this angle, we can think of Gadamer's dialectics of image as *Urbild-Abbild*. But it is not a matter of influence. Hegel captured a profound structure of reality, and thus all of the terms implicated here (e.g. form/matter, outer/inner, whole/parts, force/expression) have been used in the history of art because of their ability to explain every appearance in image.[28]

For those who wonder if Hegel had ever thought to speak literally about the dissolution of appearance, it would be enough to refer to a short chapter, expressly dedicated to the 'dissolution of appearance'.[29] But this short chapter makes no sense if considered out of its context. To summarize better what is going on here, it may be useful to refer to an internal movement, which is already present in the initial account of *Schein* and which unfolds its dialectics according to a triple movement of self-suppression/sublation.

First, the internal movement unfolds as self-suppression of the determinations of reflection:

> The determinations of reflection should have their subsistence in them and be self-subsistent. But their self-subsistence (*Selbständigkeit*) is their dissolution (*Auflösung*), which they thus have in an other; but this dissolution is itself this self-identity or the ground of the subsistence that they give to themselves (*SL*, 390; *GW* XI, 69–70).

Here is revealed not only the logic that governs these determinations but also the whole structure built on them. At stake here is not an abstract becoming that 'swallows' everything. Rather, we are dealing with the position of every foundation in the resolution of identity as an abstract 'autonomy' (*Selbst-ständigkeit*). The resolution becomes again position and identity, but of a higher kind. Nevertheless, the self-suppression/sublation of single reflexive determinations is not enough, since these, taken as a whole, constitute the reflection-as-such.

Second, we see the self-sublation of reflection itself: 'this positing – Hegel claims referring to the positing of the Essence as Ground – is the reflection of essence that *sublates* itself in its *determining*; on that side is a *positing*, on this side is *the positing of essence*, hence both in one act' (*SL*, 387; *GW* XI, 65). Hegel calls the process of *reflexion* a '*reine Vermittlung*', a *pure mediation*; it precedes the movement of the *real mediation* (*reale Vermittlung*), operated by the ground. This 'pure mediation' is also called 'the reflective shining [*das Scheinen*] of one in an other'.[30] Thus, reflexion as a whole (as *das Scheinen*) is really reflective only 'in an other'. The necessity of the genitive case for every 'image' is rooted in this: an image is always an 'image *of*' something else.

Third, the same movement of self-sublation is marked more specifically by the work of ground. Immediately after the beginning of this chapter, we read:

> *Ground* is itself *one of the reflected determinations* of essence, but it is the last, or rather, it is determination determined as sublated determination. In foundering to the ground [*zugrundegeht*], the determination of reflection receives its true meaning – that it is the absolute repelling of itself within itself; or again, that the positedness that accrues to essence is such only as sublated, and conversely that only the self-sublating positedness is the positedness of essence. In determining itself as ground, essence determines itself as the not-determined, and only the sublating of its being determined [*das Aufheben seines Bestimmtseins*] is its determining. (*SL*, 386, *GW* XI, 65; my italics)

Ground is (a) *die letzte*; (b) *Reflexionbestimmung*, but more precisely it is (c) an *aufgehobene Bestimmung*, which is such only as *aufgehobene*, as *sublated*. The meaning of *aufgehobene* is linked here to *zugrundegehen*, demonstrating that it is not simply *removed* elsewhere, but it sinks into itself. In the ground, the accomplishment of the '*Reflexionsbestimmung*' is declared. Ground is the quintessence of the determinations of reflection because it embodies the most intimate reflexive logic: *being a counter-blow*, which means 'to be posited' only as sublated. Only a 'sublated-position' really belongs to the essence.

Following the text, this 'being-posited as sublated' designates the ground. But if we stand out of the movement in which we are immersed, we may clearly see that this is the mechanism of the whole *Scheinen*: otherwise, it would remain a motionless being-posited, i.e. not the reflective determination as a counter-shock[31] but a being as a pure and abstract determinacy. The appearance as shine is the coming-out of the essence of being as such and *also* the return of shine in itself. 'As *ground*, therefore, [essence] *posits* itself *as essence*, and its determining consists in just this positing of itself as essence'.[32] Hence, ground is undoubtedly the culmination of *Schein* and therefore of reflection itself. The climax consists on the one hand in the development of the otherwise illusory shine in truth and on the other hand in the emergence and the construction of the pathway of the essence through its own negativity: denying its negation, i.e. denying the inessential shine with which it had posited itself as something other than being. In fact, this logic of negativity that finds its first reflexive accomplishment in the ground constitutes the most intimate character of the essence as the ability to conceive the truth as *the necessary position of self-withdrawing illusion*. This logic is at the foundation of every essential appearance and therefore every true image as an existing appearance.

Glosses on glosses could be added interpreting the classical art or romantic paintings according to Hegel's thought, but no historical phenomenon could ever better provide us with a unique definition of the essence of the image than the one provided in the chapter on the *Wirklichkeit*: image as manifestation of the effectivity of the essence – and this definition captures in a nutshell all the clarifications I presented above:

> Being as shine is not *nothing* [*das Nichts*] *but reflection*, reference [*Beziehung*] to the absolute; or it *is* a shine in as much as that which *shines in it is the absolute* [*das Absolute in ihm scheint*]. This positive exposition thus halts the finite just before its disappearing: it considers it an expression and an image of the absolute [*Abbild des Absoluten*]. But this transparency of the finite that lets only the absolute transpire through it ends up in complete disappearance, for there is nothing in the finite which would retain for it a difference over against the absolute; as a medium, it is absorbed by that through which it shines. (*SL*, 468; *GW* XI, 164)[33]

Notes

1 It is quite symptomatic that one of the few studies on images in Hegel's philosophy is presented in the frame of an intellectual history of iconoclasm (Besançon 1994); and indeed, Hegel's quotation significantly opens the whole work. A much more appropriate approach has been pursued by Rebecca Comay (2014), giving a better determination of what iconoclasm means in certain Hegelian contexts.

2 See, for example, his visit to the *Neorama* of Paris (*Briefe* III, 199); or, on the quality of his portraits that were spread around Germany in engravings (Pinkard 2001: 536). See also his correspondence with Goethe and Schelling on the experiments on the properties of light and colours (e.g. the letter of the 2nd of August 1821 in: *Briefe* II, 275ff.).

3 An exceptional importance, for instance, is his overture in his 1821 *Philosophy of Religion* lecture manuscript: LPR III, 62; VPR III, 1.
4 See *EI*, §3; here, Hegel argues that images are forms of the content of consciousness and that only through them we become aware of this very content. Furthermore, he adds, 'what is in itself the same, can take on the look of a different content'. Thanks to images, a dialectical process begins with the purpose to realize the passage from what is sensuous to the thought. He also claims that as representations, images may be regarded as *metaphors* of concepts (§3 R). This *transitive property* of metaphor (in Greek: μετα-φέρω, to *carry over*), attribute of image and representation, is one of the most precious elements to keep in mind.
5 For instance, a statue could be a *Stand-bild*, a *Marmor-bild* or a *Bild-säule*. Every artistic product gives us different determinations of the artistic image production.
6 In Hotho's edition of *Aesthetics*, it is the third chapter of the symbolic art form, but in reality – and in the new edition of the single lectures is clear – presents many contradictions. It is sufficient to see how in *Kehler [1826]* it is the fourth step, called '*Freiwerden des Geistigen und des Sinnlichen*' – which properly indicates its true content – and thus presents itself as an autonomous conceptual treatise, without any link with the development of the three previous forms. In *Hotho [1823]*, it was instead the third chapter, and therefore a kind of reunion of the previous two moments. The forcing, which should be attributed to Hotho, is evident when he first calls the second chapter '*Trennung der unmittelbaren Einheit*' and then, probably not knowing how to define the third, he calls it '*Rückkehr aus der Trennung [...] in die Einheit*', even if it has nothing to do with the previous one. In fact, here there is no 'return' to any 'unity' as Hotho claims. This is why Paolo D'Angelo rightly called this section 'a chapter fundamentally wrong in its planning' (see D'Angelo 1989: 162).
7 Aristotle 2012: 1448b 10ff.; Umberto Eco (2012: 592ff.) pointed to the visual terms used by Aristotle in his *Poetics* while addressing metaphor: 'Metaphor is manifested (*phaínesthai*) when it is under exam (*skopeîn*) a possible convergence or analogy.'
8 A generally adequate distinction, suggested by the binomial 'image/picture' (Mitchell 2005: 85), if investigated further, shows how one term implies the other; the precedence of the one or of the other seems a question of method: in *Aesthetics* an abstract notion 'takes body'; in the *subjective spirit*, Hegel leads us to thought, starting from intuition, through an abstractive process, an '*Auflösung*', a *dissolution* of the empirical connection of the manifold determinations of the object (*EIII* §456 A).
9 In the *Phenomenology of Spirit* Hegel uses as synonyms 'image' and 'representation': *Die Vorstellung oder das Bild hat aber seine Wirklichkeit an einem Anderen, als es ist*. (A representation or image, however, has its actual existence in something other than itself.): PS, 273; GW IX, 246.
10 On the ontological valence (*Seinsvalenz*) of *Bild*, i.e. how the *Urbild* is such only *because* of an *Abbild*, see Gadamer 1986: 139ff. Such an inversion (the effect that

realizes the cause) would be happily approved by Hegel, according to his doctrine of essence.
11 *Freiwerden des Geistigen und des Sinnlichen*, see *Kehler [1826]*, 89.
12 Rosenkranz wanted to move these forms of expression into the section on poetry (see Rosenkranz 1840: 192). The first topic discussed here is the Aesopical fable, therefore a *Greek* and not a pre-Hellenic genre. Nonetheless, even this form features specific issues regarding the image, as Lessing remarked (Lessing 1759: 113ff.).
13 D'Angelo 1989: 166; it will be useful, therefore, to declare from the beginning that this 'bring to image' does not belong specifically to poetry, as Rosenkranz would like, nor to the symbolic art in an exclusive way; for that reason, this complete 'jarring' is not translated into a systematic problem for us. Systematically, the activity of *bringing to image* and to intuition has its own place, not in poetry or in painting, but in the Subjective Spirit as 'symbolizing Fantasy' (*EIII*, §457 A).
14 VGP I, 79 (my translation).
15 Hegel notes that 'the title [...] specifies [...] an image, otherwise it could be understood as a living description (*lebendige Beschreibung*)'; see *Kehler [1826]*, 105.
16 *Kehler [1826]*, 106: 'In the image, the meaning is given by the context [Im Bild ist die Bedeutung zwar durch den Zusammenhang gegeben].'
17 *Kehler [1826]*, 108.
18 *Kehler [1826]*, 109; rightly, the editors point to the influence of Kant's *Critique of the Power of Judgment* (Kant 2000: §2, §5; see *Kehler [1826]*, fn. 214, 272f.).
19 On the necessity of transparency for the production of the visible, see *EII*, §317f.; for a systematic treatise of his theory of visibility, see Papoulias 2017: 186–282.
20 LA I, 409f.; TWA XIII, 525.
21 'For this reason we demanded of paintings at the very beginning that it should provide a portrayal of character, the soul, the inner life, not however in such a way that this inner life shall afford a recognition of itself directly in its external figure but only as it develops and expresses what it is through *actions* (*durch Handlungen*)'; see: LA II, 854; TWA XV, 89.
22 See also LA 307; TWA XIII, 398: 'A safe stronghold our God is still', more often translated as 'A Mighty Fortress is our God', is a hymn composed by Luther, famous also for its adaption by J. S. Bach (*Cantata*, BWV80).
23 There are cases in which the purpose to reach seems to be the production of 'an object that tells of the loss, destruction, disappearance of objects' (J. Johns, cited by Didi-Huberman 1992: 15). The specific moment of transition from intuition to thought and the way that an image could actually represent it, it has always been central for many authors and artists in the last centuries. G. Didi-Huberman dedicated many works to this (Didi-Huberman 1998, 2013). Following the Hegelian thought, we could easily recognize not only the truth of saying 'if [images] burn, they are real' (according to Rilke's words: *wenn es aufbrennt, ist es echt*), but also *why* they should 'burn' *in order to be real*.

24 An attempt for a systematic treatment of Hegel's theory of light as an organic whole has been presented in Papoulias 2017: 150–260. For the purpose of this chapter, the most relevant issue here is that Hegel, after a long development of the notion of visibility, stresses the 'iconoclastic' power of light being able to fade out its very own products, i.e. the colour; see *EII*, §320 A.

25 Deleuze, treating visual issues as the 'simulacrum' in Plato, remarked that 'the dual denunciation of essences and appearances dates back to Hegel' (Deleuze 1990: 253). The opening chapter on 'Shine' is also an extraordinary announcement of what Hegel will finally obtain after the harsh critique against the Kantian notion of the 'thing-in-itself' (see *SL*, 427f.).

26 See *SL*, 470, where '*Schein als Schein*' is translated as 'the reflective shine as reflective shine', which is a little bit more than what is actually said, as long as 'reflective shine' is at once the 'shine [*posited*] as shine'. At the end of the same paragraph, Hegel provides an alternative formulation: 'es ist nur, was es *ist* […], als Scheinen, das *als Scheinen* gesetzt ist.'

27 For instance, the same movement of self-dissolution is always repeated towards the end of every section: ground (the relation between ground and grounded is finally reversed), essential *relation* (*Verhältnis*) and lastly absolute *relation* are closing, respectively, the first, the second and the third sections.

28 The fruitfulness of these notions could be seen in many works on art theory. From Ruskin (1857) to Wölfflin's polar-oppositions (Wölfflin 2015: 320ff.), from Constructivism to Functionalism *et al.* (see Di Napoli 2011, e.g. 323 on 'configuration' as a 'system of forces').

29 See *SL*, 447. We could recall here that even in the *Aesthetics*, every artistic period ends up with its own dissolution; see *LA* I, 421, 502, 593.

30 Or 'the movement of nothing through nothing back to itself': *SL*, 387.

31 According to Yovel's translation of the Hegelian use of the term '*Gegenstoß*' (Yovel 2005: 180).

32 *SL*, 387; *GW* XI, 65.

33 I slightly modified the translation on the grounds of my remark at the beginning of this chapter: an *Abbild* is never a simple *copy*, but the necessary image-appearance of the original (*Urbild*) imageless.

References

Alpers, S. (1983), *The Art of Describing: Dutch Art in the Seventeenth Century*, Chicago: University of Chicago Press.

Aristotle (2012), *Poetics. Editio Maior of the Greek Text with Historical Introductions and Philological Commentaries*, ed. L. Tarán and D. Gutas, Leiden-Boston: Brill.

Aristotle (2016), *De Anima*, trans. Ch. Shields, Oxford: Oxford University Press.

Baxandall, M. (1972), *Painting and Experience in 15th Century Italy*, Oxford: Oxford University Press.

Besançon, A. (1994), *L'image interdite: une histoire intellectuelle de l'iconoclasme*, Paris: Fayard.

Boehm, G. (1994), 'Die Wiederkehr der Bilder', in Id., ed., *Was iste in Bild?* 11–38, München: W. Fink.

Comay, R. (2014), 'Defaced Statues: Idealism and Iconoclasm in Hegel's Aesthetics', *October Magazine* (149), MIT, 123–142.

Creuzer, Fr. (1819), *Symbolik und Mythologie der alten Völker, besonders der Griechen*, Bd. I, Leipzig-Darmstadt: Heyer & Leske.

D'Angelo, P. (1989), *Simbolo e arte in Hegel*, Roma-Bari: Laterza.

Deleuze, G. (1990), *The Logic of Sense*, trans. M. Lester and Ch. Stivale, London: Athlone Press.

Di Napoli, G. (2011), *I principi della forma*, Torino: Einaudi.

Didi-Huberman, G. (1992), *Ce que nous voyons, ce qui nous regarde*, Paris: Les éditions de Minuit.

Didi-Huberman, G. (1998), *Phasmes. Essais sur l'apparition, 1*, Paris: Les éditions de Minuit.

Didi-Huberman, G. (2013), *Phalènes. Essais sur l'apparition, 2*, Paris: Les éditions de Minuit.

Eco, U. (2012), 'Metafora e conoscenza nel medioevo', in *Scritti sul pensiero medievale*, Milano: Bompiani.

Gadamer, H.-G. (1986), *Hermeneutik I: Wahrheit und Methode*, in *Gesammelte Werke*, Bd. 1, Tübingen: J.C.B. Mohr.

Grave, J. (2010), *Caspar David Friedrich. Glaubensbild und Bildkritik*, Zürich: Diaphanes.

Kant, I. (2000), *Critique of the Power of Judgment*, trans. P. Guyer and E. Matthews, Cambridge: Cambridge University Press.

Lessing, G. (1759), *Fabeln. Drey Bücher. Nebst Abhandlungen mit dieser Dichtungsart verwandten Inhalts*, Berlin: Voss.

Luther, M. (1525), *Wider die himmlischen Propheten, von den Bildern und Sakrament*, Wittenberg: Cranach & Döring.

Mitchell, W.J.T. (1994), *Picture Theory: Essays on Verbal and Visual Representation*, Chicago: University of Chicago Press.

Mitchell, W.J.T. (2005), *What Do Pictures Want? The Lives and Loves of Images*, Chicago: University of Chicago Press.

Papoulias, Ch. (2017), 'Iconoclastia endogena dell'immagine. Una teoria dell'immagine nel Sistema del sapere di G.W.F. Hegel', Ph.D. diss., Università del Piemonte Orientale, Vercelli.

Pinkard, T. (2001), *Hegel: a biography*, Cambridge: Cambridge University Press.

Rosenkranz, K. (1840), *Kritische Erläuterungen des Hegel'schen Systems*, Königsberg: Bornträger.
Ruskin, J. [1857] (1904), 'The Elements of Drawing: In Three Letters to Beginners', in E. T. Cook and A. Wedderburn (eds), *The Works of John Ruskin*, vol. XV, 25–232, London: Longmans, Green & Co..
Schmidt, K. (1997), *G.W.F. Hegel: 'Wissenschaft der Logik–Die Lehre vom Wesen'*, Paderborn-München-Wien-Zürich: Schöningh.
Souche-Dagues, D. (1990), *Hégélianisme et dualisme. Réflexions sur le phénomène*, Paris: Vrin.
Wölfflin, H. (2015), *Principles of Art History: The Problem of the Development of Style in Early Modern Art*, Los Angeles: Getty Publications.
Yovel, Y. (2005), *Hegel's Preface to the Phenomenology of Spirit*, Princeton & Oxford: Princeton University Press.

14

The Silence of *Logik*: Hegel after Kojève

Hager Weslati

The reception of Alexandre Kojève's Parisian lectures on 'the religious philosophy of Hegel' (1933–1939) occupies an ambivalent position in Hegel studies, not least because it bears a strong resonance with the critical horizon beyond which many interventions in the field are still struggling to see.

Attempts at a reasoned interpretation of the *Logic* are marked by the imprint of indecision as to whether this 'textbook' is ontology, onto-theology, a metaphysic of sorts or even an extension of the *Phenomenology*. What is at stake in the indecision is not its novelty or prominence at any particular moment in the intellectual history of Hegelianism; rather what matters the most is its contemporaneity, its *untimeliness*, and its being continuously with us as a question that situates the thought-determinations of the *Logic* and the processual dynamic of the idea in relation to being, existence and the real. Hegel's *science* of logic will remain a problem for as long as the work of interpretation is trapped in the uncertainty about what it is and how it functions (in the Hegelian system). Early in the 1930s, Kojève offered an interesting solution to this problem, contending that in order to correct Hegel's monist error, the *Logic* must be defined as ontology of 'given-being' (*être-donné*), which is nothing other than 'the being-of-which-one-speaks' (*l'être-dont-on-parle*). Consequently, the task of any interpreter of Hegel is to 'update' (*mise à jour*) this ontology and to determine its relation to empirical-existence or the *Dasein* (as developed in the *Phenomenology*), and to the *metaphysics of the real*, i.e. to 'objective-reality' or the *Wirklichkeit* (as defined in Hegel's *real-philosophy* and philosophy of spirit).

De la médiation dans la philosophie de Hegel (1945) and Jean Hyppolite's *Genesis and Structure of Hegel's Phenomenology of Spirit* (1974) set the tone and orientation for an entire field of Hegel studies, which has been since then up in arms over the 'violent' interpretation that Kojève imposed on the reading of Hegelian texts. What is less known perhaps is the fact that before and after his brief teaching career on the margins of French academic philosophy, Kojève, who had no particular interest in Hegel, was applying the principles of his own philosophical system to the study of (Western and Eastern) philosophical discourses. Broadly speaking, the Kojevean system, which is still largely unknown, aims to evaluate and correct the adequate description of given-being, objective-reality and empirical-existence in other philosophical systems through the double-slit lens of action and discourse.

The present chapter sets the argument of ontologizing the *Logic* in the wider context of the Kojevean system of knowledge with the aim of outlining the consequences of this argument for the philosophical discourse, political action and the disciplinary practice of logic across the analytic-continental divide.

The primal scene of the concept

A careful reader of Kojève is constantly reminded of the fact that there are two types of philosophers (in the world in which we live): those who speak about everything and anything, including what their predecessors have talked about, and those who *speak about themselves speaking* about that which they are speaking about in the world in which they live. Kojève tried to abstract from this feedback loop a general orientation for his own philosophical system, whose completion, it is worth emphasizing, predates his close reading of the early and mature Hegel, while deliberately sidestepping the lectures and posthumous work mediated by his students.

If the philosophical discourse can begin with any random question, there is no restriction on its development into endless chatter as on its potential retreat into silence.[1] Kojève punctuates the two extreme ends of the philosopher's discourse with the question 'what am I?'

Seeking to raise the bar of the philosopher's expectation above the unsatisfactory answer 'I am a thinking being', Hegel proved that philosophy can aspire to the absolute idea on condition that it addresses and resolves the conflation of being and thought. To that end, 'Hegel's science' applies the phenomenological method to describe 'the totality of real Being as it "appears" (*erscheint*) or shows itself to [a] real [human being] who is a part of the Real, who lives, acts, thinks and speaks in it' (Kojève 1969: 213).

But since philosophers want to talk about this totality in its *realized* aspect, and not just about how it *reveals* itself, the Hegelian system allows them to 'rise to the ontological level' (Kojève 1969: 214). The *Logic*, Kojève contends, precisely serves this purpose through an adequate description of the dialectical structure of being *without applying any method*. Mediation or dialectic is not a method of thought, 'it is not an artifice of philosophical exposition: dialectic is the very structure of concrete reality itself' (Kojève 1970: 21).

Committed to the imperative of distinguishing dialectic from method as early as the lectures of 1934–35, Kojève underscored the necessity of attributing method to phenomenology, while reserving the notion of dialectic to the temporal-discursive force of the negative in being and to the power of resistance that is proper to the very (temporal) structure of the real.[2] With the distance of more than eight decades, such claims appear visionary and prescient in comparison with a long and unsettled debate around Hegel's method. Frank Ruda, for instance, revisits these debates in a desperate attempt to refute the lack of materiality and resistance in Hegel's 'narcissistic' and irresistible reason. Deploying all sorts of critical acrobatics from Foucault to Freud, Ruda hoped to rescue the *Logic* from 'the unavoidable submission to the method of speculative dialectical thought' (Ruda 2018: 18). Ruda's concern was that such a 'method' always terminates in empty idealism with neither materiality nor resistance. Conversely, for Kojève, only interpretations that conflate method and dialectic are prone to seeing in the unfolding of the Hegelian absolute idea a path to pure idealism or pure realism.

Throughout the *Lectures*, Kojève insists repeatedly that there is no *Logik* or an ontology 'without a prior *Phenomenology* or an anthropology that reveals [human being] and History' (Kojève 1947: 409). He was, however, equally emphatic in pointing that the transition from the phenomenological to the ontological level is neither a *descent* into nor *transcendence* towards different *ontic* forms of silence, be they aesthetic contemplation (or onto*graphy*), religiosity and mysticism (or onto-*theology*), mathematized or symbolized beings (or onto-*metry*).

In his comparative reading of the Kantian and Hegelian systems of knowledge, Kojève was particularly attentive to the sound of the thinking activity, underscoring the different paths the philosopher can take in her or his search for an answer to the 'what am I?'

First, there is a man called Hegel:

[He is] a man of flesh and blood who *knows* that he is such. Next, this man does not float in empty space. He is seated on a chair, at a table, writing with a pen on paper. And he *knows* that all these objects did not fall from the sky; he knows that those things are products of something called human *work*. He also knows that this work is carried out in a human *World*, in the bosom of a Nature in which he himself participates. And this World is present in his mind at the very moment when he writes to answer his 'What am I?' Thus, for example, he hears sounds from afar. But he does not hear mere *sounds*. He *knows* in addition that these sounds are cannon shots, and he knows that the cannons too are products of some *Work*, manufactured in this case for a *Fight* to the death between men. But there is still more. He knows that he is hearing shots from Napoleon's cannons at the Battle of Jena. Hence he knows that he lives in a World in which Napoleon is acting. (Kojève 1969: 34)

Conversely, the reader of Kant's third *Critique* is left with the impression that artworks are produced in the same way plants produce flowers or birds produce songs. Kant who 'did not have a particularly artistic temperament' claims to be able to analyse in detail human and natural artistic activities without evoking struggle or work with which he is surrounded day and night (Kojève 1973: 89). The conclusion to the *Phenomenology* is written against the background of industry and war, work and struggle, all in stark contrast with the growing silence of Kant (Eco 2014). The problem of conceptualizing the relation of time to the concept is, according to Kojève, a clear line of philosophical demarcation between Hegel and Kant:

> For Kant, Being is in conformity with the Concept, and the 'mediation' by Time merely allows one to move from one to the other without modifying either the one or the other. And that is why Kant cannot *explain* this conformity of Being and the Concept: for him, it is a given, that is to say, a *chance* (*transcendentale Zufalligkeit*). Hegel, on the other hand, *explains* this conformity (which for him is a *process* of conforming) by his dialectical ontology: Being *becomes* conformable to the Concept. (Kojève 1969: 147)

Because Hegel's science has work to do, because it trans-*forms* before it con-*forms*, it does not allow for a Kantian lapse into a silent or non-discursive mode of being; for in addition to its phenomenological method, and ontological dialectic or dialectical ontology, this science also allows the philosopher to posit the 'what am I?' at the level of the dialectic of the real. According to Kojève (1969: 214), Kant confined a major part of this dialectic to the unknowable thing-in-itself, depriving the philosopher from the possibility to 'ask [him/herself] what the objective Reality (*Wirklichkeit*) that is, the real (natural and human) World must be in order that' existence is revealed and shown in this or that other way, and for the dialectic of being to be necessarily realized in a specific way. Kojève describes this aspect of the philosopher's 'what am I?' as being metaphysical in nature, with *Philosophie der Natur* and *Philosophie des Geistes* as its corresponding textual fragments in Hegel's science.

Hegel's premature synthesis

What does the attribution of dialectic to being and the real entail? Why does Kojève insist that there is no such thing as a dialectical *method* and that the only method available to the philosophical discourse is a descriptive phenomenology (in the manner of the first Husserl, as Kojève claims) - a method put in place precisely to see, speak about and accompany the dialectic at work? The answers to these questions are evoked in Kojève's comments on circularity in the Hegelian system. Hegelian '"Science" or "System" is [...] a *circular* description of the realised or *closed* totality of the real dialectical movement' (Kojève 1947: 533). It was not the dialectic, but rather the idea of circularity, the *encyklos*, Kojève believed, which is 'the *only* original element' to speak of in Hegel's philosophy (Kojève 1969: 93).

For Hegel, the system of knowledge is not a static edifice; rather it is a movement that determines the truth of its logic and science by the determinations of the concept, starting with the speculative sentence announced in the *Phenomenology*. Kojève accepted and defended this idea from the very first lectures till the end. However, the more he accepts Hegel's circles, in the *Phenomenology*, in the *Logic* and in the *Encyclopaedia*, the more he spins out of them, because in addition to the circles specific to the processual development of the concept at the level of existence, being and the real, 'the system in its *entirety* [...] must also be circular. Now, it is precisely there that the non-circularity of Hegel's system is perfectly obvious' (Kojève 1969: 98).

For Kojève it was important to understand the *Phenomenology* as the presupposition of the *Logic*, and as an adequate point of departure to attend the point of view of absolute knowledge, but he identified a flaw in the system as the circle of circles. This flaw has something to do with the *unmediated* leap from the phenomenological method to the dialectic of being in the *Logic*. Without passing through a *middle term*, such a leap would ultimately lead to the equation of history with the history of philosophy. For Kojève this is unacceptable, and because Hegel placed his metaphysic *at the end* rather than in the *middle* of the system, his approach to the history of philosophy turned out to be 'the history of necessarily failed attempts to realise the totality of *thought* before having realised the totality of *existence*' (Kojève 1947: 406).

Kojève believed that Hegel's (monist) ontology was a 'failure' because it provided the foundation for the natural sciences without justifying his anthropology or his phenomenological description of finite human agents as annihilators and negators of given-being. We thus ended up with a long span of time during which Western ontology was unable to 'find a way beyond the impasse of Hegelian ontology [...] but guided by Husserl [...], Heidegger reopened the ontological question [which Hegel left suspended]' (Kojève 1993: 38). But even Heidegger's intervention was, according to Kojève, inadequate insofar as it sought to eliminate all that is related to negativity, and by so doing, Heidegger was also unwittingly refuting the work of his own *Dasein* (Kojève 1993: 42). What then is missing from these successive aborted attempts by the philosophical discourse to move beyond the impasse of Hegelian ontology (as expounded in the *Logic*)? How can these attempts be resumed and to what end? Kojève situates part of his work towards the completion of this task in relation to the first three paragraphs of the 1812 *Logic* (1990c: 246-248). But beyond this endorsement, his main objection to Hegel is formulated against the sequence *Phenomenology* → *Logic* → *Encyclopaedia* (philosophy of spirit).

The excluded third

Angelica Nuzzo's dramatization of 'how Hegel's *Logic* begins' emphasizes the silence of the *Logic*, while projecting the effectual moment of its 'realization' or 'actualization' as meaningful discourse *outside* the *Logic*, i.e. in and as *real-philosophy*. For Angelica Nuzzo, when 'the pure thinking speaks, its voice immediately vanishes into nothingness', because 'within the *Logic* there is no otherness to mark the difference necessary for the logical voice to be heard' (Nuzzo 2010: 26). In the absence of otherness, the 'logical voice' falls on deaf ears; it comes to nothing. But in the *unmediated* 'transition from the *Logic* to *Realphilosophie*', Nuzzo contends, the situation is resolved as follows: 'speaking is no longer submerged in silence or merely self-referential; the word is now heard as a living utterance in the real medium of the world' (Nuzzo 2010: 27).

Unmediated leaps from the *Phenomenology* to the science of logic, from existence to being and from being to the real are strongly contested in the Kojevean system. In one of his earliest attempt to think the articulation of being to the real in his own philosophical system, he sounds much less optimistic than Nuzzo about 'the real medium of the world', which he describes using the metaphorical imagery of the swamp.³ In this world, we will have to 'rely on finite, transitory, and unstable' forms of life:

> Fleeing from enemies, a person relied on [his] horse, and it broke its legs; a person entrusted her money to an honest friend, and [he] died, etc. etc. [...] human beings are given to themselves in a world of finite individuals ending, dying and killing each other. (Kojève 2018: 76)

According to Kojève, the *Logic* is first and foremost (ontological) discourse or discursive being.⁴ A more adequate interpretation of Hegel, in his view, must account for the transition from the *Logic* to the *Phenomenology* and from the *Phenomenology* to the *Logic* as a processual progression that passes through the philosophy of spirit as its *middle* rather than third or final term. This movement captures the ontological and metaphysical dialectic and speculation at work 'from the identity or perfect coincidence of the Subject and the Object, of the Concept and Reality, of *Bewusstsein* and *Selbst-bewusstsein*, to their opposition or "difference" (*Unterschied*)' (Kojève 1969: 170). In its gist, a Kojevean reading of Hegel is, therefore, an attempt to reposition the Hegelian *Geist* in the intermediary plane of the system where the non-discursive moments of difference and opposition are at work rather than synthesized, neutralized or resolved.

If neither the *Logic* nor the *Phenomenology* is ascending to *Geist* in the sense of a higher totality of being, or a transcendent totalizing reality, the function of the ontological and phenomenological parts of the system is to bring within their fold, into their midst, that which other philosophical systems either placed outside of their bounds or chose to deliberately ignore or pass under silence. Kojève's entire philosophical legacy is concerned with identifying and analysing this systematic middle term in different philosophical systems; his aim is clearly articulated as an attempt to put an end to the conflation of thought with being, being with the real, the real with existence. But none of this would be possible without pinning down being, existence and the real to their respective temporal and non/discursive structures.

> For Hegel 'Spirit *is* Time' (*Geist ist Zeit*), and time is 'the concept which empirically exists' (*der daseiende Begriff selbst*). There is therefore neither creative activity (= negation) nor conceptual thought outside of time. What is 'outside' of time is at the very most space, i.e., the purely natural world, or static Being (*Sein*). (Kojève 1970: 37)

Hegel's equation of time and the concept meant that he went against the entire tradition of dualist Western philosophy that divides the totality of being into subject and object, or thought and reality. What is new in Hegel is that 'no one has ever thought of dividing the totality of being into space and time' (Kojève 1969: 154). This is the very kernel of Kojève's interpretation of Hegel in the *Lectures*, which is one and the same thing as his own philosophical system. What then is at stake in the Kojevean project to orient critical attention to the temporalized and discursive modes of being expounded, first, in Hegel's *Logic* and then in his two-part (nature/spirit) *Real-philosophy*?

In the last years of the *Lectures*, Kojève notes that the autonomy of the object in Hegel underscores his acceptance, against Fichte, of Schelling's 'absolute necessity of "realist metaphysics"' (Kojève 1969: 152). However, the true causes of Kojève's insistence on replacing thought and even being with discourse or being-of-which-one-speaks cannot be deduced directly from his readings of Hegel, and neither can they be attributed exclusively to the influence of Heidegger as most of Kojève's critics believe. With Kojève, we are constantly reminded that the thinking activity of Hegel or Kant was unable to see beyond the horizon of Newtonian physics.

The full picture of this argument has long been hidden from Kojève's readers in his twofold philosophical engagement with, on the one hand, the neo-Kantian logical principle of the *Bewusstsein überhaupt* and, on the other hand, the 'fourth subject' discovered by modern physics as *Experimentaler überhaupt*. Unlike the subject of common sense, the mathematical subject and the gnoseological subject of the neo-Kantians, or even the Cartesian subject who does not say who thinks when it thinks, the subject of modern physics 'belongs to the same ontological region as the one to which its object belongs […], not as pure spirit situated outside the world, but as integral part of the world of its knowledge' (Kojève 1990b: 165).

The principle that must be safeguarded against the neo-Kantian *Bewusstsein überhaupt* is the autonomy of being, existence and the real. Therein lies one of the most distinctive aspects of Kojève's authentic philosophical system. He believed that the history of (Western) philosophy was marked by a failed struggle to obliterate those distinctions in such a way that being is conflated with thought, existence reduced to the real, being to existence and so on.

It took philosophy centuries to acknowledge that being is nothing other than the being-of-which-one-speaks; it equally took philosophy centuries to finally acknowledge that existence is not one and the same thing as being. Now the real issue for Kojève is not simply these two forms of misrecognition, but rather it was the suppression of the real, the belittling of the likes of Democritus in the (Western) philosophical tradition that is truly troubling.[5]

Being and algorithm

If some contemporary disciplinary practices of logic show more enthusiasm for mathematizing their subject matter than for speaking about it, it is difficult to tell whether their pursuit is philosophy or something else.

According to Kojève, Hegel's ontology as outlined in his science of logic, must first and foremost speak; it is discursive, and its thinking activity cannot be silent, lest it turns into aesthetic or religious (mystical) contemplation, or into the discipline of modern physics, where everyone is advised to 'shut up and measure!' Similarly, in other spheres of thinking activities, the mathematical or a musical symbol, for instance, does not need to speak. It is perhaps for this reason that, unlike philosophers, mathematicians have seldom considered the foundational problem of logic as a deterrent to getting on with the job of producing axioms. 'Philosophy answers the question: How should the world be so that what is in fact in it – i.e., as given in intuition – would be possible – i.e., logically possible' (Kojève 2018: 155) This formula, 'how should the world be … in order to … ', is present across Kojève's early and late manuscripts. The ontological and phenomenological discourse must not be self-contained, as they must not turn into a reflective mirror for one another. In one of his early manuscripts, Kojève evokes Hegel's deductions and 'abstract constructions' (2018: 164) in the *Logic* as 'an empty game of concepts (interesting as *Gedankespiel* [thought-game]) […] a conceptual game of words […] [that ultimately] replaces philosophy' (Kojève 2018: 162). Between the language of being (or ontology) and the phenomenological description, there is objective reality, an intermediary plane of forces, action and interaction, where often nothing speaks.

If the deadly silence of (Dostoyevskian) suicide and political crime haunted Kojève's thought from the early thirties until his early ontological writings in the early fifties, a similar region of silence cast its oppressive shadow over Hegel's philosophy between the *Logic* and the *Encyclopaedia*. For Hegel did not hear only the sound of Napoleon's cannon shots; he was equally attuned to the silence of madness and the 'intimacy of suffering' (Berthold-Bond 1995: 63), too close to home, in his sister Christine's illness and the frenzy (*Wahnsinn*) of his friend Holderlin.

Mute or silent logic is perfectly valid in the world in which we live. Such logic is at work everywhere, from the algorithmically curated content of our social media newsfeed to the intelligent machines that switch our lights on and off when ordered to do so. Perhaps a philosophical rendition of the 'internet of things' would not be far removed or more far-fetched than Hegel's definition of communication in 'the formal mechanical process' (*SL*, 635–636). Should we be worried when logic becomes inaudible or silent, or when it does not have the ear of the other? Kojève thinks we should, and throughout his brief teaching career as in his mostly solitary post-war writings, he warned against the potential dangers of a silent being, and a form of thought coded, transmitted and stored in meaningless signs, symbols and contradictory pseudo-notions. He establishes a direct link between these forms of silence and the return of theo*logy*, the end of politics and the bad infinity of a para-thesis without a synthesis where meaning is lost between infinite chatter and the silence of violence.[6]

Kojève did not see much difference between denying the possibility for the philosophical discourse to be realized in time from scepticism about the idea of the perfect state. These forms of denial come down, according to Kojève, to the obliteration of the time of projects that can be realized through human action and discourse. And once the path of philosophy or the idea of the (perfect) state are abandoned, we might as well 'take flight into some Religion or other … [in] some inhuman perfection (aesthetic or other), [in the ideas] of race, people, or nation' (Kojève 1969: 97).

The logic of tyranny and the tyranny of logic

Kojève can put Kant back to work, teach him how he can 'overcome his low self-esteem' (1973: 127) once his philosophical system of 1790, an open system similar to the sceptic's discourse, is transformed into the Hegelian system of knowledge of 1806 (1973: 102). Kant was not much of a challenge for Kojève or Hegel. Their true nemesis is evoked in their respective disappointment at the failure of prominent 'men of action' in their time to recognize the coincidence of philosophical self-comprehension with the self-comprehension of power. The absolute idea remained suspended in its one-sidedness, as it could not 'hear itself speak in its self-comprehension' (Dunayevskaya 2002: 179). Kojève evokes this silent moment in the *Lectures*:

> After the fall of Napoleon, [Hegel] declared that the Prussian state (which, in other respects, he detests) was the definitive or perfect state. And he could not do otherwise, given that he was convinced about the circularity of his system. (Kojève 1969: 98)

Like Hegel, Kojève followed the speculative sentence to its logical conclusions only to realize that the world in which he was living was far from satisfactory, and like Hegel before him, he knew that he had to get back to work, conceding that today 'the state that Hegel had in mind [...] is still far from having an "empirical existence" (*Dasein*) or from being an "objective reality" (*Wirklichkeit*) or a "real presence" (*Gegenwart*)' (Kojève 1969: 192). There is a widely popularized reading of Kojève, mostly inferred from anecdotal footnotes, as the philosopher of the end of history and even as 'a divine madman' (Rosen 1987: 105). However, a more attentive reading of his philosophical system will not hold any promises for a revolutionary Bacchanalian revel or a revolutionary Sabbath where everyone is anecdotally 'Japanized' or 'Americanized'.

Hegel examines 'the difference between the concept and its realization' in the first moment of the synthetic cognition, with reference to three examples or 'bad specimens' for the concept's determinedness in ephemeral and inadequate external representations of nature and spirit:

> In a bad plant, a bad animal type, a contemptible human individual, a bad state, there are aspects of their concrete existence that are defective or entirely missing [...] [while] a bad plant, a bad animal, etc., remains a plant, an animal just the same [...] in the case of the physical human being, the essentiality of the brain is missing in the instance of acephalous individuals; or, in the case of the state, the essentiality of the protection of life and of property is missing in the instance of despotic states and tyrannical governments. (*SL*, 712)

Can we understand Hegel's *Logik* in the contemporary (analytic) sense of a theory, a method or some sort of software that detects and corrects errors in the concept and its realizations in nature and spirit?

In the *Lectures* and in his later manuscripts, Kojève reframed his cautionary notes about Hegel's logical deductions, which appear in numerous notes in his 1931 manuscript (posthumously published with the misleading title *Atheism*), as the dialectic of truth and error. The science of logic must be different from biological and mechanistic teleology because in the natural world, Hegel's 'bad specimen', a malfunction or a sick body, would be eliminated. The situation is different in the human world. Human beings and their errors, including their 'despotic states', can endure in nature and *in time* without being evacuated by the logical truths of nature or spirit. And it is for such a reason that Kant can live forever in peace on his island of pure understanding, while 'Neurathian sailors [can] remain on their boat, using whatever resources they have [...] to patch the hole and continue sailing' (Sher 2016: 27).

There are three prominent examples that Kojève likes to use to illustrate the anthropogenic aspect of human error and the very existence of the Anthropos as error from the standpoint of nature (or given-being). The first example is directly inspired by the *Phenomenology*. A random time of the day is recorded on a piece of paper, for instance: 'it is now eleven o'clock.' What is written is true only when the recorded time in writing corresponds to the time shown on the clock. The passing of time will, therefore, alternate the truthfulness and falsehood of that which *was* written and is being read at different times of the day and to infinity as long as time and humans who read and write exist.

In the second example, Kojève evokes the preposterous error, which lasted over centuries, of a medieval poet talking about flying humans. But the poet's error became true after the invention of planes. In this case, error becomes truth because human work transformed the natural given and created the technology that made flying possible. If in the second example error became true, in the first example, there is no way out of the alternation of error and truth, unless of course we find a way to arrest the passing of time. In the third example, Kojève invites the audience of the *Lectures* to suppose that a person wants to murder a king. This act is defined by the primacy of the future; it *will* be an error if it fails, in which case the murderer will be treated as a criminal. If, however, the act succeeds, the criminal *will* be hailed as a hero and what began as an error (of judgement or character) will become a historical truth. In principle, the cycle of error and truth will continue as long as 'the idea we have of ourselves independently from our existence in the world differs from [our] reality in the world [*Gegenstand*]' (Kojève 1947: 399).

In the concluding statement of the 10th lecture, Kojève claims that 'the material support of the perpetual movement of the concept is henceforth in the Book which is called "*Logik*"(1947: 410). At the same time, he was reluctant to accept Hegel's absolute identification of history with the history of philosophy, firstly, because self-consciousness does not always tend towards extension (1947: 398), and secondly because other forms of satisfaction, delusional or inadequate as they may be, are available to anthropogenic life. There is the irreflected inertia [*gedankenlose Tragheit*] of the 'moron' who endures history like a stone endures the laws of gravity; there is the Nietzschean 'blonde beast' who is devoted to action but has no philosophical leanings; and there are intellectual beasts, the Hegelian 'Eitelkeit', the empty 'I' of individualist, a-political and a-social characters who believe that they are 'beyond the fray' and whose thinking activity is determined by their well-knowness or celebrity.

Kojève, however, thinks that the most serious objection to the expansion of self-consciousness can come from the religious person, always referring to an external consciousness 'he [or she] is opposed to every form of change in human life, he [or she] is always opposed to social revolution' (1947: 404). Kojève concedes that 'theological absolute knowledge can be perfectly satisfactory for many people' and that there are no necessary or vital reasons for them to look for any other forms of satisfaction (1947: 296).

Out of all scholarly authorities on Heidegger or Hegel among his contemporaries, Kojève singled out critical readings authored by Jesuit fathers Alfred Delp and Henry Niel to review, respectively, in 1936 and 1946. In his review essay of Delp, Kojève states unequivocally that 'theologizing' interpretations of Heidegger's 'destruction' of Western ontology would be as erroneous as any attempt to find a path to god via Hegelian 'mediation'. *The only choice, the truly free choice, is between theism and atheism.* This choice remains, historically speaking, free and open, while it bears no direct consequences on biological life or subjective consciousness.

Kojève will reiterate the radical atheism of his ontology, and by implication, his reading of the *Logic*, in his review essay of Father Henri Niel's (right) Hegelianism. In the conclusion to the article, Kojève states that the refutation of Hegelianism is not a question for a dialectic understood as verbal struggles. Contrary to what Niel thinks:

> History has not refuted *Hegelianism* [...] it has not decided between the 'leftist' and 'rightist' interpretations of Hegelian philosophy [...] [because] it is as work ('economic system'), revolutions and wars that the polemic between 'Hegelians' has been taking place for nearly 150s years [...] history will never refute Hegelianism, but will limit itself to choosing between its two opposed interpretations [...] The future of the world, and therefore the meaning of the present and the significance of the past, depend in the final analysis, on the way in which the Hegelian writings are interpreted today. (Kojève 1970: 41–42)

Shored up with his attentive reading of the position of the *Logic* in the Hegelian system, Kojève's ontological writings blur the lines between the continental-speculative approach and its analytic counterpart. The one thing he was adamant not to budge on was the divide between left and right Hegelianism. Kojève described this divide as a radical distinction between theism and atheism in the (Western) philosophical tradition, and more generally, as an irreducible difference which is ontologically inherent to the politics of *doing* philosophy. However, what he feared the most was not a philosophical showdown in the manner of the Kantian miracle of the Marne (1968: 28), so much as an emerging 'republic of letters' reminiscent of Bayle's *Historical and Critical Dictionary*, one which will be populated with bored stoics, unhappy sceptics and religious 'loyal citizens' lost to the bad infinity of verbal struggles.

Notes

1 It was this Kojevean observation that Stanley Rosen would later use to frame his *Idea of Hegel's* Science of Logic (2013). Rosen who was too familiar with Kojève's work, and met with him on numerous occasions during his studies in Paris, does not mention or acknowledge Kojève at all in this book.
2 In the Kojevean system, the real (objective-reality or the metaphysical plane of the system) has a temporal dual structure (space-time) but no discursive mode. Conversely, the plane of empirical-existence (or phenomenology) is discursive, has a multiple monadological structure, and the temporal mode of extended-duration (dureé étendue), while given-being (or ontology) is systematically defined as homogenous, discursive and in the temporal mode of spatio-temporality. Kojève's insistence that objective-reality is non-discursive was known to the close followers and attendees of the *Lectures*. This is, for instance, the central issue and subtext of Eric Weil's *Logique de la Philosophie* (1950) and Jean Hyppolite's *Logic and Existence* (1952).
3 The imagery of the Swamp is reminiscent of Lenin's critique of Emperio-criticism, which Kojève is undoubtedly familiar with.
4 In his 'Introduction' to the *Science of Logic*, George di Giovanni emphatically insists on the discursive dimension of the *Logic*: 'the *Logic* itself', he claims, 'is a discourse about discourse – the only discourse which, because of its subject matter, can attain perfect completion and which, therefore, defines the norm of intelligibility against which all other types of discourse, all of them more or less open-ended in their own sphere, are to be measured' (*SL*, xxxv).
5 Hegel's 'Remark' at the end of the section 'The One and the Void' (Ch. 3, 'Being-for-Itself') echoes the prejudice of the philosophical tradition with regard to classic and modern philosophers of atoms and the void: 'Physics, with its molecules and particles, suffers from its use of the atom, the principle of extreme exteriority, and therefore from an extreme lack of the concept, as does also the theory of state that starts from the singular will of individuals' (*SL*, 134).
6 Kojève devoted his entire post-war writings to a close study of the notion of the 'para-thetic' in the history of Western philosophy. He claims that readers of Hegel failed to identify the fourth term in his philosophical system. This fourth term is situated between the thesis-antithesis and the synthesis. The philosophical para-thesis extends from neo-Platonic eclecticism down to Kant and Bayle and can continue endlessly. The para-thetic has an equivalent in the history of religion, the

state, right, science and the social sciences, art, moralism and so on. The central question in Kojève's philosophy is not how history ends, but rather why history never ends.

References

Berthold-Bond, D. (1995), *Hegel's Theory of Madness*, New York: State University of New York Press.

Dunayevskaya, R. [1974] (2002), 'Hegel's Absolute as New Beginning', in Peter Hudis, Kevin B. Anderson and Boulder Lanham (eds), *The Power of Negativity: Selected Writings on the Dialect in Hegel and Marx*, 177–190, New York, Oxford: Lexington Books.

Eco, U. [1998] (2014), 'On the Silence of Kant', in *From the Tree to the Labyrinth: Historical Studies on the Sign and Interpretation*, trans. Anthony Oldcorn, Cambridge, MA: Harvard University Press.

Hyppolite, J. [1946] (1974), *Genesis and Structure of Hegel's Phenomenology of Spirit*, trans. Samuel Cherniak and John Heckman, Evanston: Northwestern University Press.

Hyppolite, J. [1952] (1997), *Logic and Existence*, trans. Leonard Lawlor and Amit Sen, New York: SUNY.

Kojève, A. (1947), *Introduction à la lecture de Hegel, leçons sur la Phénoménologie de l'Esprit professées de 1933 à 1939 à l'École des hautes études*, ed. Raymond Queneau, Paris: Gallimard.

Kojève, A. (1968–1972) *Essai d'une histoire raisonnée de la philosophie païenne*, vol. I, and vol. II, Paris: Gallimard.

Kojève, A. [1947] (1969), *Introduction to the Reading of Hegel: Lectures on the Phenomenology of Spirit*, ed. Allan Bloom, trans. James H. Nicholas, Jr., Ithaca and London: Cornell University Press.

Kojève, A. [1946] (1970), 'Hegel, Marx and Christianity', trans. Hilail Gildin, *Interpretation*, 1 (1): 21–42. Originally published as 'Hegel, Marx et le christianisme', in *Critique*, n. 3–4, August-September 1946, pp. 339–366. [Review essay of Henri Niel, *De la médiation dans la philosophie de Hegel* (1945).]

Kojève, A. [1952] (1973), *Kant*, Paris: Gallimard.

Kojève, A. [1932] (1990b), *L'Idée du déterminisme dans la physique classique et dans la physique moderne*, Paris: Le Livre de poche.

Kojève, A. [1952] (1990c), *Le Concept, le Temps et le Discours*, Paris: Gallimard.

Kojève, A. [1935] (1993), 'Note inédite sur Hegel et Heidegger' Rue Descartes, no 7, 1993, p. 29–46. Deleted notes from the review essay 'Alfred Delp, Tragische Existenz. Zur Philosophie Martin Heideggers' in *Recherches philosophiques*, vol. V, 1935–1936, p. 415–419.

Kojève, A. [1931] (2018), *Atheism*, trans. Jeff Love, New York: Columbia University Press.
Niel, H. (1945), *De la médiation dans la philosophie de Hegel*, Paris: Aubier.
Nuzzo, A. (2010), 'Dialectic, Understanding, and Reason: How Does Hegel's *Logic* Begin?' in Nectarios G. Limnatis (ed.), *The Dimensions of Hegel's Dialectic*, 12–30, London: Continuum.
Rosen, S. (1987), *Hermeneutics as Politics*, New Haven and London: Yale University Press.
Rosen, S. (2013) *The Idea of Hegel's Science of Logic*, Chicago: University of Chicago Press.
Ruda, F. (2018), 'Hegel, Resistance and Method', in Bart Zantvoort and Rebecca Comay (eds), *Hegel and Resistance: History, Politics and Dialectics*, 15–35, London: Bloomsbury.
Sher, G. (2016), *Epistemic Fiction: An Essay on Knowledge, Truth, and Logic*, Oxford: Oxford University Press.
Weil, E. (1950), *Logique de la philosophie*, Paris: Vrin.

Index

Ab-bild 203. *See also* image
absolute
   absolute idea 70, 79, 135, 136, 142, 147, 158, 171, 218–19, 226
      and dialectical method 181–3
   absolute knowledge 79, 86, 158, 221, 229
   absolute negativity 31, 33, 35, 53, 75, 82, 86
   absolute religion 140, 143 (*see also* religion, consummate)
   absolute spirit 2–3, 77, 86, 103, 108–9, 140, 145, 180, 190, 201
abstract
   autonomy 209
   determinacy 210
   form of recognition 66 (*see also* recognition)
   idea 91 (*see also* idea)
   identity 164
   legal person 138 (*see also* legal person)
   and logic 18–20
   particularity 95 (*see also* particularity)
   personality 144 (*see also* personality)
   rationalism 176 (*see also* rationalism)
   reality 67 (*see also* reality)
   rights 164
   self-consciousness 145 (*see also* self-consciousness)
   and the 'I' 67
   thinking/thought 7–9, 55, 161, 173
   universal 91, 128, 130, 156 (*see also* universal)
   universality 92 (*see also* universality)
   universal labour 124 (*see also* labour)
   will 135
accidental/accidentality 44, 46, 48, 135
actual idealism (*attualismo*) 4
actual soul 208
Adorno, Theodor Ludwig Wiesengrund 3, 34–5
aesthetics 119, 201, 205, 207–8

Agamben, Giorgio 6
algorithm 225
allegory 202
Alpers, Svetlana 204
animal 17–18, 21, 118, 120, 131, 142, 161, 173, 227
anthropology 68, 153, 219, 222
   in Hegel's philosophy of subjective spirit 139, 142–3, 208
   habit within 82–3
appearance
   contingency of 17
   and image 202–3, 206–11
   and immediacy 78–9
   of the given 79
   and the Hegelian image 13
   as the Kantian *Erscheinung* 148, 159, 163, 165 (*see also* phenomenon)
   of the sensible 31
   of the true concept 67
Aquinas, Thomas 152
Aristotle 16–17, 28, 33, 36, 102, 163–4, 202, 207
   and *Metaphysics* 48–52, 178
art 4, 108–9, 112, 201–3, 206–7, 209, 211
Augustine of Hippo 150–4, 156, 165

Bach, Johann Sebastian 180
Baxandall, Michael 204
beauty 147
beginning (*Anfang*) 2, 4, 33, 36, 61, 67, 76, 78, 80–1, 86, 90–1, 94, 136, 182, 190
Begriff. *See* concept
being 6, 13, 44, 47, 107, 203, 219–22, 224, 227
   and algorithm 225–6 (*see also* algorithm)
   being-for-itself 30, 33, 64, 144
   contingent/necessary being 49–57
   and essence 27–39, 48, 192, 208, 210
   and immediacy 75–86, 127
   logic of 196

as shine 211 (*see also* shine)
and thought 11, 17–19, 75, 142, 148, 218, 223
Beiser, Frederick 152
Bewusstsein überhaupt 223–4
Bienenstock, Myriam 112
Bloch, Ernst 3, 171–2, 180
Bobbio, Norberto 6
Bodei, Remo 5
Boehm, Gottfried 201
Böhme, Jacob 150, 152, 157, 164–5
Bonaventura (Giovanni di Fidanza) 152
Borges, Jorge Luis 84
Brague, Remi 153
Brassier, Ray 43
Bruaire, Claude 172
Brucker, Johann Jakob 154
Bruno, Giordano 154
Bubbio, Paolo Diego 145
Buddhism 197
Burbidge, John 43, 47, 49, 53

capitalism 126–7, 132
Cassin, Barbara 13
categories
    mathematical 28
    modal 44–5, 47, 49, 52–3, 55, 57
certainty 27, 63–4, 95, 194
    of consciousness 193
    self-certainty 66–7
    sensory certainty 79
Cesa, Claudio 6
Chamley, Paul 117
check (*Anstoß*) 31–2, 119, 123
Chiereghin, Franco 5–6
China 196–7
Christianity 140–1, 143, 145, 147, 152, 156, 185–7, 192, 196
civil society 126, 164
concept 7, 10–11, 16, 18, 28–9, 45, 54–6, 62–7, 69–70, 77–8, 89, 92–3, 95–6, 108, 117, 128, 136–7, 141, 157, 160–2, 172, 179–80, 182–3, 188, 192, 194–5, 197–8, 221, 223, 225, 227–8
    of actuality 162 (*see also* effectual reality/actuality)
    of being 33 (*see also* being)
    of *dynamis* (*see dynamis*)
    of essence 32 (*see also* essence)
    and experience 188
    of form 15–23 (*see also* form)
    of freedom (*see* freedom)
    of God 159, 164, 172, 189 (*see also* God)
    of habit 75–86 (*see also* habit)
    logic of 142, 144, 196
    mediation of 165
    and objectivity 77
    of otherness 34
    of person and personality 136, 138, 143 (*see also* person; personality)
    primal scene of 218–21
    of *Realität* 50
    of reality (*see* reality)
    of recognition (*see* recognition)
    of reflection 29–30, 34, 38, 47 (*see also* reflection)
    of religion 185–98 (*see also* religion)
    of shine (*see* shine)
    singularity of 89–98, 137
    speculative 190
    of spirit 82, 94, 140
        of objective spirit 106, 110
    of subjectivity 136 (*see also* subjectivity)
    of the subject (*see* subject)
    of universal 90–1, 93
    of will 94, 95, 97, 153
conciliation 186, 198
Confucian ethics. *See under* ethics
consciousness 10, 27, 62–3, 66, 68, 70, 79–81, 85, 106–7, 110, 140, 142–3, 158, 173–4, 175, 183, 188–96, 229. *See also* self-consciousness
    mythological 187
    religious 185
    subjective 229
content
    absolute 185
    of absolute idea 181
    of effectual reality 50 (*see also* effectual reality/actuality)
    of formal logic 15–21 (*see also* form/formal)
    of habit 83
    of Hegel's logic 140
    infinite 12, 186
    of knowledge 27, 31, 76, 78

logical 91–2, 94, 175, 179, 181
of mind 142, 144
of necessary being 51, 53
of objective laws 85
of philosophy of religion 143, 171, 187–95
of philosophy of right 90–1 (*see also under* philosophy)
of shine 32 (*see also* shine)
spiritual 79
and the 'I' 65, 90
of the notion/concept 50
of the world 67
of universality 91 (*see also* universality)
volitional 93, 95–6
contingency 10, 17, 43, 97, 126
effectual contingency 43–58
Copernican Revolution 12, 148–9, 165–6
correctness (*Richtigkeit*) 18
counterthrust (*Gegenstoss*) 191
creation 12, 107, 120, 126, 140, 142, 159, 172, 179–81
Creuzer, Friedrich 202
Croce, Benedetto 4–5, 171–2
cultus 193–5

D'Angelo, Paolo 202–3
das Logische 16, 175–6, 178
De Boer, Karin 46
definition 17, 21, 33, 35, 179
  of communication 226
  of *dynamis* 36 (*see also dynamis*)
  of God 172 (*see also* God)
  of image 203, 211 (*see also* image)
  of personality 135, 137–9, 141, 143 (*see also* personality)
  of positing 29 (*see also* positing)
  of social fact 109
  of the absolute 172 (*see also* absolute)
  of universal will 90
  of work 119–20 (*see also* work)
De Interpretatione 48
Della Volpe, Galvano 3, 5
De Negri, Enrico 5
derangement 82
Descartes, René 61–2, 68, 152–3, 156, 171
desire (*Begierde*) 61–2, 66–7, 90, 94–8, 119–20, 123–4, 131, 142, 153, 175, 197, 205

determinateness 32–4, 36–8, 65, 92
determinations of reflection 38–9, 47, 53, 209–10
devotion (*An-dacht*) 185, 189
dexterity 83
dialectic 3, 7, 36, 38–9, 64, 67, 78–9, 96, 136, 139, 147, 172, 179, 198, 209, 219–21, 223, 227, 229
  reform of the Hegelian 4–5
  transcendental 148, 151, 154
dianoia 39
Di Giovanni, George 4
Dihle, Albrecht 153
Dilthey, Wilhelm 2, 108–10
Ding 28, 47
Doctrine of Essence 29, 77, 203, 208
dogmatism 46, 81, 186
Doz, André 179
Durkheim, Emile 109
Düsing, Klaus 62, 142, 172
dynamis 35–6, 48, 50

Eco, Umberto 220
effectual reality/actuality (*Wirklichkeit*) 1–2, 6–7, 9–10, 44–5, 47, 50, 53, 77, 208, 211, 217, 220, 227
Egypt 197, 203
Einbildungskraft. *See* imagination
empirical
  evidence 143
  observation 109, 190
empiricism 63, 79
Enlightenment 2, 186
Esposito, Roberto 6
essence 10, 17–18, 27–39, 44, 48, 52–3, 55, 70, 76–8, 97, 124, 127, 140–1, 172, 179, 188, 192, 196, 202–4, 206–8, 210–11
  logic of (*see under* logic)
ethics 4, 78, 104, 107
  Confucian 196
  ethical life (*Sittlichkeit*) 85, 103, 106, 195
existence (*Dasein*) 29, 31, 33, 46–8, 50–1, 53, 56–7, 65, 69–70, 77, 81, 83, 85, 92, 107, 123, 125, 129, 139, 141, 165, 177, 181, 190, 195, 206, 208, 218, 220–4, 227–8
  coexistence 94, 96

existentialism 3
experience (*Erfahrung*) 1, 3, 6, 7–8, 12, 28, 39, 45–6, 64, 66, 69, 79, 118, 120, 147, 149, 153–4, 160, 162, 186–7, 192–8
    aesthetic 206
    religious 188–90, 192–3
exteriority 46, 47, 55, 57, 65, 68–70, 75–6, 83, 84, 173, 230

faith 131, 165, 171, 185, 206, 208
fantasy 197, 205, 207, 213
feeling 12, 62, 64, 68–9, 86, 87, 109, 119, 147, 173–6, 185–6, 189, 195, 205
    self-feeling 83–4
Ferguson, Adam 120–2, 131–2
Ferrarin, Alfredo 59, 62, 70–2, 179
Feuerbach, Ludwig Andreas 111, 168
Fichte, Johann Gottlieb 31–2, 61–2, 69, 70–2, 94, 106, 154, 158, 224
fideism 165
finalism 62
Fischer, Kuno 4
form/formal 5, 8, 10, 15–23, 27, 30, 33, 38–9, 45, 47–9, 50, 51, 53, 56, 61–72, 75, 77–83, 85, 89, 97, 103, 108, 111, 118, 120, 124, 127, 138, 142, 144, 161, 172–83, 193, 198, 203–4, 209, 219–20, 224, 226
    formalism/formalistic 19–20, 100
    formal logic 10, 15–16, 18–19, 21–3, 142
    formal modality 47–9
freedom 44, 54–8, 65–9, 76–7, 82, 85–6, 90–1, 97, 99, 100, 132, 138, 144–5, 148, 177, 185–6, 193, 205
free will 90, 96, 99, 100, 139, 153
Friedman, Milton 131–2
Friedman, Russell L. 152, 156
Friedrich, Caspar David 206
Fulda, Hans-Friedrich 139

Gadamer, Hans-Georg vii, 3, 37–8, 40, 209
Gentile, Giovanni viii, 4–5, 14
God 12, 28, 46, 49, 55, 98, 136, 140–69, 172, 176, 178, 179–81, 185–6, 188–9, 192–5, 197, 206–7, 213, 229
    knowledge of 12, 147–9, 158, 166, 169, 185, 194
    proofs of the existence of 195
Goethe, Johann Wolfgang von 180, 204–5, 208, 211

Göschel, Carl Friedrich 171, 180
Gramsci, Antonio 5, 9, 14
Grave, Johannes 206–7
Greek religion. *See under* religion
ground (*Grund*) 28–30, 32, 39–40, 48–9, 52, 55, 59, 62, 64, 68, 126, 137, 141, 187, 194, 206, 208–11, 214
Grundloses 49, 52

habit viii, 10, 11, 68, 75–87, 123, 173
Hartmann, Nicolai 11, 103, 106–10, 113–14
Hegel (interpretations)
    post-Kantian interpretation 12, 148
    revised metaphysical interpretation 149, 158, 166
    traditional metaphysical interpretation 149–50, 158, 166, 177
Hegel (works)
    Encyclopaedia (of Philosophical Sciences) 7, 10, 45, 61, 66–7, 171–2, 174, 181, 190, 192, 197, 202, 221–2
    Encyclopaedia Logic 155, 162
    Faith and Knowledge 147, 149
    Lecture on Logic 172
    Lectures about the Proofs of the Existence of God 46
    Lectures on Aesthetics 202, 208
    Lectures on Logic 44, 63
    Lectures on the History of Philosophy 16, 157
    Lectures on the Philosophy of Spirit 68, 71, 117
    Outlines of Philosophy of Right 89, 103, 112
    Phenomenology of Spirit 5, 13, 28, 61, 66–7, 79, 117, 123, 125, 138–9, 142, 154–5, 158, 186, 190, 191, 196, 197, 217, 219, 220–3, 228
    Philosophy of Nature 101, 181, 208
    Philosophy of Spirit 79, 81–2, 101–3, 117, 119, 138, 173, 181, 217, 222–3
    Science of Logic 1, 4, 7, 10–11, 15–18, 27, 36, 43–4, 47, 50, 54, 60, 63, 67, 89–91, 101, 135–6, 141, 158–9, 162, 170–2, 175, 177–80, 182, 192, 208, 217, 222, 225, 227
    The Spirit of Christianity 147
Hegelian school 2
Hegel-Renaissance 3, 5

Heidegger, Martin viii, 3, 6, 37, 50, 60, 106, 222, 224, 229
Henrich, Dieter 3, 56–7, 64, 71, 73, 146
hermeneutics 3, 6, 7–8, 12, 187, 192, 198
history of religions 140, 186–7, 192, 197
Hobbes, Thomas 101
Hodgson, Peter C. 198–9
Hogemann, Friedrich 172
Holy Spirit 140, 143–4
Honneth, Axel 70, 73
Hösle, Vittorio 172
Houlgate, Stephen 40, 43, 47, 49, 53, 63, 98, 100
Hume, David 79, 87, 122
Husserl, Edmund 4, 221–2
hypokeimenon 28–30, 33
hypothesis 20, 27, 37

iconoclasm 201–2, 211
idea 2, 3, 8, 16–18, 27–8, 60–72, 76–80, 82, 91, 93, 97, 99–100, 108, 110, 120–1, 125, 130–1, 135–6, 140, 142–3, 147–8, 150–3, 155–66, 168, 171, 173, 180–2, 184, 186, 196–7, 205, 207–8, 217–19, 221, 226, 228
  absolute (*see under* absolute)
idealism 4, 5, 31–2, 56, 73, 100, 106, 112, 127, 148, 152, 159, 169–70, 219
  idealist metaphysics 159
I/ego 31, 65, 68–9, 90, 92, 156
image (*Bild*) 12, 13, 78, 84, 121, 164–5, 173, 179, 180, 201–14
imagination 174, 207, 213
immanent universal 17
immediacy 31–8, 40, 52–3, 63, 67, 68, 75–87, 93, 119, 123, 125, 127, 146, 155, 165, 196, 203
inclination 80
India 196
individual thing(s) 17, 46
inference 17–23, 35, 79, 151, 159–60
infinity 66–8, 92, 140, 143, 226
inner recollection (*Erinnerung/Anamnesis*) 27, 84, 207
insight (*Einsicht*) 94, 97, 103, 186
internalism 104–5
intuition 75, 84, 142, 149, 158, 160, 162, 168, 173–5, 183, 187
  intellectual 158
  intuitive understanding 147, 158

Italian Hegel studies 2–5, 8
Italian neo-idealism 4–5

Jacobi, Friedrich Heinrich 62–3, 154, 169, 185
Jaeschke, Walter 61, 73, 180, 184, 198–9
Jesus Christ 147, 164, 206
Johnson, William Ernest 159, 161, 169
Jones, Campbell 127, 129
Judaism 196–7, 203
judgement (*Urteil/Urteilung*) 32, 38, 59, 71, 94–5, 97, 130, 160–2, 168, 177, 191, 197, 228

Kant, Immanuel 7, 10, 12, 22, 27–31, 37–40, 44–6, 50, 53–4, 58, 60, 62, 75, 87, 94, 96, 112, 146–63, 177, 184–6, 198, 213, 219–20, 224, 226–7
  Critique of Judgment 147, 149, 213
  Critique of Pure Reason 7, 38, 44, 148, 151, 159, 162
Karlstadt, Andreas Bodenstein von 202
kath'auto 32–3
Kervégan, Jean-François 79, 87
knowledge 8, 15, 18–19, 27, 31–2, 36, 43, 56, 64, 70, 73, 76, 78–9, 81–3, 85, 90, 111, 127, 129, 138, 140, 145, 147–50, 155–6, 158–9, 160–3, 166, 173, 175, 185–6, 191, 193, 201, 218–19, 221, 224, 226, 229
  of God (*see under* God)
Kojève, Alexandre ix, 13, 61, 73, 217–31
Kreines, James 149–50, 158–9
Krohn, Wolfgang 15, 21–2, 24

labour 110–11, 118, 120–4, 126
  abstract universal (*see under* abstract)
  individual 122
  universal 118, 122–4
language 3, 6–7, 13, 21, 27, 34, 64, 123, 158, 166, 179, 181, 184, 225
law of non-contradiction 18, 58
Left Hegelians 2, 150
legal person 138–9
Leibniz, Gottfried Wilhelm von 31, 38, 46, 49, 58–60, 160–3
Lenin, Vladimir 230
Lessing, Gotthold Ephraim 213
light 208, 211, 214
Locke, John 120

logic
    of being 30, 33–4, 40, 142, 196
    contemporary philosophical 15, 20
    of essence 27, 29, 39, 40, 44–5, 142
    logical truth 68
    subjective 16, 22, 44, 57, 65–6, 136
Longuenesse, Béatrice 12, 75–6, 147–51, 158, 164–5
Losurdo, Domenico 117
love 144
Löwith, Karl 172
Lugarini, Leo 5–6
Luhmann, Niklas 43
Lukács, György (Georg) 3, 117, 124
Luther, Martin 61, 152, 202, 206

Mabille, Bernard 43
Malabou, Catherine 43, 118
Mandeville, Bernard 121
Marcuse, Herbert 3
Marius Victorinus 156
Marx, Karl 3, 5, 102, 110–11, 120, 122, 126–8, 130
Marx, Werner 61
Marxism 3, 5
Massie, Pascal 48
matter 18–19, 28, 36, 38–9, 55, 119–20, 174, 181, 209
measure 28, 196
    measureless 28
mediation (*Vermittlung*) 29, 31–3, 35, 57, 76–80, 83, 85, 97, 118–20, 138, 140, 143, 165, 183, 189, 210, 219–20, 229
Megarians 49
Meillassoux, Quentin 8, 43
memory 83–4, 207
metaphor 12, 31, 68, 202–6
metaphysics 10, 16, 27, 36, 104, 108, 147–51, 158–9, 162–4, 176–8, 182, 185–6, 189, 217, 224
method 5, 11, 70, 76, 89–90, 101, 112, 177, 181–3, 191, 218–21, 227
Michelet, Carl Ludwig 139, 143
Mitchell, William John Thomas 201
modal categories. *See under* categories
modality 10, 44–6, 49–50, 52–4, 56
    modal actualism 162–3
    modal possibilism 162
    real modality 49, 52–4
modernity 43, 51, 152, 164

Montesquieu, Charles-Louis de Secondat, Baron de 111–12, 131
moral law 153
moral philosophy 148, 152, 164
Mordacci, Roberto 43

Nachdenken (reflective thinking) 174–5
natural
    language 21
    religion (*see under* religion)
nature 16, 28, 43, 57, 61, 68–70, 76, 78, 80–3, 85, 90, 94, 120, 122, 126, 131, 142, 155, 157, 171–2, 174–6, 178–9, 181, 190, 192, 220, 227–8
    second 11, 79–80, 82–3, 85–6, 142
necessity 11, 43–5, 49–57, 85–6, 90, 92, 94–6, 148, 188–9
need 10–11, 66, 90, 117–23, 125–32, 175, 197
negation 6, 29–37, 44, 52, 64, 137, 157, 161–2, 182, 211, 223
negativity 6, 30–5, 50, 53, 65–6, 70, 75–7, 82–3, 86, 155, 182, 211, 222
Neo-Platonism 154
Newton, Isaac 208
Nohl, Hermann 2
Novalis (Georg Friedrich Philipp Freiherr von Hardenberg) 154
Nuzzo, Angelica 182, 222

objective spirit. *See under* spirit
objectivity 10, 43, 63, 68, 75, 77, 81, 84–6, 159, 189, 197
Old Testament 153, 156, 163
ontic 57, 219
ontological 3, 12, 19, 27, 45–6, 53, 57, 86, 109, 175–7, 180–1, 203–4, 208, 219–20, 222–5, 229
ontology 28, 35, 46, 56, 58, 108, 127–8, 182, 217, 219–20, 222, 225, 229
organism 11, 65, 155, 204

pantheism 203
    pantheism dispute 154
Papoulias, Haris Ch. 201
Pareyson, Luigi 6
particular 11, 64–5, 69, 90–8, 110, 117–18, 122, 124–5, 127–30, 136–7
particularity 63–7, 69, 91–7, 128–9, 136–7, 143, 145, 195
Peckhaus, Volker 15

person 12, 104, 126, 135–6, 138–9, 142–4, 156–7
personality 12, 65, 135, 145
phainomenon 31
phenomenon 31, 64, 75, 77, 106–7. *See also* appearance
Philo of Alexandria 151
philosophy
  of history 3, 196
  of mythology 187
  of nature 3, 6, 11, 101, 173, 181, 196, 208, 221
  of praxis 5
  of religion 12, 139, 143, 145, 185–6, 188, 190, 193–4, 196, 197
  of revelation 187
  of right 3, 89–91, 94, 97–8, 135, 138–9
Pinkard, Terry 61, 123, 148
Pippin, Robert 61, 102–5, 112, 148–9
plasticity 11, 83, 86, 117–19, 126, 127
Plato 3, 28, 31, 34, 36, 39, 151, 153–4
  Republic 29
  Sophist 31, 35, 39
Platonism 151–2, 154, 165
Plotinus 151–2, 154, 156
Pluder, Valentin 61
Pöggeler, Otto 3
political economy 10–11, 110–11, 117–19, 121–2, 128, 132
positing (*Setzen*) 10, 29–30, 32, 37, 39, 78, 81, 85, 92, 197, 210
  positing reflection 31, 35–8, 192
possibility 28, 44, 45, 47–53, 55, 79, 84, 131, 136, 160, 162–3
post-Kantian interpretation of Hegel. *See under* Hegel (interpretations)
predicate 17–18, 28, 49–50, 159–61, 177–8, 182
presentation (*Darstellung*) 36, 147, 188, 193
presupposing reflection. *See under* reflection
presupposition 16, 27, 29, 32, 37–9, 62, 67, 160, 182, 192–3, 221
principium essendi 28, 39
principium fiendi 28, 39
principle 10, 28, 36, 39, 49, 64, 68, 89–90, 94, 104, 136, 145, 160–2, 182, 193, 201, 224
  of contradiction 161

  of determinability 161–2
  of thoroughgoing determination 161–2
Proclus 152, 154
proofs of the existence of God. *See under* God
property 46, 50, 84, 120, 138, 161, 182, 202, 205, 227
pros heteron 32

qualified post-Kantian interpretation of Hegel. *See under* Hegel (interpretations)
quantity 28

Ramdohr, Basilius von 206
rationalism 104, 112, 176
Ravaisson, Jean Gaspard Félix 80
Rawls, John 152
Realität 50
reality 1–3, 7–9, 11, 19, 28, 38, 46, 48, 51, 56, 66–7, 76–80, 97, 107, 136, 153, 159, 163, 173, 175, 177, 187, 191, 195, 197, 209, 217–20, 223–5, 227
real modality 49, 52–4. *See under* modality
realphilosophy 135, 137, 139, 141, 143–4
  realphilosophical personality 135, 144
reason 3, 16, 27, 37, 39, 57, 67, 70, 79, 103, 105, 128, 144, 148, 151, 153, 159–60, 165, 172, 177, 179, 182–3, 219
reciprocal action 44
recognition 61, 66–7, 85, 102–3, 144, 155, 164–6, 197
recollection (*Erinnerung*) 27–8, 84–6, 207
Redding, Paul 149, 165
reflection 30–1, 34–9, 45, 47, 52–3, 76–8, 80, 86, 90, 93, 174, 191, 208–11
  presupposing reflection 37, 38, 192
reform of the Hegelian dialectic. *See under* dialectic
religion 12, 78, 103, 108–9, 112, 140, 143–5, 165, 174, 180, 185–98, 226
  consummate 187, 197
  determinate 187, 196–7
  Greek 153
  natural 195
  Roman 196, 197

representation (*Vorstellung*) 40, 61, 63–7, 81, 86, 91, 94, 142, 165–6, 172–5, 177, 179, 180, 183, 186, 189, 197, 202–4, 207–8
Republic. See under Plato
revelation (*Offenbarung*) 144–5, 195, 207–8
revised metaphysical interpretation of Hegel. *See under* Hegel (interpretations)
Riedel, Mansfield 101, 110–11
Right Hegelians 171
Ritter, Joachim 15
Roman religion. *See under* religion
Rose, Gillian 7
Rosen, Stanley 227, 230
Rosenkranz, Johann Karl Friedrich 142, 213

Sache 28
sacrifice 195, 198
Sainsbury, Mark 20
scepticism 31–2, 165, 226
Schelling, Friedrich Wilhelm Joseph von 154, 158, 171, 187, 224
Schiller, Friedrich von 131, 205
Schleiermacher, Friedrich Daniel Ernst 185, 187
Schmidt, Klaus 209
Schneewind, Jerome 152
scission 186, 195, 198
the self 113, 153, 192
self-consciousness 10, 12, 61–8, 125, 136, 141–2, 145, 155, 228–9
self-determination 30, 63, 102, 112
sensibility 43, 148–9
Severino, Emanuele 6
shine (*Schein*) 30–5, 37, 77, 203, 206, 208–9, 210–11
Siep, Ludwig 143
sign 207, 226
simile (*Vergleichung*) 12, 179, 202–6
singular 11, 17, 68, 90, 92–3, 97–8, 106–7, 123, 136, 141
singularity 10, 18, 22, 43–4, 51, 56–8, 64–5, 94–6, 124–5, 137, 142–3, 195
Smith, Adam 121
society 109, 121, 125–6, 131, 139, 142, 144, 164, 187
Sophist. See under Plato

Souche-Dagues, Denise 208
soul 28, 68–9, 70, 82–4, 142, 152, 154–5, 165, 178, 186, 207–8
Spaventa, Bertrardo 4
speculation 1, 6–9, 80, 97, 136, 223
    speculative philosophy 8–9, 12, 117, 141, 177
    speculative proposition 191
    speculative reason 144
Spinoza, Baruch 154, 171
spirit 4, 6, 8, 11, 57, 65–7, 70, 75–6, 80–3, 94, 97, 100, 119, 124, 126, 135–6, 140, 157, 171–6, 178–9, 180–1, 186–7, 189, 190, 192–8, 201, 205, 217, 222–4, 227
    absolute 2–3, 72, 77, 86, 103, 145, 180, 190, 201
    free 138–9, 142
    objective 10–11, 77, 85–6, 101–3, 106–11, 138–9
    practical 139
    subjective 10, 61–2, 68–9, 82, 85, 107, 138–9, 141, 143, 186–7, 189–90, 196–7, 207, 212–13
spontaneity 75
state 78, 85, 98, 107, 131, 144–5, 164, 226–7, 230
Steuart, James 117, 119, 121, 131
stoics 156, 161, 230
Strauβ, David Friedrich 2
subject 3–4, 6, 8, 11–12, 15–16, 19, 32, 49, 54, 63, 77–8, 82–3, 103–4, 105–6, 107, 118–19, 136, 138, 139, 142–3, 157, 177–8, 180, 182, 185–6, 188, 194–5, 198, 223–5
subjective logic. *See under* logic
subjectivity 43, 54–5, 62–3, 67–8, 71, 76, 81, 85–6, 97, 102, 135–6, 139, 145, 164, 189, 190–1
sublation (*Aufhebung*) 7, 29, 36–7, 40, 49, 53–6, 65, 86, 139, 144, 208–10
substance 17, 33, 44–5, 54–6, 66, 68, 70–1, 77, 82, 85–6, 152, 155, 171
substantiality 45, 54, 70
suppositio 29, 39
syllogism 15–16, 197
    disjunctive 151, 159–60
symbol 197, 206, 225–6
symbolism 12, 202

Taoism 196
Tarski, Alfred 21
Taylor, Charles 102–3, 105, 113, 153
Tertullian 156
Textbook of Chemistry 40
theodicy 131, 153
theology 11, 140, 150, 152–3, 164–6, 171–2, 180, 185, 189, 218–19, 226
thing in itself (thing-in-itself) 75–6, 214, 220
thought (*Denken*) 62–3, 172–8, 189
thought-determination (*Denkbestimmung*) 64, 181, 217
traditional metaphysical interpretation of Hegel. *See under* Hegel (interpretations)
transcendental
  ideal 148, 159, 160–2
  logic 22, 39, 46
transition 28–9, 34, 36, 38, 49, 54, 90–4, 105, 118, 127, 138–9, 152, 159, 187, 202–7, 219, 222–3
Trendelenburg, Friedrich Adolf 4, 179
Trinity 140, 143, 152, 156–7, 163, 165
truth 12, 17–21, 29, 36, 52–6, 61–2, 66, 68–9, 78–9, 81–2, 84, 86, 96–7, 111, 143, 155, 158, 172, 179, 188–9, 190–5, 203, 208, 211, 221, 227–8

understanding 143, 147, 151–2, 158–9, 163, 174, 197, 204, 227
universal 1, 8, 11–12, 17, 62–4, 69, 70, 77, 83–6, 90–8, 185–6, 189, 192, 194–5, 198

universal basic income 130–1
universality 12, 40, 43, 56–8, 64–9, 71–2, 91–6, 98, 121, 125, 128, 130, 136–8, 143–6, 155–6, 183, 195
universal labour 118, 122–4

value 68, 120, 177, 180, 183, 186, 202
Vattimo, Gianni 6
Verra, Valerio 6
Verstandeslogik 18
Viellard-Baron, Jean-Louis 172
visual culture studies 201, 204
voluntarism 165
Vorlesungen über die Geschichte der Philosophie. *See under* Hegel (works), *Lectures on the History of Philosophy*
Vorstellung. *See* representation

Wahl, Jean 62
Werder, Karl Friedrich 4
Westphal, Kenneth 158
Whitehead, Alfred North 8, 9
Wirklichkeit. *See* effectual reality/ actuality
Wolff, Christian 46, 49, 51–2, 101
Wölfle, Gerhard Martin 53
work 117–32
worker 118–19, 125–6
world history 140–1, 145

Zander, Folko 58–9
Žižek, Slavoj 43